Francis William Newman

The Soul, its Sorrows and its Aspirations

An Essay Towards the Natural History of the Soul, as the True Basis of Theology

Francis William Newman

The Soul, its Sorrows and its Aspirations

An Essay Towards the Natural History of the Soul, as the True Basis of Theology

ISBN/EAN: 9783337182915

Printed in Europe, USA, Canada, Australia, Japan

Cover: Foto ©Lupo / pixelio.de

More available books at **www.hansebooks.com**

THE SOUL,

ITS SORROWS AND ITS ASPIRATIONS:

AN ESSAY TOWARDS

THE NATURAL HISTORY OF THE SOUL, AS THE TRUE BASIS OF THEOLOGY.

BY

FRANCIS WILLIAM NEWMAN,

FORMERLY FELLOW OF BALLIOL COLLEGE, OXFORD, AND
AUTHOR OF
"A HISTORY OF THE HEBREW MONARCHY."

"He that believeth hath the witness in himself."—*John.*
"We too believe, and therefore speak."—*Paul.*

𝔖𝔢𝔟𝔢𝔫𝔱𝔥 𝔈𝔡𝔦𝔱𝔦𝔬𝔫.

LONDON:
GEORGE MANWARING, SUCCESSOR TO JOHN CHAPMAN,
8, KING WILLIAM STREET, STRAND.

M.DCCC.LXII.

PREFACE

I HAVE been at a loss for a title to this Essay, which, while short enough, would fairly warn the reader of its character. I at first entitled it, an Essay on the Positive Foundations of Practical Religion; and afterwards, On the *Directness* of Knowledge in Things Spiritual: but gradually found that it was necessary to go into such details concerning the Pathology of the spiritual organ, that I might possibly seem to have entrapped the reader into a more experimental discussion than he could have calculated on. My present title, I think, gives fair warning to those who dislike such books; and at the same time sufficiently well explains the end in view.

By the Soul we understand that side of human nature upon which we are in contact with the Infinite, and with God, the Infinite Personality: in the Soul therefore alone is it possible to know God; and the correctness of our knowledge must depend eminently on the healthy, active and fully developed condition of our organ. While the well-being of Man is the chief reason for coveting a knowledge of God, and all sound theology must aim ultimately at a practical end, the *direct* object of this Essay is nevertheless more scientific than practical. A Natural History of the Soul demands some notice of its diseased as well as its healthy state, and of its growth from infancy towards maturity. How this is a basis for Theology will appear of itself.

The analogy and contrast between Moral and Spiritual knowledge deserves remark. A long period passed in the history of mankind, during which Morals were regarded as something essentially Dogmatic, and indeed to a considerable extent Arbitrary and varying with political institutions. The Morality of every great national system was long supposed to depend entirely on the external authority which promulgated it : only in the later stages of mental culture is it clearly discerned, that Ethics, as a science, is as unchangeable as the ethical nature of man. Thenceforward the idea that there can be anything arbitrary in morals faded away; and the authoritative sanction which is superadded to moral precepts became valued, not as that which is essential to guarantee their truth to a cultivated moral nature, but as that which (like parental command) enforces action while the moral sense is in its infancy. And this was perhaps the very feeling of the great apostle Paul towards the law of Moses. He venerated its precepts, as a mature man those of his aged schoolmaster; whose rod he no longer dreads, though he sees it to be wholesome that he once dreaded it : but after Faith was come, he was no longer under the Schoolmaster. So also, that in spiritual things each worshipper sees by a light within him, and is directly dependent on God, not on his fellow men, is an axiom pervading the thought of every New-Testament writer.

In Morals, it is something to gain external right conduct, even if there be as yet no internal love of goodness or insight into its nature; hence the Dogmatic principle derives there a real practical value, which is developed in LAW. It is important to keep people from mutual violence, even by an armed police or by arguments addressed to selfishness : and such constraint of the conduct by fear or by other lower motives, is a part of necessary training. It is a highly valuable result, if a man avoid falsehood and impurity, though he may know no better reason than his father's or his priest's command. But there not only is no spiritual *object* in his worshipping God solely because a father or a priest commands it, but the very statement is intrinsically absurd. That is not worship at all, which is rendered in obedience to mere dictation ; for worship is a state of the Affections, and these are not under the controul of the Will. A man who desires to worship, but has little heart for it, can only say to God, "Draw me, and I will follow after Thee ;" and he must needs have some heart in him, to say as much as this. At the suggestion or order of another we may present our bodies in a church or at a confessional, (which, if done without insight, is *a moral, not a spiritual, obedience,*) but it is essentially impossible to worship God spiritually unless we are drawn and led by forces internal to the Soul itself. The coming of the Spirit into a system of LAW, is that which intrinsically converts it into GOSPEL. It is useful to have spiritual teachers : and if they be wise, it is wise to listen reverently to them : but their lessons have not been successful, until the learner has gained an eye for seeing the truth ; and believes no longer because of his teacher's word, but because *he has an Anointing from the Holy One, and knoweth all things.* And this is the sole object of spiritual, as distinguished from moral, teaching,—*to minister the Spirit* ; to impart spiritual eyesight, and spiritual forces. Those truths, and those only, are properly to be called Spiritual, the nature of which admits of their being directly discerned in the Soul, just as Moral truths in the Moral Sense : and *he* is a spiritual man, not who believes these at second hand, (which is a historical or dead faith,) but who sees internally, and knows directly. To guide towards the method of ascertaining these, is the object of the present treatise : and whatever may at first seem to be digressive, is nevertheless intended to conduce to a greater fulness of insight into this cardinal point.

The *First* Chapter treats of the Infancy of the Soul,

under that rudimentary Religion, which we may possess without conscious reflection on self;—that in which we contemplate the great external realities of Faith, as if we had no personal relations towards them. It ends with the establishment of reverence towards a Personal Deity, when Morals and Religion at length coalesce. The *Second* Chapter concerns the spiritual phenomena called out by the sense that we ought to be what we are not, in the presence of God. It ought (if it were scientifically complete) to include all the dreadful results of Remorse and capricious or gloomy Asceticism; but I shrank from the odious task as needless, and have depicted only a few strongly-marked, but not fanatical experiences, issuing in happy results. The *Third* Chapter exhibits the soul struggling after a sense of its Personal Relation to God, with the happy and remarkable results of its success, and its means of recovering this sense, when lost. The *Fourth* treats of the Ideal of spiritual excellence, and of the Aids from without towards attaining it. The *Fifth* discusses the grounds on which the soul forms Hopes and Aspirations concerning a future life; and the *Sixth* closes with reflections on the state and prospects of practical Christianity.

If these pages shall save any persons from the desolating negations which are abroad, and show those who know not on what to rest their faith, to what quarter they must look for solid ground; and still more, if I shall have stimulated independent thought in men of holy feeling and devout practice, and shall have made them meditate solemnly on the insufficiency of our present Theology to evangelize any portion of the professedly unbelieving world;—I ought to regard this as recompensing me for the very serious moral effort, which it has cost me to publish this book.

March 1849.

PREFACE

THE best men cannot agree theoretically concerning Religion, while they differ on Metaphysics and Logical speculations: but their difference of judgment does not imply any want of candour, nor any mutual contempt. This belongs to an inferior order of mind and heart, which desires an excuse for thinking ill; and to such it is wholly fruitless to enter into explanations. But, as far as possible, to hinder any really candid persons from being misled by hostile reviewers, who find it easier to pretend that I contradict myself, than to aid towards positive truth; I must add a few words to clear up my moral estimate of the Jewish and Christian Scriptures.

The books so denoted differ extremely in moral value, as also in literary importance. Nevertheless they form, in some sense, an organic whole, since the later books grew out of the earlier ones; the more puerile conceptions were gradually laid aside or transformed, and new ideas also were brought in gradually, and were grafted on to the old stock. We can therefore speak of the religion as having a certain Unity of its own, in spite of the enormous diversity between Genesis, Leviticus, Isaiah, and John.

This Unity seems to me mainly to depend on the belief of the SYMPATHY of the most High with his devoted servants, and his desire of their Moral Perfection.

In this belief I think that there resides a prolific germ, which makes the Bible a book of vast worth and a root of goodness to those who wisely venerate it. The doctrine may be found, *occasionally* expressed, in the best of the Greeks or Romans; but it *pervades* the Bible, and therefore is constantly re-appearing in every form of Christianity.

Nevertheless, there are numerous errors, not merely external, but moral and spiritual, in the Bible; some peculiar to certain parts, others pervading the whole. These need not much affect the value of the book to those who know that it is imperfect, and who habitually seek to separate its pearls from its chaff. But to those who imagine the whole book to be infallible, its errors become always hurtful, often dangerous and sometimes fatal. As in every sect, if the founder be venerated too much, his weakest points of character and his most foolish opinions become typical to his followers; so the errors of the Bible are precisely what must become characteristic of those who bow to it fanatically. Its errors indeed are no more self-coherent than error in general; hence *many* schools of error are necessarily propagated from it. Of these, by far the worst is the Papal school, which has ended by dethroning the Bible, but was founded on a slavish adoration of its letter.

Individuals may rise to the highest pitch of moral excellence as yet possible to man, while holding to a theoretic confession of the infallibility of the Bible. But it is my conviction, that the Protestant world *collectively* can no more make progress without overthrowing this dogma, than the Papal world without overthrowing the collateral superstition of the Pope's infallibility. In the case of any recent writer, we all understand that to idolize him is to convert every accidental error of his into a fountain of pestilence: and, however great our veneration of his wisdom, we know instinctively that to proclaim his words infallible would be profane and dangerous beyond calculation.

And here I complain, that men put Falsehood for Truth,

in charging *presumption* and *audacity* on those who shriuk
from investing a human book or a human person with divine honours. To take on ourselves the responsibility of
avowing that all the words bound up between certain lids
are Absolute Truth,—to guarantee all the consequences
that follow from such a dogma,—*this* is extremely auda-
cious; as everybody at once feels it if applied to any
new example. The audacity and presumption of bidding
men to run all risks of pernicious error, in accepting the
words of a book as *all* divine, certainly is not obviated by
the fact that the book is old and foreign, and its origin
thereby somewhat obscured.

CONTENTS.

CHAPTER   PAGE

I. Introductory Remarks 1

II. Sense of the Infinite without us . . 7

III. Sense of Sin 45

IV. Sense of Personal Relation to God . . 77

V. Spiritual Progress 106

VI. Hopes concerning Future Life . . . 135

VII. Prospects of Christianity 148

THE SOUL,

ITS SORROWS AND ITS ASPIRATIONS.

CHAPTER I.

INTRODUCTORY REMARKS.

AGAINST the earlier editions of this Essay, objections have been urged, which seem to be based on doctrines in Morals or Metaphysics different from what I acknowledge. I have therefore determined to prefix consecutively some judgments on these subjects which recommend themselves to me. Of course nothing new is pretended : any real novelty would strongly imply error.

1. To acknowledge the *Unity* of the human mind, is no reason against speaking of separate Faculties. Even if, at all times, in all actions, all parts of the mind act together, it is not the less certain that different men have different excellences and different abilities, and that the parts of the mind have in them a different prominence, and are differently blended. Therefore we are forced to say, one man excels in Imagination, another in Logical Analysis, a third in Moral Discrimination, a fourth has a genius for Combination, and so on. But in thus recognizing Special Faculties, we do not disintegrate the mind.

2. Demonstration, or Proof, consists in so connecting a hitherto doubtful proposition with one or more that are undoubted, as to assure us of the truth of the former. Hence First Principles

B

cannot be demonstrated; for if they could be referred to others
more evident, (or earlier known,) they would not be *first* principles.   Of course therefore, the foundations of all science
transcend formal logic.

3. First Principles commend themselves to us as *Presumptions*,
by their apparent reasonableness.   They are confirmed, *first*, by
general acceptance,—or by an acceptance widening with men's
intelligence; *secondly*, by the perpetual harmony of the results
drawn from them by severe reasonings and manifold combinations.

4. No alledged first principle can be even plausible, when it
is arbitrary and wilful.   Some persons are so infatuated, or so
dishonest, as to argue, that "since we must have *some* first principles, and cannot prove *any*, we may as well assume one, as
another."   But certainly we must not assume any which manifestly refutes itself.   A man would seem to be joking, who proposed for belief, as the first principle of all human knowledge,
that the Grand Lama of Tibet is omniscient, or the Archbishop
of Paris infallible; for we have certainly no more *à priori* knowledge of these personages than of a thousand others; and it is
mere wilfulness to prefer Paris to Canterbury, or the Lama to the
Sultan.   Yet it is very common in certain schools of religion, to
pretend that the infallibility of "*the* Church," or "*the* Bible,"
can be, and is, A FIRST PRINCIPLE of human knowledge; when
even the Unity of the many societies collectively called the
Church, and of the many books collectively called the Bible, is by
no means *à priori* clear; and when, at any rate, the Church is
not the only community in the world, nor the Bible the only
book; when therefore it is *primâ facie* quite as plausible to claim
infallibility for every other community, and every other book,—
if no reasons are to be given.

So far from admitting such propositions even provisionally, we
must evidently disbelieve them until proved, and must necessarily
demand an exceedingly cogent proof of that which has so little
à priori to accredit it.

5. Inconsistency is a certain proof of Error; and in fact, Error
is so easily incoherent, that we can hardly believe it ever to possess absolute harmony.   In proportion therefore as our doctrines
admit of combination and application, so as to bring them within
the regions where they *might* be confuted, if false,—does our
confidence in their truth accumulate, if no confutation is met.
Truth can have no confirmations, except as we attain some power
of detecting error.   Therefore, without a development of incredulity, there can be no single step towards wisdom and permanent knowledge.   Yet the non-detection of incongruities can

never demonstrate that there are none to be detected, or that our conceptions agree with an external reality. If any one chooses to imagine human life to be a self-consistent dream, it is useless to argue with him, for we certainly shall never refute him.

6. Some assume as a first principle, that the Mind is made for Truth, or, that our faculties are veracious. Perhaps the real first principle here rather is, that "no higher arbiter of truth is accessible to man, than the mind of man." When people treat this as a *proud* sentiment, they do but show confusion of thought. On the contrary, it avows the sober proposition (which is certain, if anything can be), that man is finite, tied down within his own sphere, limited by his limited faculties; this is, in other words, to avow that he has no inlets or tests of truth, other than those faculties afford.

To oppose this by asserting that the infallibility of Church or Bible is a first principle, *needing no proof*, is wilful and ridiculous, as has been said. To oppose it by asserting such infallibility, while yet allowing that the infallibility *needs to be proved*, is to blunder grossly. For no proof can have a certainty higher than the accuracy and veracity of the faculties which conduct the proof.

If, by divine enlightenment, individuals receive what is equivalent to *new* faculties, they may become proportionably more capable of discerning and attaining truth. But such new faculties, if intended as an inheritance of all mankind, are not to be disowned as not *human*; nor can we dispense with testing by the old the soundness of the new; nor can any one, on the ground of his possessing such new faculties, claim belief, at least without first proving to men's ordinary understanding that he does possess them in some peculiar and exclusive measure.

7. Moral Truth is developed by experience and reasoning combined with the faculty peculiarly named Moral; which alone can pronounce on the *relative value* of inward impulses, desires, and pleasures, and alone decides that we *ought* to follow the higher and nobler. Morality cannot be resolved into the pursuit of the greatest happiness for the greatest number: first, because it remains to settle *what is* Happiness; secondly, because it remains to answer: why *ought* I to seek any man's happiness? To say that it is my interest, is not identical with saying that it is my duty.

A meaner soul chooses a meaner thing as its best. If one man regard Ease, a second Power, a third Knowledge, a fourth Active Excitement, a fifth Love, as the chief good, neither observation nor argument can mediate between them. The mind itself decides which *ought* to be preferred; and in enunciating the word *ought*, assumes its moral position. If any one deliberately prefers selfish profligacy to kindness and justice, and would rather have a jocund and boisterous course, with the chance of its being a short one, than any tranquil happiness, this is nothing but a difference of Taste, until a moral judgment interferes, to pronounce the one *wrong* and the other *right*; nor do we make him virtuous, by merely inducing him to choose another sort of selfishness.

The brutes in general act by *unconscious impulse*: a mere rational agent will act also by *conscious impulse*, which we call Motive: but a moral agent is guided by convictions of Duty.

8. For the growth of the Moral faculties human society is needful, and human history is profitable; but no one particular society is needed, nor any particular history. Human Morality could not be altered by the disappearance of a nation or an individual out of history; for it depends, not on what this or that man is, but on what human nature collectively is. A remarkable individual or nation may at certain times by example have stimulated new moral thought in our race, but their personality does not enter Moral Science. It may be true that "Moses was the meekest of men;" it may be equally true, that his conduct led to new views of the virtue of meekness : but no proposition of moral philosophy ought to contain the name of Moses. Its propositions are general; those of History are special, or relate to individuals.

Nor can Morals be made argumentatively to depend on facts of remote history, without disowning the universality of moral obligation. This universality assumes a direct and homely knowledge of right and wrong. If I am to obey the Ten Commandments *on the ground that* a divine voice pronounced them from Mount Sinai (and not because I and you and collective humanity discern them to be right), every one of us needs to ascertain a very distant and obscure matter of history, before he is under obligation to obey the decalogue.*

All the same remarks apply, as to the essential difference between a Historical and a Spiritual proposition.

9. The Moral faculty has been above described, as that which pronounces on the relative worth of our different impulses or attractions, and enunciates the *duty* of selecting the higher. By

* Of course the above is mere illustration. The Fourth Commandment of the Decalogue is without validity for Gentiles.

the WILL is understood, the inward power which actually makes a selection. Thus, if we are simultaneously impelled,—to do what is just,—to gratify a friend,—and to gain lucre or honour; —and it be impossible to secure more than one of these ends; by an act of the Will we choose and adopt one of these.

If no power of choice existed in man, but he were determined by an externally imposed necessity, it would be absurd in others to blame him, and a very superfluous self-torment to blame himself. Yet we know, that without self-reproof, there can be no deep-seated or fruitful virtue. In proportion therefore as the existence of active Will is disbelieved, practical virtue is impaired.

The same follows in another way; namely, since no man will make an effort, unless he believes that there is power within him. No sane man will struggle to break a chain which he believes will defy his utmost exertions. No insane man will move a limb which he fancies to be paralyzed. If we have no power of Will, to choose and to reject, and thereby to determine and guide our action, self-discipline and self-control are really impossible; *nor will he, who believes it to be impossible, ever attempt it.*—Those who call themselves Necessarians have of course some good qualities without cultivation: others have been cultivated by them from childhood, before they became converts to this creed; many virtues have thus become *habitual* to them: but from the time that they adopted the doctrine of Necessarianism, they have inevitably ceased to *cultivate* virtue, except at intervals while forgetting their creed and believing as other men. If any one could hold the creed from childhood, and the belief were always active, he neither would nor could attempt self-guidance, and would be a mere creature of desire.

10. Though the Will is a real power, it is limited, like other powers; and it grows up out of insensible beginnings. Moreover, it is either weakened or superseded by Habit. In a vicious habit, the Will is oppressed or paralyzed; in a virtuous habit, all effort of the will is superfluous: right action is carried on, as in preserving the balance of the body, without exertion or struggle, and the moral strength is reserved for other service.

A perfect state of the Will does not suffice for right *conduct*: knowledge, experience, and other intellectual combinations are often requisite to decide *what is* right, in external affairs.

11. Wherever there may be foresight of action, we recognize the existence of Law, which implies, not Compulsion, but Certainty. In the movements of inanimate matter, all now recognize pervading Law. At the other extreme, where a perfect Will resides, there also is Law; for it is certain that it will act aright;

and another mind sufficiently powerful would be able to predict its doings. The Habit of right action, is a Law made by itself, for itself.—But where Will is imperfect, and where there is a struggle, an element of uncertainty proportionably interferes, and instead of one Law, there are two or more Laws crossing and clashing. This is not the sphere of divine harmony; it is the sphere of human conflict and partial lawlessness: and to look for certainty in it, is very gratuitous.

CHAPTER II.

SENSE OF THE INFINITE WITHOUT US.

ALL human knowledge, like human power, is bounded; and it is then most accurate, when we can sharply draw the line which shows where ignorance begins. In actual life, our region of sensible light, where the common understanding guides us, is always encircled with a dimmer belt, beyond which are glimpses of partial light, and then, infinite darkness; but, though we do not pass suddenly from positive knowledge to absolute ignorance, we are, in every direction, distinctly aware of both states. To different minds, moreover, the sphere through which the understanding ranges, varies exceedingly; and many adults, especially in savage nations, remain all their lives like children.

It is thus a condition of human existence, to be surrounded with but moderately diffused light, that instructs the understanding, and illimitable haziness, that excites the imagination : and this being our natural and necessary case, the question suggests itself, whether the obscurity, as well as the light, is adapted to call forth any sentiments within us, or in any way tend to the perfection of our nature. And happily, the reply to this question immediately suggests itself, upon referring to the case of children. How lovely in a child is that modesty, which springs from an unaffected consciousness of ignorance; especially when joined with a belief that others know. When new knowledge puffs up, and amiable diffidence is lost, all feel that a bad exchange has been made. If so, we attain one fixed point. We perceive that the region of dimness is not wholly without relations towards our moral state. There is a proper effect which it ought to produce upon us, and which deserves to be more closely analyzed.

The case of the child will still farther aid our examination. Reverence towards parental judgments not only is approved as salutary, in order to gain the advantage of a wiser guidance; but in itself, especially in the earlier years of childhood, commends itself to all as a beautiful and excellent state of feeling. A very young child has no measure whatever of a parent's wisdom : it is to him unbounded. He neither knows, nor expects ever to know, the limits of it; and, therefore, his reverence is capable of being absolute. A whole world of sentiment is wrapt up in the relations felt and acted upon by such a child; sentiment, which none are brutish enough to fail to appreciate. Not all the knowledge, nor all the wisdom, nor all the prudence and self-control, nor all the manly independence, which a child of five years old could, under human limitations, attain, would compare in value to the loving reverence, sure trust, and unreflecting joy which such a child may exercise towards a parent, whose wisdom and goodness appear to him illimitable.

Are then these exercises of heart a source of happiness and of moral perfection in infancy, and are they *not* desirable for the adult ? Or are they desirable, yet not possible, for those, whose understandings have opened wide enough to see that all human minds are limited, all human hearts shallow, and that no object worthy of absolute reverence comes within the reach of sense ? Certainly it is no artificial dogma, invented by priests or needing enforcement by princes, that the man who has reverence for nothing has a hard, dry, and barren soul. In the English tongue, indeed, the very word *Soul* appears to have been intended to express that side of our nature, by which we are in contact with the Infinite. The Soul is to things spiritual, what the Conscience is to things moral; each is the seat of feeling, *and thereby the organ of specific information to us*, respecting its own subject. If all human Souls and Consciences felt absolutely alike, we should fitly regard their enunciations as having a certainty on a par with the perceptions of Sense : only, as Sense is matured in an earlier stage, and is less dependent on higher cultivation than the Conscience and the Soul, the decisions of Sense are undoubtedly far easier to ascertain—not therefore more certain when ascertained.

In the child and in the savage, as the Conscience is but half developed, so is it manifestly with the Soul. The former is built up out of certain rudimentary sympathies and perceptions, co-operating with an experience of human tendencies, under the stimulus of which the moral powers expand, until moral Truth is at length discerned by direct vision. The Natural History of the Soul is far less simple, as must be expected of a higher organ : its diseases also are more hidden and more embarrassing, and in consequence its pathology will assume an apparently disproportionate part of a true theology. For if Theology is "a science of God," it cannot omit to treat of the bright or sullied state of the mirror, in which alone God's face is to be seen. How to keep it ever bright, is the problem for every practical Christian; to unfold the practical rules in connection with an extended knowledge of the entire man, so as to reconcile Passion, Prudence, Duty, Free Thought, and Reverence, is perhaps the highest form that the problem can assume to the Theologian.

In order to see the whole from its commencement, it is well to begin from the study of the elementary phenomena out of which are evolved the ideas of something boundless beyond us—of Supernatural Power—of Divine Existence—and finally of One Infinite God; and, in passing, the collateral degraded types of each new sentiment or judgment will be remarked upon.

1. AWE.

The child of a good and wise parent, before attaining an age when it can meditate on the parent's finite powers, is certain to learn that there is One higher still, worshipped by him with prayer and praise. This is at first, and for some time, mere hearsay, destitute of any religious power on the heart, until a higher idea of infinity is attained. The gloom of night (*deadly night*, as Homer terms it), more universally perhaps than any other phenomenon, first awakens an uneasy sense of vastness. A young child accustomed to survey the narrow limits of a lighted apartment, wakes in the night and is frightened at the dim vacancy. No nurse's tales about spectres are needed to make the darkness awful. Nor is it from fear of any human or material enemy: it is the negation, the unknown, the unlimited, which excites and alarms; and sometimes the more, if mingled with glimpses of light.

A moral feeling blends with the sense of the awful unknown and infinite, when Death comes before a child's mind, especially if it fall upon one known and loved; and at a more adult age its effect is proportionably increased. Whither is our beloved one gone? Does he exist? Can he hear us? What a world of possibilities are presented to the imagination! Tender hope suggests that the spirit of the deceased still hovers about us, still watches us, still loves to know that we remember him. Yet what sharpness of thought can pierce this veil and *prove* that any of these things are true? There may be a brighter scene beyond the grave, at least for those who are so kind or brave as our lost one; or it may be, that while his shade flits about in air, it is nothing to him; it is but a delusive ghost, in which he is not at all. Such are probably the alternatives which present themselves to the untutored mind: a misty and infinite region of possible existence is opened to it; and as often as evil conscience goads a man, he becomes less brave in the contemplation of death.

Among places and circumstances, perhaps the darkness of *Groves* may be made prominent, as conducive to religious awe. The very name of a grove in Latin (*lucus*) is implicated with religion. The grove of the Eumenides was to an Athenian the most awe-striking of places. To the ancient Germans, groves were the proper temples of the gods. Among the Hebrews likewise, as with their Canaanite neighbours, the tendency to worship in groves was enough to overpower positive commands to make offerings in Jerusalem only. Nor will any one wonder at this, who knows what it is to walk alone by night under thick trees. A good conscience, and a heart not unused to pious communings, is only enough to repel painful tremors, except in those whom habit has deadened; and even these—though brave and stout men—unless fortified by intelligent devoutness, are liable to sudden panic. We must repeat, it is not bodily enemies that they dread; but a sense of the infinite, the unseen, the unknown—pierces through and perhaps unmans them.

So much having been obtained as a foundation, Awe, if it cannot be and ought not to be annihilated, ought to take some moral form. But even in this early stage numberless deviations take place, and mark especially the rudest Paganism. We may embrace them under the general name of Fetishism, which here claims attention.

In its simplest form, Fetishism ascribes divine virtue to some common object; to a stone, a beast, a tree, or a scrap of writing. Any of these may be made a god, an amulet or talisman; or may vary from the one character to the other. The worshipper dares not use his common sense, which would reject these absurdities; because his soul is sufficiently awakened to suggest that there is an occult power in nature transcending his reasoning faculties. He has gratuitously, indeed, attached the power to a definite object; but he is not trained to observe *within what limits* he is to follow his understanding, and *where* it is salutary to trust his imagination and faith to go beyond it; hence the fear of offending something divine paralyzes his powers. Natural phenomena probably in many cases commence such delusions. The falling of a meteoric stone is a highly exciting event. Such a stone, in an ignorant people, is certain to be revered, perhaps worshipped; and then is likely so to break down the objections of common sense, as to increase the predisposition to similar prostrations of soul. To knock off a bit of the fetish as a talisman, might seem too daring; but to adopt for such a purpose a piece of stone similar in appearance to it, would be an easy progress. If one man has a talisman, others wish for it, and a premium is offered for the manufacture of charms. While a nation is in this state of ignorance, some or other event is almost certain to commence such superstition; and any commencement suffices to ensure a continuation. Among the savages of Africa, of Asia, of America, the form of the result varies, but the spirit and the spiritual consequences are the same. The incipient cravings of the soul are in a certain way satisfied, but so as to arrest their farther development. To the unknown and the infinite, no moral element, nor in fact even any personality, has been ascribed. Nay, it has been reduced into a finite sensible shape. One fragment of Deity has been as it were embalmed for awe; but it has no life nor life-giving power.

In the same stage a gross and hard-drawn picture of an after-life is often adopted with firm belief. An unseen world is imagined, probably under ground, where the nations of the departed reside; and in this Tartarus different souls have a better or worse lot. So far there is little amiss; but next enters the idea, that men on earth can in some way affect the state of the dead. The simplest and most amiable form of the thought is, that offerings of meat and drink, of flowers and wine, at the grave of the deceased, allay his appetites and soothe his feelings. Out of this grows an *art* of propitiating the dead, perhaps also of consulting them; and a class of men arises who profess skill in this art; they are the primitive priests or necromancers. As their credit takes root and their science unfolds itself, they are at length supposed to have power over the under-world. Their favour is purchased by costly gifts, and the warriors alternately tremble before them or trample them down.

With the advance of cultivation, when the idea of a world of spirits has become familiar, Fetishism in many cases rises out of its primitive sottishness into a belief in spirits of magic. Arab superstition is in this respect a step higher than African. The *genii* of the Arabians appear at one moment as acted upon by spells or talismans, at another as the unseen powers, in fact spirits, who animate them. Here the human mind has proceeded to add personality to the occult influences, but has not been able to disentangle the supernatural persons from the sacred object or fetish, and has systematized moreover the belief in a science which gives to man a control over these powers. To the genii in general no pre-eminency of moral character is ascribed. Nevertheless, so soon as personality is allowed them, it inevitably follows to conceive of some as better and some worse; hence the doctrine of *good* and *evil* genii: out of which in due time is certain to grow the Persian idea of two great spirits, good and bad, and ultimately that of Monotheism, if general cultivation proceeds.

But even in the midst of enlightened science and highly literate ages, errors fundamentally identical with those of Fetishism may and do exist, and with the very same results. As the savage adores the darkness without seeking or longing for light, so the cultivated man sometimes by a morbid sense dreads the light, lest it should interfere with the gloom which he thinks necessary to religious awe. Not satisfied to take God's world as it is, he makes as it were an artificial darkness in order that he may be more religious; as if there were danger lest the human mind should exhaust the mysteries of the universe, and leave no room for wonder and reverence. Of course it is not meant that the individual is conscious of this; yet bystanders may see that there is in him a positive dread of clear notions, a suspicion that one who knows what his own words and professions mean cannot be reverential, a tendency to confound enigmas with mysteries, and to inculcate (under new names) a belief in charms and magic. A wafer blessed and water sprinkled by a priest are often invested over the breadth of Europe with magical virtue; and the words of a creed, reverentially recited by one who does not profess to understand them, are believed to have power in heaven and hell. A "purgatory" of fire is imagined, where souls have their guilt burnt out of them in long time, unless indeed the mass-chanting priest give to these unfortunates an earlier release. On his unction and absolution the state of dying men depends; for he keeps the keys of the courts above—we know not why or how, but because God has willed it. The priest may be both ignorant and wicked, yet he holds these celestial powers by virtue of his office, and his office by a magical investment derived from a man perhaps neither better nor wiser than he. The ordained and consecrated are all *fetish*: it is irreverent to pry closely into their pretensions.—In proportion as such fantasies prevail, religious growth is stunted. To abandon the common understanding becomes a necessary virtue; after which, moral enormities may be incorporated with the system without revolting the worshipper. If the whole religion were of this kind, it would be as debasing as any possible Fetishism; and such things now stand their ground only because they are generally combined with purer and holier principles; the influence of which for good imparts undue credit to these besotting superstitions.

2. WONDER.

But if such errors are escaped, the pure and reasonable result of Awe upon the soul is a pervading and active sense that we are as motes in the sunbeam, lost in immensity; insects of an hour, enveloped with mystery, knowing neither whence we came nor whither we go. And this feeling of Awe is soon blended and softened by the sentiment of the Sublime and the Wonderful mixing with it. Of all natural objects the starry heavens probably impart the most vivid conception of boundlessness, and the fullest feeling of sublimity, while the night itself, in which they are seen, aids their impression on the soul. Some, however, live in mountainous countries, or within view of the sea, and have, even in the day-time, magnificent objects in sight. Here it is natural to expect that the sentiment of the sublime would be more effectually cultivated; but it is not always so. Far more depends on the susceptibility of the soul, than on the scene habitually presented to us; and perhaps a stranger is more powerfully affected by the majesty of sea and mountain, than those who see them habitually.

Nevertheless, it cannot be doubted that the ideas of the Sublime and of the Wonderful, however excited, rise in more or less energy in all human bosoms long before we attain adult age, and are characteristic of the species. A man without these ideas would be as great a monster as a man without love or power of laughter; such a one, if in human form, would deserve to be judged an idiot. And herein lies the fundamental union of Poetry and Religion. Hence is it that the ancient Bard, Vates, or Prophet, united the characters of poet and religious teacher; and in fact to feed upon the higher and sublime poetry is virtually an exercise of the soul—a preparation at least for actual religion. Its similarity to religious meditations is in many respects evident. As the same hymn of praise and love may be daily recited and wearies not; as no new information for the understanding is coveted; so the same lines of the poet eternally delight—the more

perhaps because they are old. We dwell upon each word, and
find the imagination more and more stimulated; it is a never-
ending feast; for the wise poet does not limit his hearers to his
own mind, but leaves room for them to range beyond him if they
can.

There is indeed an elementary religion, a certain religiosity,
implied in the perception and enjoyment of the Sublime.   The
soul, awakened to a sense of the boundlessness of the universe,
of its own essential littleness and inferiority, combines an aspiration after fuller knowledge with a devotional self-prostration in
the presence of that *power*, *principle*, or *person*, out of which we
and all that we see has proceeded. Perhaps in this stage no
definite judgment is formed, whether the power be, or be not, a
conscious designing mind, or whether one or many; in fact, all
these hypotheses may be embraced alternately with the changes
of feeling, while (through the absence of self-inspection) the
person is unaware of it.   There is also an elementary religion
in speculations about an after-life, so long as they proceed from
the feelings of the soul, and not from metaphysics or inventive
fancy.   To explore that dim abyss with wondering thoughtfulness, though no conclusion be reached, is a profitable exercise of
soul, which enlivens the conscience, and rectifies our views of
earthly interests. *Moral* reverence in all this is not yet formed,
yet the Wonder is reverential.   Curiosity is not forbidden, but is
sobered; inquiry is encouraged, if it be in an earnest and grave
spirit; but in conjunction with these, there is the humility of
conscious ignorance and littleness, and astonishment at powers to
which no limit is seen.   Such is the second stage of healthy
development.

But of this likewise we find numerous degraded types, in
which the rising religion is marred.   Curiosity having once obtained leave to pry into things and powers which surpass the
understanding, becomes sportive, and luxuriates in fanciful invention, wholly unmoral, and into company with which nothing
can force the conscience.   Of this we have eminent instances in
the gods of Greece, and in the fairies of the German and Persian
tribes.   To indulge in mere *play* with the ideas of things infinite,
appears to be more fatal to religion than any other corruption.
It can hardly be esteemed an alleviation of the evil, that the form
moulded by wild fancy soon gets some hereditary sanction, and a
fixed aspect, after which it is believed as a veritable likeness; for
the more intense the belief of notions which destroy all reverence
for the unknown and supernatural, the more hurtful the result. So
long as a man is giving loose to such fancy, he is depraving his

own religious faculties by egregious trifling ; and a nation eminent
for the tendency, can have depth neither in its religion nor in its
conscience, which are forcibly kept apart. Perhaps it may be
thought severe to pass this judgment on the Ionian tribes of
Greece ; yet even if the result was checked by other causes, there
is still too much truth in the remark to be withheld. In the
same way, the writing and reading of fairy tales, in prose or
verse, if I do not mistake, exerts whatever influence it has in the
direction of deadening the religious sense.* Those who people
the vague, unseen, and infinite world with beings not much
superior to us, and in a moral aspect often inferior ; who become
as it were familiar with these creations of their fancy ; not only
can feel no reverence to *them*, but just in proportion as they
realize the ideas, incapacitate themselves for any reverence at all.
Puerile wonder remains as the deepest sentiment possible to them.
A man may, no doubt, read the *Midsummer Night's Dream*, and
get no harm from its fairy personages ; for the simple reason
that they touch only the outside of his nature, excite no deep
interest, and, however beautiful, are altogether frigid. But if
the tale stirred him up deeply—if it seized firmly on his imagination—and, much more, if it were actually believed, it would
proportionably exhaust the sources of real devoutness. Under
the same head will be included the grotesque devil-stories, and
other legends of the Middle Ages. It has often been remarked
how emphatically degrading must be the religion of an Italian,
who whips the image of his saint when he has failed to obtain a
request. But this is only a particular instance of the general
proposition, that familiarity is antagonistic to devotional awe, and
that we cannot make the world of spirits a place of amusement
to the superficial fancy, without impairing our susceptibility to
its sober and profound influences.

The old religions, which sinned on this side, sometimes had a
counterweight in the fantastic melancholy of other fictions. The
sympathy of the Greek with Ceres for the disappearance of her
daughter, and with Niobe for the slaughter of her beautiful
children, was perhaps rather tender than reverential ; but the
awe inspired by the Eumenides was true and deep ; and, in the
opinion of Müller, the belief connected with the infernal gods
was the only purifying part of the Greek religion. No earthly

---

* Of course supernatural imagery may be a *vehicle* for pure and impressive sentiment; nay, may be of a grave and impressive character
itself, as in Mr. Robert Landor's recent tale, called "The Fountain of
Arethusa." I speak solely of such inventions *as cannot be forced into
contact with the conscience*.

enchanter could deliver the guilty soul by celebrating mass. Yet the dreadful alternative of gross superstition is this, that the graver view tends to cruel and horrible rites, while the fanciful and sportive sucks out the life-blood of devout feeling.

Between these two extremes—which were the besetting sins of Carthage and Gaul on the one hand, of Greece on the other —the Romans and the Egyptians appear to have held a wiser mean. Both the latter nations had the principle of reverence so deep, that they were susceptible of grovelling superstition even when their cultivation was considerably advanced. Egypt is regarded as the native land of secret doctrines or mysterics; and such things seem to have been highly congenial to the Romans. The credulity of both appears to us astonishing; yet dark and bloody rites were foreign to them, and at the same time they were far removed from puerile familiarity with their deities. Nevertheless, each nation fell at last into another, equally fatal, corruption; into the worship of a hard hereditary ceremonial, unprompted by feeling, unrenewed by fresh inspiration. Thus the infinite became degraded into the finite, the divine into the petty or the bestial. The death of a cat, or the drinking of a chicken, were made of prime religious importance; and though no gossiping poets dissolved their piety into lascivious dreams, the Hierophant and the Pontifex congealed it into grotesque shapes, immovable and lifeless as stone.

3. ADMIRATION.

The human mind opens in some degree to a perception of Beauty, as early as to that of Awe; but Awe, as a sentiment, reaches its beneficial limit in a low stage of cultivation. The sense of Wonder also exists in much intensity, at a time when that of Beauty is little developed. Indeed this last advances but slowly towards perfection, and always perhaps falls short of it. Herein we see, that Beauty, though it exists in limited dimensions only, and seldom can inspire Awe—for Respect, Admiration, Rapture, rather than Reverence, Awe, Devoutness, express our feelings toward beauty, of whatever kind—still, Beauty has one element of infinity; what is more, it is received by a single grasp of the soul, by an intuition which cannot be analyzed; and, as we contemplate its higher specimens, we can feed upon them untiringly, finding no end of admiration and delight.

In those great scenes of the visible world, the sublimity of which impresses us, we also generally discern much beauty. In the starry heavens indeed, there is sameness; yet the eye only, and not the mind, gets weary in gazing on them. The tranquillity of their beauty never becomes insipid, though there is so little variety. Very different is the sunlit landscape; in which the characters of beauty are too numerous to be counted, no one spot giving a view like the rest, nor one day like another. Yet here also, in that which changes least, as the falling of the cascade or the rolling of the sea, there is no satiety of admiration. How close to devout exercises of soul is this feeding of the heart on beauty, the epithets and metaphors of every language testify. We need therefore to examine the relation which it bears to religion.

As Awe is softened into Reverential Wonder, when the understanding is sufficiently enlightened to save us from vain and degrading fears, so the latter sentiment warms into Admiration, when we discern the Beauty which invests the infinite world. As a glimpse of life beyond the grave, and a glance of the eye into the depths of space, are adapted to calm stormy passions so a tranquil resting of the soul, on whatever form of beauty, tends to impart cheerfulness, elasticity of spirits, and mute thankfulness, towards—perhaps we know not *whom*. The child who gazes on the colours of the sunset, on the light which ripples with the water, or on the deep blue of the sky, is often ready to bound with speechless and unanalyzed delight. Nor need adults any higher beauty to call forth the same feelings, though the magnificent scenery of some favoured spots is appreciated by them with still keener zest. Thus, in short, to call forth the heart into admiration, *and prepare it for love*, is the appropriate function of all natural beauty.

How far the beauty of the human countenance can here be included, is a question which may move debate. The living face of man is undoubtedly an infinite depth, inasmuch as it depicts character; but this concerns expression only, and is therefore but partially dependent on mere feature and primitive form. It must indeed be admitted, that meek and majestic features, a pure soul shining through the eye, a self-collected spirit seen in the general harmony of the countenance and in the absence of everything spasmodic, exert a strong *moral* action on the spectator; and, in so far as religion consists in a quickening of the conscience under a sense that a superior intelligence is gazing upon us, the sight of a human face—even sculptured or painted—may be called a religious influence. Such is that of a mother to her infant. But this influence is not that of beauty, though it is heightened by beauty. We must disentangle the two things. A countenance of great purity and love *must* have a certain sweetness of its own,

but not dependent on feature: on the other hand, the most
beautiful features that ever were, may be insipid and inexpressive,
as those of many Venuses and Madonnas. Such beauty does not
even draw admiration from the cultivated; and when it does in
any, the limit is soon reached; satiety succeeds; the matter has
thus no place in our present discussion. But as, in the few instances in which it is our privilege to see a living face beam with
the highest moral qualities of man, the mere sight is kindling to
every good and holy emotion, so pictures or statues, which skil-
fully represent such countenances, are themselves, (up to a certain
limit not easily reached,) a moral and spiritual power.

It is not from these that idolatrous mischiefs are to be feared;
no populace ever became degraded by gazing upon them. The
many representations of the countenance of the Man of Sorrows,
on which the eyes of the Middle Ages were fed, varying no doubt
greatly in merit, were yet on the whole highly conducive to
spiritual improvement. On the contrary, the stupid and debasing
idolatry was found in connection with some staring large doll,
tricked out in tawdry finery and called a Virgin—such as still
infests Continental cathedrals—or with some daub of a picture,
neither having nor supposed to have artistic excellence. Such
things were made fetish, and the worship of them was attended
with nearly the same influences as the worship of a stone fallen
from Jupiter. They had not even elevating reminiscences; for
no one fact was imagined concerning the Virgin which tended to
quicken the conscience.*

But though the painted or sculptured countenance is, under
certain circumstances, a spiritual power, yet, as being a work of
art, it in all cases puts us beneath the artificer, and may even
keep us down to his level. This was strikingly illustrated in Greek
sculpture. A statue of exquisite beauty, representing some hero, or
an Apollo, *because* of its beauty seemed to the Greeks a fit object of
worship. We still have before us many of the finest performances
of their sculptors. We know distinctly enough what an Apollo,
what a Mercury was; and we can accurately appreciate the influence of such worship. None of the qualities of mind which we peculiarly call spiritual, were expressed at all. Meekness, thankfulness,
love, contentment, compassion, humility, patience, resignation, dis-
interestedness, purity, aspiration, devoutness; little of all these

---

* The preposterous ascription of perpetual virginity to a married
woman tends to promote, not true purity, but fantastic error in elder people, impure curiosity in younger ones. The abuse of the word *chastity* to
mean *celibacy* is bad enough; but this is so much worse, that I fear to
express my feelings about it.

was felt or understood by the sculptor; and how then *could* he communicate them? Those who adored his work could not rise to a higher adoration; such is the danger besetting those who allow themselves to cultivate devout feeling by aid of human art. We must not indeed disdain that occasional stimulus; but much less must we habitually have recourse to it, or make ourselves dependent on it.

The same remark, I believe, will apply to Church architecture. That the canopy of heaven elevates and sobers the heart, preparing it for devotion, if devout in itself,—few will deny. It needs not much susceptibility farther to confess, that a lofty cathedral, when suitably constructed, has an effect similar in kind to this; and that, other things being equal, it is better adapted for prayer, (though not for preaching,) than a well-lighted room, with low and flat roof. It is then evidently our wisdom to use such an advantage, when it offers itself. But on the other hand, since nearly all depends on the judgment of the architect; since many fail utterly, and produce only clumsy piles of masonry more or less ambitious, or gorgeous palaces more or less tawdry, but in no way appealing to the religious sense; it will only degrade our worship, if we force our hearts into sympathy with their false conceits, and invest their influence with a *quasi*-religious sanction. It is deplorable to hear how the form of a mullion or of a capital, the adorning of a pulpit or communion table, to say nothing of other finery or fancies, is elevated into religious importance, with reference to churches which all the ornaments and all the architectural lore in Europe can never invest with religious beauty; which are either as thoroughly *industrial*, in their primitive conception, as any square meeting-house, or are built on some hereditary pattern with no moulding idea. Mediocrity—as in poetry, so in church-architecture—must utterly fail to *elevate* the soul; patch the work as much as we will. Considering how rare access to churches of the noblest kind must always be, tenets of religion which dwell much on such a help to devotion are likely to gravitate into mere fetish superstition.

An opposite danger is often remarked to accompany the use of *all* the fine arts as handmaids to religion; namely, that the would-be worshipper is so absorbed in mere beauty, as never to rise into devotion. Music, Painting, Architecture, are by him appreciated as such; and if *criticized* as such, then farewell to their religious influence. That the danger is real and imminent, the history of Italy and of modern Rome proves. What Romanist will claim for Rome a high place in his religious world? and yet where else have these influences acted on so great a scale for so loug a time? On the whole therefore, we must assign an exceedingly subordinate place in religion to *that* beauty which the hand of man produces. Its author is not divine enough; it is dangerous to make much of his work. Only when it is so glorious as to rise above criticism, can it lift us higher than our common level.

The worship of beauty in days of chivalry was in some sense more elevating; that is, oftentimes no visible thing was worshipped, but a mere ideal of the mind. When a Spanish knight devoted himself to promote the honour of the Virgin, or even if a human mistress was his idol, yet as he perhaps had never had more than a transient glimpse of her countenance, his own imagination was the chief source whence her beauties were drawn, and this imagination was stimulated by whatever other female beauty met his eye. If we measure religion by its efficacy upon the conscience, this knightly religion was very feeble indeed; yet, as supplying a principle of action which rose out of an ideal, it was not without analogy to religion, and perhaps was as good as the worship of Apollo.

Far better is the modern enthusiasm for romantic scenery and all the beauty of nature; for that is a real infinity and constantly mingles itself with the awful and sublime. He who has a keen sensibility for this beauty, is not forthwith to be called a religious man; yet he has a temperament on which true religion may be happily superinduced, with more substance and grandeur of devotion than is to be found, where *only* the moral sentiments are in any active life.

But here we reach a point at which it is suitable to review the connection of these primitive affections of the soul—Awe, Wonder, and Admiration—with its moral state. As regulating our social conduct, Morality embraces both Self and Not Self; and in every possible development it recognizes both Interest and Duty as leading ends of action. When they do not clash, the virtue which pursues Interest is called *Prudence*; when they do clash, then to pursue Interest is stigmatized as *Selfishness*. But the essential difficulty of the moralist is, that he has no command of the impulsive forces of man, such as to help each of us in sacrificing Interest at the shrine of Duty: hence the mere moralist, in a sort of despair of generous virtue, is tempted to recommend self-sacrifice on selfish grounds; and the moral system, which began with the profession of exalting Duty, ends with an idolizing of Self. Thus few men indeed are ever made more moral (in any but a *prudential* sense) by treatises on morality.

Is there then in human nature no direct antagonist to Self? Undoubtedly there is. The first aid against it is gained from Domestic affection. To gross and barbarian natures, love for Woman, not uninspired by some perception of beauty or grace, is probably the first school of practical virtue : so too do all the domestic relations tend to the same result—the sacrifice of self to another. He who lives without any such ties, is shorn of a great aid towards the mortification of self ; and unless he cultivates a peculiarly enlarged benevolence, falls morally below the average of his class and country.

Nevertheless the domestic affections rather *multiply* Self than annihilate selfishness, and often reproduce it in a less odious but more intense form. They are quite insufficient to the general demands of morality. But another and far more implacable antagonist to Self is found in Enthusiasm ; which is generally a passionate love for some idea or abstract conception : and whatever form it may take, its impulse is capable of animating the man to any or every sacrifice of Self. But not to speak of separate enthusiasms, one universal enthusiasm belongs to man as man ; namely, that which is called out by a sense of the Infinite, wherein we feel Self to be swallowed up. All the *generous* side of human nature is nurtured and expanded by the contemplation of the Infinite. Hence is it, that a sense of the Sublime and Beautiful, though it be not yet Religion, supplies to Morals an important part of that, which it is reserved for Religion to give in full power and divine harmony. Hence the glorious effect of high poetry, and of all that excites pure and beautiful imagination, on the youthful mind. Therefore is it, that to weep with Andromache, to shudder for Hector, to tremble at Achilles, to admire Alcestis, to rejoice with Admetus, constitute a better moral training than Paley's Philosophy or Aristotle's Ethics can give. Whatever throws the heart out of Self and swallows it up into some noble or beautiful Idea, affords to the moralist precisely that which he wants, but cannot get within his own science. He may, as it were, build an elegant Engine, but he has to look elsewhere for Heat and Moving Power. Enthusiasm is the Life to morality ; and to excite a pure and reasonable Enthusiasm is, as will be seen, the great moral end of Religion.

4. SENSE OF ORDER.

But to return from this digression.—Quite differing in kind, though now and then coinciding with the sense of Beauty, is that of Order. The same stars, which strike the eye of the savage as so beautiful, impress the diligent observer still more powerfully as the type of all Order, Unchangeableness, and thereby of Eternity. With the cultivation of the intellect and of scientific astronomy, immense additional weight accrues to this view. The recurrence of the seasons, as of day and night, presents itself to the mind as the most fixed and indubitable certainty in the universe. It suggests, ere long, that other departments of the world follow laws of equal fixedness, even if less known to us. The winds and the waves, long before their subjection to law is proved, are assumed to act really under similar limitations. Thus the supremacy of Order over the universe is recognized.

Accordingly, κόσμος (Order) was the name for the Universe introduced among the Greeks after the birth of philosophy, and exceedingly modified the wild conceptions suggested by the then current mythology. If the powers or principles by which Nature is as it were animated, have personal consciousness and design, yet at least they have nothing approaching to caprice and fickleness. Be that which we call Deity, mind, be it feeling or be it life, at any rate unchangeableness is its most striking attribute. The recognition of this fact is the turning point and passage from barbarian, or puerile, to cultivated or manly religion. After this step has been made, the religion cannot possibly remain what it was. It may lose in simplicity and depth, or it may even gain as to both: it may recede or it may advance; but to stand still is impossible.

The first great change which the perception of Universal Order brings about is the abolition of Polytheism. Where many gods are a national belief, all of these are thenceforth regarded as separated by an immense chasm from One who is Supreme; —that is, if the notion of their distinct personality is retained at all. He is farther discerned to stand in the *same* relation towards *all* nations of men and all worlds; His principles of action to be the same in every age; and now also, perhaps for the first time, a distinct conception of His *Eternity* comes in. Whatever of moral character be in other respects ascribed to Him, constancy *must* be ascribed; henceforth therefore contemplations and imaginations concerning the Infinite put on the coherent form of Thought and Speculation. A man's religion ceases to be a result of unreflective emotion: it has become self-conscious. Thus also it has fallen, more or less, under the control of his understanding, and he is a moral agent in regard to it, which he was not during his time of barbarism : and with

his more adult condition, he has assumed new powers and en-
counters new dangers.   A new element has been admitted,
which will either dilute and as it were dissolve all the rest, or by
blending with them happily will give to the religion definiteness
of form, consistency, and notions which can abide the criticism
of acute incredulity.   As before, we stop to consider the degraded types incident to this stage of development.

Whatever is habitual to us, is ill adapted to rouse attention or
excite Wonder.   No one wonders that a rock remains at rest ;
and though, as long as we know no other cause of motion than
muscular force, the movement of the sun and stars does seem
wonderful, yet their regularity certainly abates largely from the
feeling.   After it has appeared that a magnet will cause steel-
filings to move towards it ; much more, after we are convinced
that stones fall to the ground, and planets move round the sun,
for the same reason as steel-filings are drawn to the magnet, the
mind is forced to confess that Motion has nothing in it more
wonderful than Rest.   Everything appears either to remain as it
is or to change, by a *Law*.   This suggests the theory, that Mind
is not in the universe at large, since it is not wanted to account
for Motion.   If in this stage of thought a man have adopted a
moral hypothesis which denies that in the human mind any originating Will exists, and which resolves Will into other forces of
which we are not conscious ; then such a man naturally becomes
an Atheist ; for, discerning no first principle of movement even
within himself, he of course needs none out of himself.   If in
his own actions he see no marks of (what others call) Will, why
should he see them in the actions of Nature ?

Yet Error cannot be self-coherent.   The Atheist of this class
discerns Law and Necessity in his actions, and does not therefore deny that he has a Mind himself : why then should Law and
Necessity in the universe imply that there is not a Mind there
also ?   Grant that the human mind has no Will ; suppose that
the divine mind is herein similar : still, that is no reason for
denying that there is mind in the universe, in the only sense in
which he has experience of mind. If he admits this, he will really
become a Theist.   But it would be truly absurd, to demand as
an indispensable mark of a Divine Mind, the very Freedom,
which, at the same time, he pronounces to be absent from the
human and impossible for *any* mind.

When Atheism depends on the Moral* error of believing that

* I do not know how to avoid calling this a *moral* error ; but I
must carefully guard against seeming to overlook that it may be still a

man's Will is never self-moving, it is to the Moralist that we must appeal for correction. But if the atheistic tendency arise solely from the impression (*produced by the uniformity of Law*) that there is no Will active in the universe, this objection appears to be suitably met by the argument for Design, to which I next proceed.

5. SENSE OF DESIGN.

In barbarian religion the idea of a personality in the Powers of Nature slips in and out ; establishes itself generally in the popular creed of more advanced nations with considerable constancy, but does not know how to justify itself on reasonable grounds : and very often, at the first touch of philosophy, crumbles into ashes, leaving only Atheism or Pantheism. The question now arises—Is this ascription of Personality to the universal Power so gratuitous as those philosophers thought ? Does the universe exhibit to us much Order indeed, but no marks of Mind ?

An imperfect moral will is uncertain and disorderly : Law is but doubtfully manifest in it. But in proportion as its highest state is attained, uncertainty disappears, and Order or Law is developed. Surely then there is no natural repugnance between Order and Mind, nor any plausibility in the argument, which endeavours to explode the idea of Mind by giving prominence to that of Law.

Here, if anywhere, we must guard against the fallacy, which pretends that a clue to truth is worthless, if it have not the form of cogent Argument. We discern *Design* in the world : *Fitnesses* are the clue by which we track it out; yet they undoubtedly do not always, and much less in every detail, indicate Design. Fruit is palatable and wholesome to man : a suitability might strike me, between an orange or pine-apple and my appetite ; but it would not be sound forthwith to infer that *this particular* fruit had been designed for me *as a particular person* —either by man or by God. Farther examination often shows antagonist fitnesses : two mouths want the same loaf, and it can-

merely speculative error, which ought not to separate our hearts from any man. If we see another to love goodness and shudder at evil, he is to be loved, although he may hold a theory, which we think logically tends to annihilate exertion *for* the good and *against* the evil. On the other hand, many a bad-hearted man is theoretically orthodox on these points.

not have been intended for both. The antagonisms are often of a less obvious kind, yet serve equally well to correct the first rash conclusion. So again, fantastical minds may carry up the detail of human arts into the divine purposes; as the well-known engineer, who before a Parliamentary Committee expressed his opinion, that "large rivers were intended to feed navigable canals." It must be admitted, that the argument from Fitness to Design may be ill applied : but the question arises—Can it never be trusted?

A lung bears a certain relation to the air, a gill to the water, the eye to light, the mind to truth, human hearts to one another ; is it gratuitous and puerile to say, that these relations imply design? There is no undue specification here, no antagonist argument, no intrusion of human artifice : we take the things fresh from nature. In saying that lungs *were intended* to breathe, and eyes to see, we imply an argument from Fitness to Design, which carries conviction to the overwhelming majority of cultivated as well as uncultivated minds. Yet, in calling it an argument, we may seem to appeal to the logical faculty; and this would be an error. No syllogism is pretended, that *proves* a lung to have been made to breathe ; but *we see it* by what some call Common Sense, and some Intuition. If such a fact stood alone in the universe, and no other existences spoke of Design, it would probably remain a mere enigma to us ; but when the whole human world is pervaded by similar instances, not to see a Universal Mind in nature appears to indicate so hopeless a deficiency in the Religious Faculty, as to preclude farther discussion. Just as, if any one had no sense of Beauty in anything, we should not imagine that we could impart it by argument, so neither here. Possibly some day, by a new developement of his character or by the contagion of sympathy, he may acquire Religious Insight; but for the present, we lament that he has it not, and hereby is cut off from the profoundest influences of humanity.

I must nevertheless here add my belief, that in modern days some have been carried into a theory of Atheism, not from any want of religious susceptibility, but just as others into Romanism; from an inability to disentangle sophistical argument, and from a desire to be honest in sacrificing their instinctive convictions to their technically erroneous reasoning. This is probably a strictly correct account of the process by which *Necessarians* are made. And as professed Necessarians are ordinarily unconscious believers in Free Will, so those professors of Atheism, who retain pure moral sympathies, do perhaps, under other names, such as Veneration of the Infinite and of Eternal Law, nourish within themselves some nucleus of religion. On no account let us exaggerate the real difference between them and us; though real it is and must be, if they forbid themselves to love and trust in a Superior Intelligence.

But to return to the marks of Design.

No stress whatever needs here to be laid upon minute anatomy, as for instance, of the eye: it signifies not, whether we do or do not understand its optical structure as a matter of science. If it had *no* optical structure at all, if it differed in no respect (that we could discover) from a piece of marble, except that it sees, this would not destroy our conviction* that it *is meant* to see. Of the physical structure of mind, no one pretends to know anything; but this does not inspire doubt whether the mind was meant to discern truth.

Why should any philosopher resist this judgment? One thing might justify him; namely, if there were strong *à priori* reasons for disbelieving that Mind exists anywhere except in man. But the case is just the reverse. That puny beings who are but of yesterday, and presently disappear, should alone possess that which of all things is highest and most wonderful, is *à priori* exceedingly unplausible. As Socrates and Cicero have pointedly asked: "Whence have we picked it up?" Its source is not in ourselves: there must surely be a source beyond us. Thus the tables are turned: we must *primâ facie* expect to find Mind in the Universe, acting on some stupendous scale, and of course imperfectly understood by us. Consequently, such Fitnesses as meet our view on all sides bring a reasonable conviction that Design lies beneath them. To confess this, is to confess the doctrine of an *intelligent Creator*, although we pretend not to understand anything concerning the mode, stages, or time of Creation. *Adding now the conclusions drawn from the Order of the universe*, we have testimony, adapted to the cultivated judgment, that there is a Boundless, Eternal, Unchangeable, Designing Mind, not without whom this system of things coheres: and this Mind we call God.

It is however right here to enter a protest against being thought to have any accurate and perfect knowledge of that Infinite Mind. Our knowledge is essentially crude and only *approximate*; and to affect the rigid form of human science is mere delusion. We attribute to God those properties of mind with

---

* See in Charles Hennell's Christian Theism, p. 34, &c., a luminous statement of the argument from *mechanism*.

which we are acquainted,—Will, Design, Forethought, and others; but it is unreasonable to imagine that we can at all more deeply sound His mind, than a dog that of his master. Hence *Religious Knowledge*, from the nature of the case, *is essentially popular*; and if the scientific mind has any advantage over the unscientific in prosecuting it, the advantage is not in the direct perceptive powers of the soul and in any greater fulness of knowledge, but, negatively, in avoiding vulgar prejudices derived from false lights. Intellectual cultivation, in itself, is here purely critical and only destructive of error: yet as such, of very high importance. If this essential imperfection in our knowledge of God be admitted, an important corollary follows: namely, that no long deductions, following logical (that is to say, verbal) processes, can be trusted in Theology. Such deductions imply full accuracy in the verbal premises. Inference may guide our thoughts to new beliefs; but we need to discern the results directly, and not *merely* to depend on our syllogisms, if we are to have the full confidence of practical truth. What mathematician will trust to a refined and lengthy process of argument, depending on empirical formulas? In Hydraulics and Pneumatics, where the first principles are only approximately known, it is requisite to keep close to experiment, and verify every speculative inference by practical trial. A system of Theology, constructed like a treatise on Mechanics, by fine-drawn reasonings from a few primitive axioms or experimental laws, is likely to be nothing but a Sham Science.

Injustice, I think, is done to the train of thought which suggests Design, when it is represented as *a search after Causes*, until we come to a *First Cause*, and there stop. As an argument, this, I confess, in itself brings me no satisfaction. It is not pretended that we understand the First Cause any more than the original phenomena: when we know not the character of His agency, how have we *accounted for* anything? or how have we even simplified the problem? A *God* uncaused and existing from eternity, is to the full as incomprehensible as a *world* uncaused and existing from eternity. We must not reject the latter theory, merely as incomprehensible; for so is every other possible theory. To believe in a divine Architect, because I cannot *otherwise* understand by what train of causation an Eye could have been made, is one thing; (does the Theist any the more understand?) but to believe in a Designer, because I see the Eye to be suited to Light, is another thing. The latter argument indeed does not in itself carry us up to a First Cause; its whole scope is to point out intellect external to man and higher than

his, which suffices to justify the popular ascription of mind and
personality to the power which is in Nature.

To carry out extravagantly, and as it were caricature, the doctrine of Design, is a rare perversity. There are however those,
who think not only to honour God, but to be peculiarly logical
and scientific, by teaching that He has designed *everything* that
happens; regardless whether any Fitnesses exist to indicate Design. Every pebble washed up by the sea, every bone imbedded
in the mud, was definitely intended by Him to lie where it lies.—
Now if those who so believe mean merely to say, that the so-
called powers of nature are actings of the divine will, the reply
is, that this is a juggle of words; for they manifestly do *not*
reveal His *moral* will. To become an agent of cruelty in tor-
menting a martyr, would be a crime: yet if nothing but the
immediate will of God, exerted as directly as by the torturer,
makes the scourge to cut and the flesh to feel, then God also is
an accomplice in the crime. This conclusion is of course inadmissible. It is evaded by remarking,—what is a certain fact,—
that He acts by general laws: which means, that He sees it to
be more important to adhere to processes which admit of mechanical, chemical and (in short) physical definition, than to guide
His proceedings by the moral right and wrong of special cases.
No other solution has ever been suggested; and this is adequate
and convincing.—But what does this imply? Why, that God's
moral thoughts can no more be detected in the detailed actions
of material objects, than the affections of a watchmaker by in-
specting a watch :—that when the flesh of a martyr is agonized
by the flames, God gives the fire power to burn him, *not because*
He wishes it on that particular occasion to burn, *but because* it is
better to adhere to a fixed system, so that the element which
burns at one time should burn also at another. Thus the qualities of matter are on the whole, no doubt, agreeable to the divine
will, and may be speciously called the actings of that will; but
the phrase is very delusive; since the sole use of it is to propagate a notion which is directly contrary to obvious fact. For in
material nature Law alone rules, and *moral considerations are,* as
far as we know, *uniformly overborne by mechanical ones.* Since
then the details of mechanical agencies evidently denote no *moral*
Will, it is a fallacy to call them Will at all. If an unmoral Will
were *all* that we attributed to God, He would be a mere me-
chanist, coming into no contact with our hearts and souls; and
we might as well be Atheists, as far as moral and spiritual things
are concerned.—On the other hand, if this doctrine of Design be
carried unshrinkingly into the actings of the human soul, (which

is the worst form of Pantheism,) it becomes a detestable moral error, in comparison to which simple Atheism is a light mistake. Every sin of every wicked man is converted into a direct act of deity; an idea than which nothing can be more blasphemous.

Yet the persons who teach this doctrine, if accepted not as logicians, but as men labouring with sentiment which they know not how otherwise to express, may be found even to kindle in us a high devotion. Who can read the Pantheism of the Orphic Hymns or of Virgil, and not be moved by them? It is when the Pantheism which would swallow up all mind and action in the divine, is proposed as an accurate and logical system, that we are justified in intense repugnance to it, as furnishing excuses for Sin.

I feel some timidity in adverting to another form of Pantheism, lest I should misrepresent what is so difficult in my own mind to grasp. I believe that some are called Pantheists, merely because they are hyperphilosophic Theists.* They have a morbid fear of attributing human qualities to God, lest they should degrade him: thus they shun to ascribe to him, not only " body, parts, and passions," but affections, judgments, designs, mind; and so his personality vanishes. Yet in fact they do ascribe to him *quasi*-affections, *quasi*-mind, and *quasi*-personality; so that their practical creed vacillates from Atheism to Theism by the infinite vagueness of the *quasi*: and perhaps, like many religionists, they have two mutually refuting creeds, which may be used as the case requires. Such men may themselves be fundamentally religious, though their doctrine seduce others into irreligion.—Concerning the Divine Nature, we know that our metaphorical language *must* be inaccurate; but it is the best we have got: to refuse to speak of God as loving and planning, as grieving and sympathizing, without the protest of a *quasi*, will not tend to clearer intellectual views, (for what can be darker?) but will muddy the springs of affection. Metaphorical language in this whole subject is that which the soul dictates, and therefore must surely express our nearest approximation to truth, if the soul be the eye by which alone we see God. Jealously to resist metaphor, does not testify to depth of insight.

As to that Pantheism which deliberately and coldly merges all human Will and action in the Divine,—which on moral grounds is so shocking,—it is at the same time so obviously self-destruc-

* I now find that there are persons who call themselves Pantheists, merely because they are Theists who have no belief concerning a finite era of Creation, but nevertheless firmly hold the intelligent Personality of the ever-acting and all-pervading Spirit. (Second Edition.)

tive even as a logical system, that it has always been wonderful to me how it can claim intellectual respect. For nothing but a consciousness of active originating Will in ourselves suggests or can justify the idea of a mighty Will pervading Nature; and to merge the former in the latter, is to sacrifice the Premiss to the glory of the Conclusion.

6. SENSE OF GOODNESS.

As soon as the intellectual belief of One Personal God has been clearly attained, the mind most rapidly superadds the idea of his *Goodness*, at least from the negative side. He is too great to be moved by petty passions; he cannot have pleasure in our misery: the only doubt is, whether he thinks of us *individually* at all: for allowing his ability, some remain unconvinced of his willingness.

The great struggle of mere intellectual philosophers has always been on this side. In the abstract they admit God's goodness, nay, his moral perfection; but doubt whether it is a part of his perfection to pay any attention to us; and, certainly, as far as *external* things are concerned, their reasonings appear unanswerable: no miracles are wrought for our convenience or welfare. What answer there is in regard to *spiritual* things, will afterwards be treated. Meanwhile, the *à priori* conviction of God's goodness is unquestioned; and is indeed so satisfactory, as scarcely to need with a cultivated mind such confirmations as the vulgar dwell upon:—our daily supplies of things needful and comfortable; the kind provision made for mankind at large; the adaptation of the night for rest, the day for action; the gift of inferior animals suited to become our servants, aid, or friends. Perhaps these arguments are in a certain stage of culture necessary, while the mind is unprepared either to see that they are defective or to understand a higher view; afterwards, far more conviction is attained from considering that *all the possible perfectness of man's spirit must be a mere faint shadow of the divine perfection.* To conceive of God at all, as an intelligent existence, and not regard Him as morally more perfect than man, is obviously absurd. Nor only so; but to volunteer limiting any of His attributes is equally absurd. Until the contrary be proved, we unhesitatingly attribute to Him boundlessness in every kind *of which we can conceive.* But on account of the last limitation, the Perfections of God are justly called a projected image of our own highest conceptions.

Philosophers however of old times dreaded to impute *affections* to God, not knowing how to distinguish them from *emotions*; both indeed being merged by the Greeks under the single term πάθη. Perhaps they rightly maintain that the two words denote difference of degree only, and thus may force us to admit that *affections* are attributed by us to the divinity, only metaphorically. Still as the metaphor is our nearest approach to truth, and (as before said) we gain nothing by inserting a *quasi*, it is best to abide by the popular phraseology. Else to what do we come? First, denying emotion to Him, we must deny affection, because that is nothing but a gentle emotion : next we must deny desire. But if he wishes for nothing, He aims at nothing, He designs nothing : thus we come into collision with what appears to the mind as fact—that there *are* marks of Design in the universe. Inverting then the argument, Design leads legitimately back to Desire, and in some sense to affection ; and we call him Benign, *for desiring the welfare* of his creatures. To endeavour to resolve God into intellect without affection, is atheism under a new name ; for mere intellect is not an active principle. If therefore the argument from Design leads to any God at all, it leads to a Good God, not too great to take interest in his creatures' welfare and perfection.

A difficulty is nevertheless encountered from the fact of human suffering ;—suffering of the good and of the innocent,—of innocent brutes as well as men. This wide-spread reality has a thousand times distressed the purest hearts ; and it would be vain to try to blink at it. But one reason why it has weighed so heavily on many, is,—that they had unduly rested the proof of the divine goodness on an opposite fact, viz. on what are called Providential Mercies. When such mercies fail, when on the contrary scourges and torment befal the righteous, an anxious embarrassment of mind follows. Especially if the received religion have taught that external prosperity is a mark of the divine favour, misfortunes falling on good men will bring a ten-fold sting. But that side of the difficulty falls away, when we find the proofs of the divine goodness, not in events and circumstances, but in primitive and essential arrangements, and in the human mind itself, as an imperfect type of the divine.

It is true, that even in the primitive structure of things, we discover much which at first shocks us. Physical pain in many aspects appears not as an accident and an abuse, but as if definitely designed. Fierce beasts are observed to be armed for inflicting misery, and the instincts of one creature are often directed to destroy the quiet and comfort of another, which may seem not to have earned hostility. On this subject whole volumes might be written, as ample arguments have been. Here it may be sufficient to remark, that the difficulty turns on the Epicurean assumption, that Physical Ease and Comfort is the most valuable thing in the universe; but that is not true, even with brutes. There is a certain perfection in the nature of each, consisting in the full development of all their powers, to which the existing Order manifestly tends; and any one who shall speculatively reconstruct the organized world and coherently follow out his own scheme, will probably end in discerning, that the present arrangements of God are better than man could have devised. As for susceptibility to Pain, it is obviously essential to every part of corporeal life, and to discuss the question of *degree* is beyond us. On the other hand, Human capacity for Sorrow is equally necessary to our whole moral nature, and Sorrow itself is a most essential process for the perfecting of the soul. Not to have discerned the relation of Sorrow to Virtue is perhaps the most striking defect pervading all the Greek moral philosophy.

More permanent disturbance of mind is caused to good men who have no extensive view of human nature, nor habit of mental analysis, from the prevailing wickedness of mankind. It avails not here to say that human goodness is only a relative idea, and that however much better men were, we should still think them bad, since our standard would have risen. In a mere moral view indeed such a reply suffices; for all tribes of men have some morality. Those who are ferocious towards foreigners, are often tender-hearted towards their own people; and the difference of savage from civilized virtue is one of degree. But religiously the case is otherwise; for there is a chasm between loving God and not loving him, serving him and not serving him. We can easily suppose such an improvement in human nature, that though all would of course be still imperfect, yet none should be irreligious: and men will ask, Why does a good God leave so large a part of mankind in irreligion? To many, this is an exceedingly severe trial of faith, because irreligion has been invested with *eternal* consequences, which binds the understanding in a net absolutely inextricable. But let the Gordian knot be cut; let it be discerned that the infinite cannot be the meed of the finite;—then, while we lament the actual state of the world, we shall not find it hard to understand that it has necessarily resulted from the independence of the human Will; which *must* be left free, and capable of resisting the Divine Will; otherwise we should not be men, but brutes or machines. Assuming then that evil is finite, transitory, and only an essential condition towards the attainment of higher and permanent good, we find nothing in human wickedness, however intense, and whatever misery it causes, to inspire rational doubt of the divine Goodness.

That there is abroad among us an unsound view of supreme Goodness, (or *benevolence*, as it is called,) cannot, I think, be denied. It is akin to that spurious humanity, which so shudders at putting a criminal to death, as to prefer keeping him alive even where there is no human hope of his being recovered to virtue, but every probability of his incurring more and more desperate hardness. The benevolent man is supposed to shrink from inflicting bodily pain on any one, whether for his own good, or as a necessary process for defending others : and where this morbid notion prevails, we must expect people to be much shocked at the broad facts of the Natural History of animals, to say nothing of Man himself. But against such errors those will never be able successfully to contend, who run into the opposite and hideous extreme, of representing God as an everlasting torturer; and would tell us that this only shows His strength of mind. Pain and Suffering undoubtedly are among God's most efficacious means for perfecting all his creatures, and, not least, man; but they must needs be with Him *means*, not *ends*, if we are to attribute to Him in any sense that which we are able to recognise as Goodness; and consequently, they must be in His plans either partial and subordinate, or finite and transitory. All Theology which contradicts this, darkens and distorts the face of God to us.

7. SENSE OF WISDOM.

As long as we conceive the Deity to possess a crude omnipotence, capable of effecting everything instantaneously by his mere will or fiat, there is no room for attributing *Wisdom* to him in regard to processes and means. To absolute omnipotence there are no difficulties, no antagonist powers; and it is uncertain whether the idea of Wisdom could then be suggested, at least as different from Goodness. We see Goodness in the choice of the *ends*, Wisdom principally and perhaps solely in the direction of the *means*. The early philosophers of the East appear to have discerned, that it is impossible to hold a belief of the divine goodness, together with this absolute omnipotence : human sin and misery are an insuperable difficulty. They however looked for the antagonist, which limits the divine omnipotence, in *matter*; attributing to it inherent perversity, of which he made the best, though the best was bad. At this we may smile : yet it perhaps was only expressing in their own dialect a thought fundamentally the same as our own, at least as far as religion is concerned. We now distinctly understand that the *human Will* is the antagonist; and how formidable a one, daily experience shows. The course of History however more and more witnesses to us of the divine Wisdom, which provides for the final triumph of Truth and Right.

This is an ocean too deep to be sounded. *We* advance farther into it than our forefathers; our distant posterity may advance beyond us ; but most eminently do we need wisdom ourselves, if we are to judge of Divine wisdom. We do nevertheless see, that the instincts of men, leading them to form family connections, to unite into States, to engage in active industry, to conquer foreigners, to carry on commerce, to indulge in luxury, to enjoy poetry, to study science,—mixed, as they all are, with every sort of imperfection, polluted with sin and crime or sullied with vanity and folly ;—still, in the long run, advance nations towards a higher and higher level. Some nations sink, while others rise; but the lower and the higher levels are both generally ascending. Such, at least in my apprehension, is the testi mony of History rightly interpreted.

Yet our belief in the Wisdom of God, as in his Goodness, is assuredly a matter of *à priori* discernment, by no means depending on learned arguments. We cannot conceive of such a Being, *and perceive that there are difficulties to be overcome, against which mere Omnipotence cannot be invoked,*—and not attribute to him Wisdom that shall ultimately overcome those difficulties. And on this turns what is called the Divine Government of the world, or, the course of Providence. Incipient speculation vainly endeavoured to trace in detail the marks of the divine government in the history of short periods and in special events. The error of this consists in overlooking the nature of the combat ; namely, that the human mind, which is to be conquered by the divine, must nevertheless preserve its liberty, and be *freely* conquered. This so nearly approaches a contradiction, that it may well be a hard and lingering struggle ; and in the course of it, the imperfect will of man has its own way against that of God so frequently, that to appeal to separate events in proof of the divine government can only mislead. Abandoning however this, Faith falls back on the *à priori* certainty that He whose Designs are visible in the structure and adaptation of the things of this world, knew *what* he was designing, and would not have done anything, except for ultimate good results. To imagine that the Creator was *under constraint* to create the world, is in fact to deny the doctrine of a personal designer and to run back into that of a blind Fate ; and as we must suppose him to have acted not only freely but with a foresight what it was that he was doing, we cannot believe in a designing mind at all without inevitably implicating it with that of Divine Providence.

An exaggerated and corrupt view of the divine wisdom is found in that spurious optimism, which extends the doctrine that "Whatever is, is best," to those details in which human folly and wickedness are peculiarly manifest. Allowance however must be made for incautiousness of language or love of paradoxical statement. Some will say that a deed of cruelty was "for the best," not meaning to include the perpetrator among those benefited. And not only so, but our very sins are often overruled to ourselves as well as to others. But to say that we "could not have done better than sin," is at once self-contradictory and morally corrupting : it was not sin, if we could not have done better.

8. REVERENCE.

The affections of Awe, Wonder, Admiration, with which religion began, did not denote any necessary or fixed belief in a personal Deity, nor any activity of mind in him who experienced them. The perceptions of Order, Design, Goodness and Wisdom, do bring in a personal Deity, but they belong to the intellect more than to the soul : and all this is rather preparation for religion, than religion itself. But after that preparation, the legitimate result is the rise of a totally new affection, the ground of which is *Reverence* towards the mighty inscrutable Being whom we have discerned in the Universe. Here the Soul once more begins to be affected, but no longer passively : it is taking its first step into self-conscious moral action : thus Reverence is the beginning of true religion. He who reverences God is a religious man, and whatever his other ignorances or defects, is an accepted worshipper.

It is hard to judge how far it is possible in an unenlightened intellect for Reverence to be directed towards the Deity without a consciousness that His eye is simultaneously upon us. One may imagine a barbarian mind to adore God, just as we might admire a mighty prince whom we saw pass by, though we knew not that he saw us. But undoubtedly this is impossible to a moderately cultivated mind ; and the most decisive moral effects produced by the devotional posture of the soul depend on consciousness that it has met the eye of God.

Nevertheless, it is not to be imagined that Reverence rises at once into high intelligent worship, and that Spirituality is forthwith generated. Ages rolled by in the history of our race without such a disentanglement of truth from error as to allow of this, and many years pass with most of us individually. The first great revolution wrought in religion, may be traced back even to Polytheistic times, as with Æschylus and Herodotus, when the union commences between it and morality; that is, when it is discerned that the great Power or Powers who preside over Nature must needs possess *Moral* qualities *similar to our own*, though every-way more perfect; after this, every elevation of the standard of human morals leads also to a more elevated conception of God's moral nature. This it is first which raises what was Paganism into rational *Religion*, and justifies us in using the word *Reverence*; nevertheless, for a long time (perhaps) the worshipper has still no vivid idea that morality concerns itself with the heart; consequently, he does not conceive of God as concerning himself with the human heart, and God abides as it were wholly outside of his nature. A man who commits murder, who gives false judgment for bribes, perjures himself, seduces his neighbour's wife, defrauds his ward, or violates the rights of friendship and hospitality—is believed to incur the anger of God: but those whose ordinary moral conduct is correct have no consciousness of guilt, and are able to yield to Him decorous and sincere reverence on every stated occasion.

Where the Will is strong, and Passions or Temptation moderate; where the person is engaged in outward action, and little disposed to self-inspection; a man is satisfied with his own attainments, and feels no inward pressure after a higher and higher perfection. This is often reproved as Self-righteousness by spiritual people; unduly, I think; for the mind of the worshipper is not engaged in a reflex act of self-admiration. Moreover, in that stage of low development of the soul, a certain self-complacency is perhaps undistinguishable from that which we call a Good Conscience: but this subject is important enough to deserve afterwards a fuller discussion. Many estimable people spend the best part of their lives in this stage, without any growth of soul, perhaps exemplary in social morals, and every way amiable, with the intellectual wish to be truly religious, but with no hungering and thirsting after righteousness. They so far rise above the description just given, as to feel that to *plan* a sin is itself a sin; but God is with them an Avenger, not a spiritual Rewarder: they reverence Him indeed, but do not at all aspire to love Him. Natural Affection and other good feelings move them more than either the pure Conscience or the Soul; spiritually they are in a puerile stage; their religious faculties are uncorrupted and immature: and, on the whole, happy is the country (if there be one in the whole world so favoured) which has the great mass of its population in this state. Religion is to them, according to its old-fashioned etymology, a bond or band; recognized indeed by their conscience, and in so far internal; yet not a living inward force. It rather restrains externally, than animates them: still, when we see what human nature is and has been, we must count this a great step forward. Of this respectable and worthy class, (if we may be allowed to borrow a harsh metaphor from a poetical book,* which is habitually explained as allegorical,) we may say: "We have a little sister, and she has no breasts." To drive away from our sympathies by haughty airs of superiority those who are only in an earlier stage of advancement than ourselves, is so harsh and so unwise, as to be a spot of Pharisaism upon us.

With the improvement of moral doctrine, Reverential worship will become more elevated; or conversely, improved religious doctrine may elevate morality. In the stage of which we treat, neither of the two has living power, and no growth can be counted on: both wait upon external influences, and morality *chiefly* depends on the political institutions and social circumstances. Yet the link between the Conscience and the Soul is already formed, and the two are now likely to thrive or to pine together.

The commonest degraded form of Reverence is that of substituting artificial mysteries for the real mystery; which is, God in God's *own direct* works: a perversion, which leads the worshipper to venerate something different from, and of course lower than, the highest ideal of the Good and Great which his soul is capable of forming: and this "something" is generally in modern days, God in *human* works. Such a corruption is evidently an inward and spiritual Idolatry; and must dwarf the soul, giving to it a rigid and unnatural form, in which it may indeed live, but can make no thriving growth. To expand the separate branches of this case, would be to enter into a universal crusade against erroneous religions in detail; but by way of preface to some admissible remarks, it will be useful to consider what is the *essence* of Idolatry, in the bad sense which the word ought always to bear.

Infinity, or the Absence of Bounds, is an idea wholly relative to the mind which contemplates it. That of which I believe that I cannot know the bounds, is practically boundless to me;† and

---

* Song of Solomon, viii. 8.
† Infinity or Boundlessness is, I presume, a negative idea, as much

if there were a being revealed to my senses, so godlike in all his attributes, that in no direction could I discover infirmity or expect ever to discover it, he might become the object of devout reverence, as exalted and as pure as that which I am capable of rendering to an invisible and eternal God.

On this account, a child even of an age at which the recognition of a God is impossible, is by no means necessarily in the state of an Atheist. At least the child of a tender and wise parent exercises towards that parent in some degree the principal actions of the religious soul;—reverence, love, trust, hope, belief. Not only is this the genuine preparation for true devotion towards God, but as it is the only possible devotion of which the child is capable, so it is the highest and best state. Moreover, we are thus led to a right view of Idolatry. Such a child, at first sight, might seem to be an Idolater; inasmuch as he worships for a god one who is not God: but this is an error. To worship as perfect and infinite one whom *we know* to be imperfect and finite, this is Idolatry, and (in any bad sense) this alone. Evidently it is degrading and pernicious to lavish acts of devotion on one whom we perceive not to deserve them; for it is an unnatural, uncalled-for self-abasement, tending to lower our ideas of goodness or greatness. Thus, to adore even with very qualified reverence a Mercury or a Bacchus, in whom no sort of moral excellence was believed to reside, is fitly stigmatised as Idolatry. But if any simple Roman, forming in his mind a certain not very high moral image of "Jupiter Best and Greatest," yet imputed to him no conduct or tempers, in which he himself discerned imperfection; then, we might indeed lament his dimness of sight, we might think him in a puerile condition, but (remaining in this respect as he is) it would be better for him to worship than not; just as the child is better for reverencing the human parent, and rendering to him whatever of adoration is within his compass. The old Jew must generally have conceived of Jehovah as a respecter of persons and of nations, and as in many ways partial, capricious, arbitrary and even fierce; in so far, the Jew misjudged, and his misjudgment was not harmless; yet this, being unknown to him,

as any can be; yet no one need therefore shrink to call God *Infinite*, or fancy that he gains any thing by substituting the word *Absolute*. Infinity, in the abstract, is only an attribute of those things which to us are infinite, as the Ocean, the Heaven, or God; and as *it plainly does not exhaust our whole conception* of any of these things, I cannot imagine how any one fears that he shall admit God to be a negation if he hold that God is Infinite, and that Infinity is a negation.

was no reason to *him* for not worshipping. Nor yet to *us*, as bystanders, can it be a reason for deprecating his worship. For a man can but adore his own highest Ideal ; to forbid this is to forbid all religion to him. If therefore *Idolatry* is to mean anything wrong and bad, the word must be reserved for the cases in which a man degrades his Ideal by worshipping something that falls short of it. As long as this is *not* done, two worshippers may indeed differ widely from one another in the depth or truth of their views concerning the Best and Highest, as Jacob differed from Paul ; in which case he who has the purer insight will have the holier and nobler religion ; yet the religion of each will be the only right thing for each, and the more ignorant of the two is Superstitious perhaps, but not Idolatrous. Indeed every one of us who is religious at all, is superstitious, exactly in the proportion in which error is implicated in his religion ; and wholly to escape this is not given to man.

But a man may lower his Ideal, and become a degraded Idolater, in other ways besides that of old Polytheism. It matters not whether I worship Mercury, while my conscience tells me that there are things in him that do not deserve honour ; or whether I force my heart to submit in devout reverence to the whole of an ecclesiastical system, against parts of which my conscience would protest. The same plea of Authority, which says to the superstitious Christian, "It is your duty to suppress the misgivings of conscience, because we have External and Ostensible claims on your faith," is equally available on the side of the Pagan Priest, for the worship of Ganesa or of Bacchus. The same boldness of simple and true faith, by which the born votary of Paganism breaks away from the errors of his national creed, to follow the revelations of God in his soul, will also *both authorize and require* the Romanist to reject the Authority of his Church, and the Protestant that of his Bible, whenever the one or the other inculcates upon him as divine that which falls beneath the highest Ideal of his soul. To do otherwise is Ecclesiolatry or Bibliolatry : this is the modern Heathenism, which, having supplanted the ancient, has for ages imitated the old craft of slandering as Atheists or Infidels (*i. e.. unfaithful, treacherous*) all who aspire to a higher and purer worship. Among ourselves, Bibliolatry makes pretensions so haughty, of being alone pure, alone pious, alone spiritual, alone infallible, that I feel it a duty to encounter the pain of exposing the erroneous foundation of men, many of whom I honour, esteem and love as the excellent of the earth.

ENGLISH IDOLATRY.

That part of English society which has most diligently cultivated religious feeling by the aid of the Hebrew and Christian Scriptures, allows wide currency to the speculative notion, that the highest attainable certainty to man (if indeed there be any other certainty at all) concerning spiritual matters, is that which the testimony of the Bible affords. This is a natural exaggeration flowing out of their just love for a noble book ; but a very little calm thought is sufficient to dispel the error, which is neither small nor harmless. No heaven-sent Bible can guarantee the veracity of God to a man who doubts that veracity. Unless we have independent means of knowing that *God knows the truth, and is disposed to tell it to us,* his word (if we be ever so certain that it is really his word) might as well not have been spoken. But if we know, independently of the Bible, that God knows the truth, and is disposed to tell it to us, obviously we know a great deal more also. We know not only the existence of God, but much concerning his character. For only by discerning that he has Virtues similar in kind to human Virtues, do we know of his truthfulness and his goodness. Without this *à priori* belief, a book-revelation is a useless impertinence : hence no book-revelation can (without sapping its own pedestal) authoritatively dictate laws of human Virtue, or alter our *à priori* view of the Divine Character. The nature of the case implies, that the human mind is competent to sit in *moral* and *spiritual* judgment on a professed revelation ; and to decide (if the case seem to require it) in the following tone : "This doctrine attributes to God, that which we should all call harsh, cruel, or unjust in Man ; it is therefore intrinsically inadmissible : for if God may be (what we should call) *cruel,* he may equally well be (what we should call) *a liar* ; and if so, of what use is his Word to us ?" And in fact, all Christian apostles and missionaries, like the Hebrew prophets, have always refuted Paganism by direct attacks on its immoral and unspiritual doctrines ; and have appealed to the consciences of heathens, as competent to decide in the controversy. Christianity itself has thus practically confessed, what is theoretically clear, that an authoritative *external* revelation of moral and spiritual truth, is essentially impossible to man. What God reveals to us, he reveals *within,* through the medium of our moral and spiritual senses. External teaching may be a training of those senses, but affords no foundation for certitude. Our certainty in divine truth cannot be more certain than the veracity of our inward organs of discernment; and must undoubtedly be far less, if it is liable to be overthrown also by historical, geographical, or psychological errors involved in the immense sweep of argument which undertakes to prove that *the Bible is infallible.*

The search after the Philosopher's Stone or after Perpetual Motion, was a less pitiful imbecility, than this modern notion that fallible man can, by selecting his own Bible or his own Church, or by demonstrating the infallibility of the system in which he was educated, get rid of his natural fallibility. It obviously cleaves to him like his own personality, and infects every decision at which he arrives. Those therefore use words of wild boasting, who with superior pity look down on another as "without chart and without compass on the deep," because he does not admit the infallibility of the Bible.

Take any practical question of detail, as, "How shall I conduct myself in this moral conjuncture of affairs?" or, "How ought I to think of God and feel towards Him?" and consider two ways of seeking for a reply. The one is to study the questions, in their practical limitation, by such direct insight as we have, or can get. The other method, is, *first* to master the infinitely greater and more arduous question, "Is or is not the Bible fallible?" and after determining in the negative, then to elicit its decisions on the points of doubt. But to *prove* the infallibility of a book that contains twenty thousand propositions, is evidently impossible by any testing of its contents,—a process which would need Omniscience in the inquirer. It must then either be simply *assumed* without any attempt at proof or verification (which is by far the commonest method), or it must be rested on *external credentials*, which, treating it as a sealed book, attempt nevertheless to establish *à priori* that all which it contains must be true. No man is qualified to judge on an arduous and complex argument, who does not see that the latter, even if admissible in principle, is beyond the powers of the many; and vastly more difficult to the few, than any (strictly personal) questions of practical life. But an intermediate method is highly popular; to set forth the excellence of a *great deal* in the Bible to which our *Consciences bear witness*; and then deduce that all persons are wicked, who deny the authority and infallibility of the book. This, forsooth, from those who pity, scorn or dread the man, who says that Conscience is, after all, the best guide! This from those, who are actually maintaining, that when Conscience and the Book come into collision, we must believe Conscience to be wrong and the Book right! for that is the whole meaning of its "authority;" since, until such collision arises, no practical trial of authority can be made. But in this way, every religious system can guarantee its infallibility to us. Romanism or Mohammedanism has many points which our consciences approve; therefore each of these systems is divine and infallible: therefore we are to believe the system in preference to conscience when the two clash! No internal and moral argument, appealing to conscience, can ever rightly supersede and dethrone conscieuce: in fact, a doctrine which aims at this, under the name of an "Authoritative Revelation," aims to destroy our moral sensibilities. If, *because* conscience approves something in the Bible, we are to revere the Bible; it must be conceded, that if in any thing conscience dissents, we must withhold reverence and approval.

Men of different complexions and blood, ages and countries, ranks and culture, exhibit a great agreement as to their decisions concerning moral right and wrong, when a question is proposed in such a form that no personal bias or special prejudice affects them. The same is approximately true of purely spiritual doctrines, in proportion as men become spiritually exercised, though it is far harder to get rid of special prejudice, rising out of their national creed. On the other hand, a vast experience proves, that even the ablest, best and wisest men are liable to the most extravagant delusions when they undertake to judge the general and broad question, whether a national religion is guaranteed to them by supernatural testimony. It is therefore a gross blunder to aim at greater certitude, by resting the truth of our special opinions in morals and religion, on our knowledge of the truth of our national creed. Most truly has it been said, that creeds are a geographical product: and Bibliolatry* is the British form of idolatry. One nation has been educated to believe the infallibility of a book, another of a church; each method is no doubt convenient for those who want to drill men's minds into uniformity; each may also have aided towards some external results, too valuable to be slighted: but to imagine that either mode of arbitrary assumption can conduce to religious certitude, is absurd.

---

* It must be remembered, that the result of the preceding analysis is, that Bibliolatry does not consist in reverence to the Bible, however great, as long as Conscience is too dull to rise above the Bible; but it consists in *depressing* Conscience to the Biblical standard. This is done to a fatal extent by thousands, in regard to the Old Testament, and by hundreds in regard to the New.

Our knowledge of God is limited as is our knowledge of the Infinite Heaven, by the susceptibility of (mental and bodily) eye-sight which he has vouchsafed to us. Up to the limit of such perfection as the human soul can attain, our knowledge of God may reach: no higher: and as He is infinite, and we are finite, there will always be in Him an immeasurable depth unsounded. Hence, I repeat, we have no *absolute* knowledge of him. But on the other hand, He has revealed Himself to us as to all things which pertain to life and godliness; and whoever despises as mean and insufficient that inward revelation of the heart, will never found any thing so enduring in its place, but will elabo-rately build mazes of false Theology for the wonder and contempt of future days. Whole tons of such rubbish have been shovelled away by universal consent: yet the idolaters of Church and Bible take no warning. The immediate practical mischief is, that instead of exercising his conscience to discern good and evil, the Bibliolater (in proportion to his consistency and earnestness) exercises only his logical intellect to interpret, like a lawyer, the written document proposed to him. Hence the saying attributed to Luther, (a man who in practice was by no means wedded to so degrading a maxim,) *Bonus grammaticus bonus theologus.* Why should any one exert the free energies of thought, why should he study to develop from within a knowledge of Right and Wrong, when, if his results clash with those of the book, he will have to trim and prune himself into its shape? It is easier and safer to crush inward sentiment, in order to receive Truth by testimony *from without*! This is the carnal and dense covert, under which every system of superstition in its turn has found shelter; and which, if it be not torn down, will in every age foster as much unclean-ness and cruelty in the church, as the moral light abroad in the world will allow.* In fact, experience shows that these evils will find apology or active support with thousands of the pious.

* It is instructive to see how in every age men adopt the specious tone of dignified rebuke and threat against religious improvement. Euripides puts the following into the mouth of Greek orthodoxy: "The Divine might is slow to come forth, but sure nevertheless; and it chastises those mortals who foster insensate obstinacy, who from mad Opinion refuse to exalt the institutions of the Gods. Subtly and perseveringly do They hide their foot in ambush, and catch the impious man. For never should we indulge convictions and meditations which are wiser than established practices. For cheap is the effort to believe that the Divinity, whatever else He may be, is powerful: and what comes from long time is esta-blished eternally and inheres in Nature." Eur. Bacch. 882—896; and to the same effect, 385—396, and elsewhere.

The *impiety* here rebuked consisted in disapproving of Bacchanalian orgies! That such rebukes often came from grave sincerity is beyond a

The alarm and anxiety felt by so many well-meaning persons at every thing which breaks down the sacredness of the Letter, would be abated by a calm retrospect at the very same event in apostolic times. *Then* also there were two classes who cast off allegiance to the Law,—those who spurned restraint on their passions, and those who were spiritually enlightened to desire and demand a higher rule. The latter are unseen or distrusted; a few of the former suffice to raise a wild outcry about "Antinomianism." Yet it was no divine voice heard by the outward ear, in the midst of clouds and flame, that abolished the Law to the mind of Paul and his Jewish fellow-converts. Believing that that Law had actually thus been once sanctioned on Mount Sinai, they yet held that it was now repealed to them by the inward gift of the Spirit, which more than fulfilled and hereby superseded the Law. For this they were regarded as impious; for this Paul underwent slander and persecution from the Judaizers, who in such doctrine saw only lawlessness and contempt of all things sacred. In the Gentile Church time has built up a new law of the letter; and now, as before, two parties revolt against it, some to use their liberty as an occasion for the flesh, others to stand fast in the liberty wherewith God has made them free, and avoid being again entangled in the yoke of bondage. The noise and rudeness of a few profligates throw quiet people into panic, and too often drive them into uncharitableness and formality. Let law abide for the constraint of the lawless:—the duties of the magistrate are unquestionable:—but let not spiritual sentiment be dwarfed under pretence of training it. Three centuries of Protestantism demonstrate, that the supremacy of the letter will never give an end of bitter controversy, nor any of that enlarged wisdom and recognition of goodness, in which we are so scandalously deficient.

doubt. Elsewhere the same speaker is made to say: "Oh! blessed is he, whose God is good (or, who is favoured by the god); Who, initiated in Divine ceremonies, Hallows his life by rule, And yields his soul to the sacred Troop, And roams with Bacchus on the mountains, In pure sanctifications."

If this surprise the English reader, let him be assured, that a future age will be equally surprised to look back on our Christian Sects; which (with small exception) labour each with deep purpose to inculcate as divine and immovable all that is in each *established*, and agree to denounce as impious any one who in good earnest gives his heart to search after "the good and acceptable and perfect will of God."

CHAPTER III.

THE SENSE OF SIN.

WHERE the traditionary impure influences of early crude religion have been happily worked off, to such a degree that the new elements are allowed to display their proper tendencies; no sooner does it become distinctly conceived that the God of nature is the God of our consciences, and that all *wrong* doing is frowned on by Him, than the two new terms Holiness and Sin are needed. To murder or to betray, are no longer merely offences against man,—which we call crime; they also offend God, and are sins. In this state were the Hebrews from even an early period; and God, as abhorring sin, was entitled by them a Holy God. Where Polytheism and its degenerate deities were honoured, such phrases could not enter the common language even of philosophers; yet, in Greece for instance, philosophers of a religious turn undoubtedly held the fundamental notion involved in them.

We cannot pretend to sound the mystery, *whence come* the new births in certain souls. To reply, " The Spirit bloweth where He listeth," confesses the mystery, and declines to explain it. But it is evident that individuals in Greece, in the third century before the Christian era, were already moving towards an intelligent heart-worship, or had even begun to practise it. The most eminent extant proof of this, is in the beautiful hymn of Cleanthes to Jupiter.* Even in old Herodotus we see the cordial response of his conscience to the sentiment which he emphatically approves,—that the Gods hate and punish the desire of sin, as itself a sin: and this is the germ of all spirituality. Thus God for the first time is acknowledged as Lord of the conscience, and is conceived of as a God who searches the heart. Thus, if the

* See Note 1 to this Chapter.

thought be legitimately unravelled, Duty, from having been finite, becomes an infinite thing; thus Sin also enlarges its dimensions proportionably, and may soon assume a formidable aspect. Yet religion by no means runs forward in one stream, and we shall have to trace its separate courses.

Two very different causes may in this stage induce deep inward distress; tenderness of conscience, and unregulated passion. God is terrible to the one as abhorring, to the latter sometimes only as punishing, sin. Both believe Him to be justly angry with them; both inquire how they shall appease Him: out of which grows the totally new phenomenon of internal conflict.

If there be any side of practical religion over the perversions of which one may groan, it is this; for there is none, as to which an unmanly or cruel superstition stands in so close contact with profound and reasonable sensitiveness of conscience. There is in fact an intense contrast between the moral Self-Despair incident to every holy nature, and the unmoral Self-Degradation of the superstitious. Yet so common has the latter been in the history of the world, so hidden in the sacred recesses of the heart is the former ordinarily kept, that the mass of a nation in which intellectual cultivation is gaining general diffusion, is apt to mistake the former for the latter; and even religious teachers, while healing the deep wounds which superstition has planted in the soul, very often skin them over with callosity. Nowhere is truth and error, right and morbid feeling, so miserably entangled: nowhere is it harder to vindicate the sensibilities of reasonable devotion, without seeming to lay a foundation for despicable superstition. But let it be remembered, that, as human characters are not purely separable into two classes, the good and the bad, so neither is human religion; and in those who are manifestly very superstitious, there may be a larger share of true devotion than in the calmer and clearer intellects which despise their follies: for clearness of thought by no means necessarily implies depth of soul, and may be joined with a very partial experience of the most impulsive principles in man.

The reader must be many times cautioned against supposing that I am about to detail processes of heart through which I imagine that all persons pass or ought to pass. No two men, no two nations, no two ages, are quite alike. A Natural History does not imply the description of any individual, but of a very few leading types which collectively represent the nature in its divergencies: and I regard these pages as only *an Essay towards* the object in question. Moreover, I am aiming principally at that, which will conduce to an understanding of practical truth and error, of spiritual realities and their counterfeits.

If the sense of sin becomes acute, so that misery follows without any action of Shame and Fear from man's knowledge of our guilt, then, whatever the character of that guilt, the heart is not yet hardened and hopelessly depraved. Total and (to human eyes) hopeless depravation is in the case of *triumphant selfishness.* In the habitual seducer of innocence, the conscious trader in vice, the avaricious poisoner, the hired ruffian,—the moral paralysis may seem complete. But not only so : in the pampered and proud man, who has long regarded his own ease and indulgence as the sole end for which he and those around him live,— the voluptuary upon principle,—(even though he commit no crime and can be taxed with no physical vice or excess),—the Soul must be so torpid, that ordinarily nothing but external calamities can rouse it. For Selfishness is the direct antagonist to the Sense of the Infinite : the former cramps us within our own miserable body, the latter spreads one abroad into the universe. The thoroughly selfish know not what Sin means, nor what God means, nor that they have got a Soul : if once they break the bounds of Habit, so as to fall into crime, mere teaching without training is utterly useless. Like fierce or crafty beasts, they need a cage and club, not a religious instructor.

The most respectable passion of which such are susceptible, is Shame after detection : but to such lamentable cases allusion is here made, solely in order to remark that Shame must not be confounded with Remorse. Shame is a moral suffering, excited by the eye of man ; Remorse* is a convulsion of the Soul, as it consciously stands under the eye of God : thus Remorse alone has anything to do with our present discussion.

Remorse for sin does certainly prhove tat the Soul is not dead ; just as the agony of a wound proves be body to be alive : in the same sense only is the one and the other to be desired. But Remorse is not a sanctifying principle : on the contrary, it is an exceedingly dangerous one ; and the Soul may die of it, as truly as the Body of acute pain. It often drives men to despair, to frenzied iniquity, and thus to final hardness of heart ; consequently, such tenets of (what is called) Religion as artificially

---

* I use this word according to what seems to me its genuine sense ; that is, *not* to mean any or all sorrow for sin, but *that* misery of self-condemnation which follows the idea that the evil which we have done is *irreparable*: thus Remorse is closely akin to Despair. Some portion of it clings to the offender even after he has attained a sense of pardon, if his offence seem to have caused irretrievable mischief *to others.*

aggravate it are a horrible calamity. Its milder action impairs
spiritual life in some natures more than all other causes : in its
coarser forms it generates Asceticism and every kind of soul-
burdening and body-destroying superstition. I find it too painful to pursue details of the latter kind, and see that it cannot be
needed : most readers know enough of these hideous perversions.
It will suffice to confine ourselves to the purely internal results
of the milder sort of Remorse, which is often called a Bad Conscience before God.

The moral uses of religion are, to enliven man's conscience,
strengthen his will, elevate his aspirations, content him with
small supplies to his lower wants, rouse all his generous tendencies, and hereby ennoble him altogether; but it can do none of
these things effectually, except when it keeps him steadily looking into the face of the Infinite and Infinitely Pure One. Now
this is to most persons exceedingly hard. The mere formalist,
in whom spirituality is quite undeveloped, does not see God as a
heart-searcher at all : and long after that stage is passed, and
men are intellectually quite alive to this point, they yet continue,
in their devotions, as it were to turn only their *side*, and a blind
eye, towards God. They speak *at* Him, but not *to* Him; for
they instinctively flinch from His holy gaze. This is ordinarily
true, even if no particular sin distresses the conscience; but if
they have been busying themselves to improve their conduct, if
they have made solemn resolutions,—and broken them,—it is
harder than ever to meet God. Especially, if with active good-
will they have tried to amend their inward faults ;—to repress
evil desire, to cultivate meekness and love;—the conscience
rapidly becomes more sensitive, and taxes them with a thousand
sins before unregarded. The evil thus gets worse: the worshipper is less and less able to look boldly up into the Pure All-
seeing eye : and he perhaps keeps working at his heart to infuse
spiritual affections by some direct process, under the guidance
of the Will. It cannot be done. He quickens his conscience
thus, but he does not strengthen his soul : hence he is perpetually
undertaking tasks beyond his strength,—making bricks without
straw ; a very Egyptian slavery. He believes that he *ought* to
love his God with all his heart, and yet feels that he assuredly
does not. Nay, he is constantly breaking his resolutions, being
too lazy to resist habit or carried away by temptation. He at
length appears like a fly in a spider's web, which is the worse
entangled, the more it struggles; so that he may well seem in
danger, not indeed of insanity of intellect, but of permanently
morbid soul. If such a case becomes known to good people

around, who have had no experience of such conflicts, they imagine that a change of air and scene is wanted, and diversion of the mind :—which may sometimes really be true, if intellectual errors concerning God have complicated the case : at least I presume there is no doubt that any prolongation of so wretched a state might disorder the brain physically, especially if it interfered with sleep. Put aside such sad and extreme cases : and let us ask, What is the spiritual cure ?

Some will reply, that he needs to believe *the doctrine* of the Atonement of Christ, and of forgiveness of sins *on the sole condition* of his having Faith in it. If this is solemnly urged upon him by those whom he loves and respects, it is more than possible that he sets about self-examination to find out whether he has got Faith or not. He perhaps always believed the proposition intellectually, and he knows that numbers of irreligious men also believe it : a mere historical Faith will not do : is then *his* Faith of the right kind ? How can it be ? for Faith works by Love, and exhibits itself in Spiritual Action ; and he sees himself defective in both. To believe that he has Faith, is to believe that he is a Saint ; but he is *not* a Saint,—a sanctified one : the more he looks inwardly on himself, the worse he feels his case to be, and the clearer the proof that he has no true Faith. But what is this faith ? is it assent to a *general* proposition ? He does indeed assent, but so do the devils. Is it, assent to the *special* proposition, that the individual M. N. is forgiven through Christ ? but the question returns, How is that to be known from any authoritative book-revelation ?—Thus confusion may well become worse confounded.

No intellectual proposition, however true, can, as such, bring Peace to a wounded soul ; though it may incidentally and indirectly guide to that *action* which alone does bring peace ; namely, to an unreserved exposure of the heart to the eye of God. This is the desirable consummation, to which all the previous distress was preparatory ; and nearly all of that distress might perhaps have been avoided, if the man had been better taught. Yet no one can say how much severe goading one or another may need, before he dares to rush as it were straight into God's* presence, consciously unfaithful and uncleansed. To many a man perhaps, his own act is as one of desperation. He faces that bright and pure Sun, which seems to scorch his eyes, and says : Slay me, O God, if Thou wilt ; I deserve it ; I am miserable ; but leave me not sinful thus. Put me to shame : I *am* shameful. Behold !

* Or *Christ's* presence ; which is with the majority only a change of name. In future this will not need mention.

I hide nothing. Thou art light: expose my darkness. I will not palliate. I am worse than I know. Show me all that I am. I cannot heal myself. If I must die, I will die in Thy Light.

Oh, wonderful simplicity of Faith! he *is* faithful, and knows it not. He has trusted himself to the Judge of all the earth; he has abandoned all self-justification: his heart is broken, and is ready to welcome Mercy undeserved: he has believed in God's good will, and in His eternal purpose to destroy sin; he has himself become a real hater of sin: and,—though he knows not why,—he is therefore already in perfect peace. He has followed conscience through cloud and storm into the fiery presence of the Eternal, till fear has dropt off in His nearness. The harmony of Heaven and Earth is begun within the man's soul, because his will is subdued to God's will; and thus Self-despair, joined to Faith, has led to peace with God. He is guileless now as a child: quiet therefore and easy, though in fullest consciousness that God is reading his heart to the bottom. Before, he thought of God as a severe judge; now, he feels that he is a compassionate Father.—*Guilelessness* is the whole secret of divine peace; and happy are any who attain it without a convulsion of soul preceding. Some hearts fight longer and harder against God's full supremacy; others perhaps yield so easily, that none of this description applies: of that we shall have more to say in the next Chapter. But come how it may, this is the thing. "Blessed is he to whom the Lord imputeth not sin; *in whose spirit there is no guile.*"

The value however of this experience to the soul is great, because it now has learned how to get peace, especially if the phenomena have been brought out so sharply, that the intellect can read the case without practical error. Unhappily, most persons mix up the theories of others and fixed traditional doctrines with their own realities; and hence entanglement and frequent mischief. But, from the establishment of this guilelessness of heart, and peace flowing out of it, a new era of spiritual life necessarily commences. God himself appears practically *in a new relation,* as a Father: for though the intellect may long ago have approved that title, the soul had previously no true filial feeling: thus the case passes over into that reserved for our fourth Chapter; which it is not convenient here to pursue. But when Peace is established, the first great problem is solved. Only by meeting the gaze of God can the impure soul be purified: this had been too terrible a process: and the soul had shrunk from it. Why? first perhaps and chiefly, because it clung to the desire of palliating its offences: it did not cast itself absolutely and totally on Divine Mercy, but tried to reserve some excuse and partial justification. Hence it never attained the position of absolute dependence and self-abandonment. It desired to do its duty to God, and have a surplus of independent rights for itself. While struggling for this, it wished to be better, but not infinitely better; wished so to act, as not to incur just reproof from God, but probably did not wish to have him as a constant resident in the heart. His All-seeing eye searching the soul was submitted to as a necessity, not desired as a glorious privilege: hence when self-consciousness reached a certain intensity, peace became impossible to one who had pure and spiritual views of the divine perfection. But now, things are changed; he says calmly, "Thou, Lord, knowest thy servant;" and wonderful to write or think, the finite impure man has complacency in the pervading presence of the infinite and pure God. Now therefore a new course of sanctification may commence: for it is only by contact with God's spirit that the human spirit can possibly be sanctified.

A striking phenomenon in the history of religion, is, the struggle between the spiritual and the unspiritual elements of human nature to retain or to evade this close contact of the worshipper with Supreme Purity. Even in early Paganism it is seen how a Jupiter or a Brahma was superseded by secondary deities,—by an Apollo, a Minerva, a Ganesa, a Vishnu, a Surya, —and these in turn by others still inferior, when long-continued reverence had elevated even a secondary name into primary rank. The same pernicious principle is familiar in Christianity under the name of *Mediation*; from which it is the just boast of the Pre-Babylonian Judaism to have kept itself entirely free. By a Mediator is understood a being higher than man, but lower than God; whose avowed office is to shield the soul, conscious of its guilt, from the painful sense of God's immediate presence; to intercept the too fierce splendour of the divine countenance, and enable the soul to transact its affairs with God through the medium of God's deputy. Conjoined with this is the idea, that God himself is too high to sympathize rightly and fully with us; that he does not accurately know our infirmities, because he has not experienced them; and that we shall meet more candid allowance, and obtain mercy on better terms, from some inferior being. These two feelings,—a guilty dread of meeting God, and an unbelief of his sympathy or fair judgment,—must combine before the Mediatorial doctrine is complete. That neither of the two ought to be cherished, or treated tenderly; that on the contrary, the attempt to invent a system of religion which should

gratify and establish them, deserves to be gravely censured and
warmly deprecated;—I see not how to doubt. To imagine that
God himself does not know our infirmities, might be called mon-
strous, were it not too puerile. To suppose that we shall meet
with more allowance from one more susceptible of being tempted
like ourselves, either dishonours God, as wanting in pure and
right mercy, or unduly comforts, with the hope of mercy, him
who ought not to be comforted. On the other hand, to spare
the sinner the intense pain of confronting his God, by shutting
out the sight of God, is to thwart his only sanctification; to
which that sight is essential. The proper business of the teacher
is not to introduce a screen, which shall intercept some of the
rays of God's glory, and hinder man from seeing the true face of
God: all the effort must be the other way; to clear and
strengthen the eye, so that it may not discolour the divine
countenance with human vindictiveness. Many talk in such a
tone about "God in Christ," as though this were a Being
essentially different from the true and real God; as though Christ
did not show them God as He is, but some assumed appearance:
which is a virtual confutation of their theory.

Now where the place of Mediator is held by priests, saints, or
a Virgin, it would appear that uncompensated mischief results:
but as applied to Jesus Christ, the doctrine of Mediation is far
more perplexed, owing to the manifold and complicated tenets held
concerning his person. There are some who teach that he was
less than God, and accordingly a fit Mediator between God and
man. Where such mediation is not a mere name, received by
tradition;—where he is effectively believed to be a more lenient
judge than God;—to me it appears certain, that the belief is
purely evil. But during the healthy outburst of early Christianity, when Jesus was first brought forward as a Mediator, a
true spiritual instinct seems to have interposed against the mischief. The reverential imagination of the Church at Antioch
sublimated its One Mediator into something spiritually undistinguishable from the morally perfect and omniscient God;—
into an ever-present heart-searching Being, with eyes of fire,
sinless and separate from sinners, an omnipotent Judge, the
breath of whose lips shall slay the wicked. For the soul to present itself before such a One, was (spiritually and morally) identical with presenting itself before God the Father. Paul consequently was able truly to say : "We all with face unveiled be-
holding as in a mirror the glory of the Lord (Christ), are trans-
figured into the same image, from glory to glory, *seeing that it is
by a Lord who is Spirit.*" For his Christ and that of the Gentile

Churches was not a man whom he had seen and heard walking in Judea, nor about whom they learned from the pages of a book; but one at whom they gazed "in the mirror" of their own souls, and with whom they sought fellowship in secret meditation. This may have been, with many, a logical Polytheism : probably enough : for the Christian Church has always zealously trampled down logic, first, in grasping at spirituality, and next in ostentatious mortifying of the common understanding. As to the case before us, the Mediation was in fact made nominal, as soon as Jesus was elevated to a moral equality with God : for, except any one held the barbarous notion that the Second person of the Trinity had more sympathy with man than the First, it was equally arduous to the soul to unbosom itself to the Son, as to the Father. In point of fact, I believe that the most fruitful and living religion in Christendom has generally been found among those who most emphatically deified Christ :—and that, —because nothing short of this can neutralize the noxious doctrine of mediation, and convert it into a mere name.

Yet it must be confessed, that no one can foresee the opposites, which result in different minds from a verbal formula, which has dared to despise self-consistency.* For instance, while one, believing that "Jesus is Jehovah," (according to the unabashed Sabellianism of modern Christians,) innocently worships Jehovah under the newer name of Jesus ; another picks out of the same ample creed a permission to expect from the human sympathy of Christ a forgiveness of sins which he could not have expected from God himself. Contradictions may be believed in alternate minutes by the same mind ; but they can never be blended into a single whole, or be received by the same grasp of the soul. Hence the fate of a formal creed which admits them, is to be torn into shreds, of which each votary carries away his favourite portion, while each in name does homage to all.

But when thus in the early Gentile Church, the spirituality, which had been endangered by the mediatorial doctrine, was saved at the expense, first, of losing self-consistency, and secondly, of incurring thorny controversies, by which to this hour enmity and jealousy, confusion and every evil sentiment is propagated ; —guilty consciences, defrauded of their mediation, sought out new mediators between themselves and Jesus, now that he was felt to be the very Being, before whom guilt shudders. But the new mediators, (of whom the Virgin Mary has carried off by far the largest honour,) have only received divine worship, and have

* See Note 2 at the end of this Chapter.

never been invested by the imagination with the purely divine attributes : hence the adoration has been a gratuitous and baneful idolatry, the scandal and ruin of Christian Churches. To these mediators petitions are addressed, which could not be offered to the All Pure God. They forgive sin on easier or on other terms than He ; and the fruit of it all, is, to make the heart of the righteous sad, and to speak peace to the wicked, while continuing in his wickedness.

We return from this digression, to the case of him, who, whether he call that God whom his inmost soul discerns, by the name of Jesus or Jehovah, yet at any rate comes into direct and positive contact of spirit with his highest Ideal of Purity. Such a one has commenced to live in the Spirit ; but oh, how many derangements do old habit and ever-young passion and the world around us offer to the progress of the new life ! However, pass we all these. Suppose the worshipper faithful and brave, never swerving from his new course ; and that, animated by God's presence, his Will assumes energy so great, that all Duty is successfully performed, all temptations scornfully trodden down, so that the kingdom of God within him seems to go forth conquering and to conquer. Are then his conflicts past, and is his peace perpetual? Ought it not to be so ? Will it not perhaps be so, when the experience of one becomes available to another, and ignorance is dispelled? Be this as it may, now certainly each man seems to learn for himself from the beginning, and discovers little by little to his great discomfort what should have been known long ago from such as Paul and Luther and Bunyan. And what is this? Why, it is discovered that the Will has no power over the Affections. While *both* were in disorder, while a man's Will was half for God and half for independence from God, he did not find this out distinctly : he then blamed *his entire nature.* But now that his Will is really subdued, he begins to discern that his impulses refuse to be guided by it, and regards therefore *one half only* of his nature as diseased.* He resolves to speak with meekness ; but he finds himself excited and bitter, if not in word, yet in heart. He resolves to be

---

* "I delight in the law of God after the inward man [The Will] ; but I see *another law* in my members, warring against the law of my mind ; and bringing me into captivity to the law of sin which is in my members." Rom. vii. 22, 23. From this phenomenon, it has been almost inevitable for Christians to conceive of the right Will as a pure and divine spirit, recently infused, and the reluctant or perverse Affection as an old or corrupt nature, for which (nowadays) Adam is made to bear the blame.

chaste ; and his thoughts become impure. He resolves to worship God in spirit ; but his mind wanders into countless imaginations. He resolves to be contented ; and his heart swells
with a foolish ambition. He resolves to be humble ; but he is
mortified that somebody gave him too little honour. He resolves to be simple ; yet he said something to make himself
admired. And so all through, "when he would do good, evil is
present with him." Many persons (perhaps most) are liable to
be reduced hereby to a state of distress, scarcely less than that
from which they had escaped : especially if, from the peace for
a short time enjoyed, they fancied they were really going to be
as perfect as they sincerely entreated to be made.

Thus men, aiming at a spiritual life, often become uncontrolled in invective against the unmanageable side of their
nature,—that very side of it in which alone activity resides,—and
denounce it as totally evil and incurable. Paul calls it *a body of
death*, to which he regarded himself as miserably tied. Indeed
it may seem to be impossible that a really vehement and passionate desire after God's perfect holiness should be excited in the
human soul, and its utterance yet retain logical coherence and be
duly measured. The same Paul who so severely lashes his nature
and declares : " I myself with the mind [Will] serve the law of
God, *but with my flesh* [Affections] *the law of* SIN :" yet distinctly
shows us that he did not regard himself as responsible for this
imperfection. For he disowns this part of his nature, as not himself : " If then I do that which I would not, it is no more I that do
it, but Sin that dwelleth in me." His comfort, his sufficient comfort, is not, that Christ has atoned for it,—(that indeed might
prove too much ; for it would apply to sins of the Will, as
well as to imperfection of the Affections,)—but, that nothing but
his Will is he himself. If his Will commands his Heart not to
covet, and yet the heart will covet, Paul declares, " My flesh
has sinned, but I have not." Of course then he had nothing to
repent of : he felt grief, vexation, disappointment, but not self-
reproach : not one sting of it ; and therefore no cloud passed
between his soul and God.

It is of great importance to discern, that what is *popularly*
called, "the total depravity of human nature," is more correctly
the essential eternal imperfection of every created existence : and
that that imperfection which is strictly necessary must not be
appropriated by us as Sin. In order to be morally PERFECT, we
should need at once infinite wisdom and affections of infinite
power ; and these are the incommunicable prerogatives of God :
hence every creature,—angels and archangels, beatified saints,

and Adam fresh from his Maker's hand,—every one is morally imperfect, and, if the vulgar phraseology were justifiable, would deserve to be called *sinful*. Perfection, like omnipotence, inheres in God alone : in this sense " HE only is Holy." It is calamitous that so grave an error as the confounding of unwilling imperfection with sin should have been built up out of passionate phrases of St. Paul when the context itself shows that what he calls Sin* was not counted by him as his own deed, nor therefore needed to be repented of. This is one out of many examples of the mischief arising from the current Bibliolatry and its developments. For in consequence, upright souls which find that they are still imperfect, fall into a bad conscience, as those who have incurred guilt; and have, as it were, to begin their inward life anew by confession and repentance : and when this has happened ten, twenty, fifty times, religion becomes a round of weary groaning. Nor is it easy to suppress the persuasion, that with many this becomes a hypocritical routine, from their ceasing to strive, and becoming blunted in feeling, by too much and too hopeless confession. On the other hand, some get to hate themselves morbidly, and to be frightened away from God's presence : and may even in some distressing instances seem to have relapsed into a deplorable state of apathetic unspirituality; differing from the untaught world only in a profound, dangerous and miserable self-despair. Self-despair joined with trust in God, is a beginning of vigorous spiritual life : self-despair without hope from God is too awful to think of.

But what then is that, of which so many devout persons speak,—daily repentance and daily forgiveness? Can it be all emptiness and morbid feeling? I am far indeed from saying so. It has been laid down above, that we must distinguish between our failures through want of power in the spiritual affections, and failures from a double mind and traitorous will; and must lament indeed, but on no account scourge ourselves, on account of the former. But there is also a third class, in a manner intermediate to these two, which is not to be overlooked; namely, when we fall short of our own discerned standard through a weakness of spiritual affection which may possibly be imputed to our own

---

* Poetry must have Saxon vocables, and devotion, like common love, spurns logical exactness. When a hymn-writer chooses to say : " Yet I mourn *my stubborn will*; Find *my sin* a grief and thrall;" &c., it is useless to bid him alter " Stubborn will" into *reluctant affections*, and " Sin" into *imperfection*; and yet this, and this only, is what he really means. Nothing is left for us, but to use interpretation, whenever is the right time for using the critical faculty :—but this is *not* during moments of devotion, as to which mere words matter little.

negligences or *indolence.*   As our experience grows, our strength ought to grow, and to plead weakness is not always an adequate exculpation.   Hence sometimes the deepest confessions come from those who feel themselves competent for higher duty : a thought which was at the bottom of Paul's utterance,—"Woe is unto me, if I preach not the gospel." It is not therefore always a mark of something extravagant, when eminently holy men appear to be carried beyond bounds in their self-displeasure.   In fact, in proportion as our sphere of knowledge enlarges, so does our responsibility ; and in the farther advance of spiritual life, it may seem that the affections themselves become virtually to a great extent at our call.   Not that we are able at will to bid them exist and act, and that, in any intensity which we chose ; yet experience shows us ways of courting pure and holy feeling ; and if we apprehend that we have neglected these, we necessarily blame ourselves.   In short, OMISSION is probably the form of guilt, which is most apt to overcloud the heart, when all the better defined sins are subdued ; especially because it is often extremely difficult to ascertain whether we are or are not to blame.

And here probably there will be no hazard in affirming, that the most spiritual men have concurred in regarding the posture of self-justification and palliation as so hurtful, that they prefer to admit their own guilt, whenever there is room to suspect it. Sins of omission may be unobserved and unknown.   Waste of time and of other talents, selfishness, indolence, cowardice, negligence, self-pleasing, nay, want of sympathy, of tenderness, of meekness, may be sins of the will in *this* sense,—that if at the time of temptation our will had been in its normal vigour, it was in our power to avoid them ; but because the mind was preoccupied by something else, we did not exert ourselves ; and in the retrospect we now cannot tell what we might have done, if a holier will had been active.   The same remark will apply to those who are called to peculiarly difficult and painful duty : as a wife exposed to a drunken husband ; a father, whose constant toil cannot save his children and their mother from famine and disease : a son or a servant, perpetually harassed by capricious and overbearing rule.   The highest human virtue, when put to such trial, will constantly confess its shortcomings.   For all such sins of Omission devout spirits mourn day by day.   Frequent confession and complaint is the impulse of their nature ; and is found necessary to keep the conscience tender, and purify the heart to receive the impressions of God's near and ever-living activity.   But this is widely different from having to

repent daily of *deliberately wilful* sin ; a thing which is absolutely irreconcilable with any but a spasmodic acting of spiritual
life, and must imply a state of frequent misery proportioned
to the spiritual light and sincerity of the individual.   It may be
conceived of in one who is struggling against some fierce impulsive passion, which every day more or less overcomes him, and
causes him the bitter anguish of apparently useless repentances.
Let us pity, and if possible, aid such a one, and throw no stone
at him : God may at length make him stand firm.   But let us
not represent his unhappy and convulsive state, as the standard
life which alone can be proposed for human attainment; or confound the diffidence of the successful warrior, who dares not claim
the crown, because he thinks that he might have pushed his victory farther, with the self-reproach of the runaway soldier, whose
back is covered with dishonourable gashes. The sacred complaint
and sorrow which holy men, when they have done their best, still
daily pour forth, may be *called* Repentance,* if so they please :
but there is in it far more of the sweet and tender, than of the
bitter. It is neither remorse, nor self-reproach ; and is little else
than the outbreaking of fervent desire for a higher perfection.

Nor must we forget the danger just now hinted at, of incurring hypocrisy, by too readily confessing as sin that against
which we do not seriously intend to struggle.   Every conventional standard of duty, to which the Soul itself makes no
response, involves this danger; and those who find they are
perpetually confessing the same sins and making no progress,
have to enquire whether they are not falling into a deluding
routine.   Under the name of dreading self-righteousness, a very
self-complacent inactivity may shelter itself : nor is it to be
endured that any should argue from prevalent half-heartedness,
that no higher sanctification than their own is attainable.   The
evil of not setting our hopes of present holiness high enough, is
not unnoticed nor left without protest† in the present day.

---

* In the phraseology of the Scripture, Repentance is the *beginning* of
spiritual life, and not a daily process.   Neither μετάνοια nor μεταμέλεια
are attributed to the healthily advancing saint.

† A small volume, called "Interior Life, *designed for those who are
seeking assurance of Faith and perfect Love,*" by Thomas C. Upham,
(8th edition, 1848, New York,) has lately fallen into my hands, and by
its general spirit has greatly delighted me.

It is remarkable to see how, in the current evangelicalism, passages
of the New Testament which expressly describe the Christian walk as
sinless, (as I John ii. 1,) are wrested by partial quotation into the very
opposite. Compare verses 4, 5, 6 ; also iii. 3, 4, 6, 7, 9, 10, 20, 21, 24 ;
and indeed many other places.

There is no real humility in exaggerating the *extent* of our necessary sinfulness, a proceeding which will always both exculpate and paralyze us. Perfection is a Limit, which can never be reached, yet towards which we may approximate indefinitely. But if sin and self-reproach must be daily incurred, then, either no peace with God is possible, or else, *a heart which condemns itself* can have and ought to have peace and confidence before Him.

A conscious uprightness is obviously necessary to any spiritual peace, nor does the heart need any other testimony than its own to the fact of its uprightness. The guileless soul knows it own guilelessness. If any one press us with the objection, that we may possibly delude ourselves, by fancying that our will is with God, when in fact it is not; for that there *is* such a thing as self-delusion;—it would be enough to reply, that a universal scepticism must not be set up,—in things Spiritual any more than in the External World,—on the mere ground that the spiritual (or the outward) senses are in some persons weak or diseased. The double-minded does deceive himself; but neither does he take pains to avoid it: nor can it be pretended that he has any testimony of his conscience to his own unreserved self-searching. The veracity of our specific senses (spiritual or external) has its establishment from the self-congruity of results, and from the collateral testimonies of other minds and of lower departments of the same mind. This is not the place to enlarge on the general topic of Certitude. But we may add, the single-minded Soul is conscious how promptly it aspires after better success, the moment that failure is discerned. It is not merely vexed at the failure, (which might denote mortified self-admiration,) nor merely asks pardon, (as if more concerned with the guilt of sin, than with its inherent evil,) but while breathing to God, "Oh that my heart were as Thy heart, and that wholly," it blends hope with sorrow. Thus complaint is not self-reproach; and instead of unprofitable dark solitary repentance, it has the light of God's countenance imparting cheerfulness and strength for a new effort.

Some have so feared immoral consequences, if a man is allowed to distinguish between "himself" and his "flesh," that they have elaborately explained away St. Paul's language, (above quoted,) as said, not of himself, but of some other man,—or of himself in his old unconverted state. Yet this appears (in fact) gratuitously to increase whatever difficulty may be in the passage. For it cannot be denied that he distinctly acquits himself: to say then that the *self* so acquitted is the old unconverted one, is a preposterous way of saving morality. But unless I mistake, the prevailing desire for some such evasion has turned upon St. Paul's use of the word *flesh* in a sense very foreign to our modern notions. To me it appears to have meant all that part of his nature, which he felt *to resist and lag behind* in his efforts after God's perfection, and therefore eminently, the affections of his heart and soul. But the modern European ear no sooner hears the word *flesh*, than it thinks of sensual and other low sins, and of offences against outward morality. Let moralists then be satisfied to lay down, what is most true, that St. Paul's self-exculpation can never be applied in regard to duties which Law demands of us. For Law is not made for a righteous man, but for the ungodly and disobedient. It is addressed to the common capacities of nature, and puts forth claims on our Conduct, not on our Affections. There are morbid or very ill-trained persons, whose wills are scarcely responsible for their conduct : unless we mean to class ourselves with these, we cannot claim any exemption. If we are unable to observe even outward duties, our feebleness of Will is clearly to be blamed, and not the feebleness of Spiritual Affections : thus we have incurred guilt.

To maintain a Good Conscience before God, and not before man only, is the first condition of all spiritual progress. If the divine life in man is to grow steadily and healthily, it is absolutely essential to have an abiding peace ; for, as was said, without this the soul will not and cannot meet the eye of its God often enough and regularly enough to feel its ever-purifying influence. But the difficulty here arises,—how are we to distinguish between the testimony of a *Good Conscience*, and the complacency of *Self-Righteousness*? It cannot be said that they are discriminated by there being no self-contemplation in the former ; for although this need not be prominent, yet it not only may exist, but probably must be more and more active with experience and self-knowledge. Yet, that self-righteousness is a real and not an imaginary evil, is very clear.—It may help us farther to investigate the subject, if we consider wherein that evil consists. Surely it is, that the moment we begin to admire ourselves, we are satisfied with the state of goodness already attained, and cease (for so long) to aspire after anything higher : thus the life-blood of the soul is arrested, and putrefying stagnation is to be feared. If so, self-righteousness is not the black and fatal mark of bad and perverse men only, but obviously besets all men at all times ; and it does not consist so much in thinking highly of ourselves, as in not caring to be better : for the humblest saint becomes virtually self-righteous, as soon as he ceases to aspire towards a higher goodness. Such a view of the case not only removes all wonder that this blight of the soul should cling so firmly to us as holy men confess, but, if I do not mistake, will show more distinctly its intimate nature.

First then, we impute Self-righteousness as a sin, chiefly where Self-consciousness has been developed; for this is the stage in which there ought to be life and growth; and its evil is, that it thwarts these. Hence it is winked at as scarcely an offence, in that embryo state of religion in which growth cannot be expected. Stagnation, or mere cold-blooded life, is the natural condition of those who are under the LAW, which is an infantine stage; as also of those who are children in years: so it seems not worth while to censure a moderate self-righteousness in such. Perhaps indeed the difference between it and a good conscience is in that stage not yet developed: hence if a mere Old-Testament saint rejoices in the testimony of his conscience, it is apt to be in a self-righteous tone. But when a warmer and more active life of the soul has commenced, then a check to its current cannot be endured without mischief, and Self-complacency manifests itself as a grievous evil.

Secondly, it now comes to differ widely from a Good Conscience, inasmuch as the self-complacent man measures his present attainments with *some arbitrary finite standard*, (which is pronounced to be *adequate*,) and admires or approves himself as a result of the comparison. The standard assumed may be the conventional routine, which in a particular religious society is held to characterize Piety; or may be a sort of average, struck from the apparent goodness of men in general, or may be an invention of his own: but in all cases the standard is finite, and is already reached by him. But the sacred happiness of a heart which knows it is known of God, is not derived from approving its own attainments, but from the very acting of its insatiable desires, and from its sympathy with the Source of life and joy. Its outcry is after Perfection. It longs after God's own holiness: for this it would give Earth and Heaven. It no sooner effects one conquest, than it aspires after another. If God would offer to make it at once and wholly perfect, it would eagerly catch at the offer. For while it does *not* renounce the world, in any such sense as not to have a thousand objects of worldly interest and desire; yet the One desire,—to please God,—so predominates over all, that for personal attainment, the soul counts all things as in comparison valueless. And (where the spiritual stage of development has been reached) the consciousness of this infinite longing to be more and more like to the Only Perfect one seems to be the essence of a Good Conscience. He who breathes forth this steady desire after God's holiness, he is upright, he is reconciled, he is humble : and is truly in peace of conscience, even when most full of sacred contrition. He has no finite standard of goodness : for although what he dimly imagines as Perfection is only a limited idea of his own mind, it is both above what he has yet reached, and it rises the moment he seems about to reach it. This state of things may even be called the exact reverse of self-righteousness,—which is stagnation : in fact, the soul is probably so far from self-complacency, as to look with much severity on its own shortcomings; because it measures them with the grace and mercy of God which it has known, and feels how much He may justly expect of it.

Those who are practically ignorant how spiritual men measure the guilt of their sins, whether of omission or of commission, are apt to attribute hypocrisy to their confessions. I do not doubt, there *is* sometimes that insincerity which is implied in imitation : there is occasional morbid exaggeration of feeling : there is, perhaps very often, an exaggeration of phrase, suggested by the mere vehemence of pure desire. But in the last case, a super-cilious pity is ill bestowed. One who (deeply and sincerely) sorrows even over abandoned and conquered sin, and over his unwilling infirmities, provided that he still maintains a peaceful conscience and sense of reconciliation, breathes a freer atmo-sphere than his critics. He has learnt to rejoice in a sense of Mercy ;—a joy which no one fully tastes, who does not think of himself as a pardoned criminal. In proportion to the tenderness of his conscience and the depth of his self-condemnation is his estimate of the wonder of that Love which has freely forgiven him. So full of sacred refreshment is this sense of Mercy, that even confession of old sin (if there be no unretrieved wrong to others which barbs his self-reproach) becomes an acceptable pain, because of the invigorating confidence in God's compassionate long suffering, which it nurtures within. Free Grace is a sound delightful to his heart, and wakes up a song of sweet and lowly thanksgiving.

Against coarse external and stupid Pharisaism, no protest is here needed : but where a spiritual standard of action is used, yet a fixed and arbitrary one which justifies self-satisfaction, a man is not necessarily proud and puffed up or overbearing towards the more guilty, and it may be very unjust to call him Pharisaic. The danger from his self-complacent repose increases, no doubt, with the activity of his self-consciousness ; and in any case, so long as it is by approving his own attainments that he escapes spiritual conflict, his heart remains comparatively as stony ground. No soft dews from heaven can sink in there, no roots of penitence strike deep into the soil, no spiritual affections bud and bloom forth under the beams of the Sun of Mercy. Only after he has felt that nothing but God's immeasurable long-suffering can suit his case, will rills of spiritual Love bubble forth out of the depths of his bruised heart. But now, if he does not in theory hold Mercy to be limited, yet he feels no need to draw largely on it himself. He is forgiven little and he loves little. Perhaps he reveres God sincerely, and approves of all that is right, holy and lovely: but his affections are not drawn out actively after God and His holiness; and so long, the most energetic spirituality does not seem to be possible in him. Nevertheless, if he is earnest, if he loves truth more than self-justifying, an increase of self-consciousness will tend to humility and to spiritual growth, not to self-righteousness, pride, stagnation, and hardness of heart.

In the present discussion, regard has hitherto been had to the progress of a Soul not deliberately sinful, but falling into an evil conscience, with all its discomforts or miseries, while striving with more or less honesty in the right direction. But what of one, which is stung by the distinct knowledge that it has again and again sinned wilfully; nay, in spite of much light and many resolutions? Suppose a man to have lived for weeks and months in conscious sin, of course unable to approach God, with soul dark and crushed, knowing that he ought to repent, and yet not able to repent. But one day, he knows not how or why, (in part, it may be, because he has *forgotten* his worst sins, so that they have ceased to trouble him,) his heart is drawn into a strange boldness, and rises into some sort of prayer or praise,—as perhaps on the occurrence of some happy external event, which gives him serenity and gladness. What is to be said of this? Is he very presumptuous? Should he be told to go and *repent first?* Is a long course of confession, probation and penance essential? This is interesting enough to deserve some discussion.

Christian writers will probably with one voice declare that a heathen at his first conversion (and by parity of reasoning, one who has all his life hitherto lived without any spiritual religion) will be right and wise in ignoring the past course of iniquity as an ugly dream. They encourage him to " put off the old man" by a single effort, and " put on the new ;" to spurn with disgust and shame, but without distinct and separate acts of repentance, the whole scene of darkness and folly; to believe that God freely forgives him everything past, and henceforth to fix his eyes and heart on all things that are pure and good and lovely. And the wisdom of this is manifest. For no man is made better by dwelling on the details of his own iniquity : either it will accustom him to evil, or it will horribly discourage him. Dark and weak as is one who just begins to breathe a purer air, and to raise his spirit towards the Father of spirits, even the fond dream that he is now all at once about to pass into blissful purity, would scarcely be more than is wanted to stimulate and confirm his new life. No one is so ignorant and cruel, as to insist that this man's memory shall rake up one by one all his misdeeds, in order to make adequate confession of them before God. In fact, if possible, he cannot do better, for the present at least, than utterly to forget them all.

Yet, strange to say, this principle is by very many reasoners quite reversed, when the case is that of one to whom a personal religion is not wholly new. If his resolutions have proved too weak for his passions, or, in spite of intellectual convictions that he ought to be religious, he has become hardened into neglect of God by the occupations of business or calls of pleasure; such a one, it is often imagined, not only has harmed his own soul, but has in some sense defrauded the most High. A ledger (as it were) is supposed to be kept, in which all his offences are duly entered ; and a special process is requisite for obliterating, one by one, the items of his gross debt. Confession of each separately to the Searcher of hearts is thought to be the smallest part of the necessary ordeal : Romish religion even adds, that the details of iniquity must be told out to a fellow-man; a practice which is not only enslaving but grievously corrupting. All this however proceeds upon an extravagant misconception of the nature of sin, as if it had in itself a permanent existence exterior to the soul, and when subdued there, had still to be destroyed somewhere else.

There has indeed been much needless discussion on the question, *How we know* of the connexion between Repentance and Forgiveness ? Neither the intellectual nor the practical answer is really obscure. *Intellectually*, we of necessity hold that the highest human perfection is the best type of the divine. Hence, where human morality is low and immature, where revenge is regarded as a sweet and lawful satisfaction, there men believe that God must (in all cases) either punish sin, or receive compensation if he foregoes vengeance. But with the growth of a purer morality in man, this notion of divine revenge is gradually modified. Every good man has learnt to forgive, and when the offender is penitent, to forgive freely—without punishment or retribution : whence the conclusion is inevitable, that God also forgives, as soon as sin is repented of. *Practically* however, it is by no means essential that a man should be conscious of this train of thought. When he has trusted God sufficiently to disclose his whole heart and cast himself freely on divine grace, he has already believed (perhaps unawares) the absolute Mercy of God, and he reaps Peace as the fruit of his Faith ; a peace which God has given, and which the theories of man cannot take away.

Much confusion has been introduced by laying down as an absolute and necessary moral truth the ambiguous assertion that "Guilt *ought* to be punished :" which is true, if it mean that guilt *deserves* punishment ; false, if it means that to leave it unpunished is an immorality. The latter doctrine would make Mercy to be a vice. All that Conscience has to depose on the subject seems to be summed up in three propositions :
1. The guilty person, whether penitent or impenitent, deserves* punishment. 2. It is right to punish him who is guilty and impenitent. 3. It is right to forgive him who is guilty, but penitent. Thus there is a sharp distinction between that which the offender deserves, and that which the offended ought to inflict. There is no inconsistency at all in the former saying to the latter, "I deserve punishment from thee, yet it becometh thee rather to show me mercy ;" which is in truth necessarily and for ever the sentiment of the repenting sinner towards God. But to forgive and to punish are not always inconsistent. Sometimes the punishment must be inflicted for the offender's own good, sometimes it comes in the train of cause and effect which he has himself originated. He may then have to say, "I will bear the judgments of the Lord, because I have sinned against Him ;" but this is quite compatible with that sense of spiritual forgiveness, which not only expels evil conscience and all boding of future wrath, but gives the heart to rejoice in Mercy.

Human laws indeed ordinarily show no mercy to penitent guilt ; but that is obviously because no magistrate can be trusted to discriminate real from feigned repentance, and because to spare the offender is thought a very small object in comparison with deterring others from crime. This cannot mislead us as to the divine judgment, when we observe that every pure and

---

* This means,—"He ought not to consider himself wronged, if punished." Even so, there is a *measure* of punishment, to exceed which would wrong him. *Excessive* punishment may be a worse evil than the offence :—a large topic for which I have no room.

loving heart grieves over this severity of human law as a necessary imperfection.   The sword which the magistrate bears is at
best a coarse and vulgar weapon; necessary indeed against outward crime, but, as it scarcely takes cognizance of the degrees
of temptation and weakness, or knows what Mercy means, no
one can without absurdity appeal to it as the type of the divine
administration.   No good man would consent to take Public
Law as the measure of his own mercifulness.   In the case of an
offence committed against ourselves, as soon as we are convinced
that repentance is sincere, we feel this at once to *justify* and to
demand of us full forgiveness; surely then God pardons man, as
freely as man pardons his fellow.   Nor is this a new discovery.
The Hebrew Psalmists unhesitatingly believed in the absolute
forgivingness of God; nay, the Lord's Prayer, in one petition,
when rightly translated, teaches, unless I mistake, that God also
may be expected to forgive, "*since even we* (men) forgive those
who trespass against us."   The truth seems to be that the desire
of Vengeance is an *instinct* implanted in us, in order to check or
destroy dangerous persons or things; and in its blind exercise,
we virtually presume that a man's past conduct is a clue to his
future.   As long as this presumption holds good, the cry for
Vengeance predominates in the bosom; but as soon as genuine
repentance has disconnected the offender's probable* future from
his past, the new instinct of Mercy rises to supplant that of
Vengeance.   Thus though Punishment is in its origin retro-
spective, yet it is so only because the retrospect is presumed to
be premonitory.   Punishment is suggested by the past, but its
aim (in so far as it can be approved) is towards the future.

There is therefore no reason to doubt, that that mode of proceeding which is confessed to be wise on the conversion of a
profligate heathen, applies equally to all other cases of wilful
sinners, as soon as any turn of mind comes, from whatever
cause.   They cannot be too quick in getting *out of* the evil
feelings and *into* holier thoughts and aspirations.   The great difficulty is to do this at all: let not artificial impediments be
superadded, by prescribing a routine of confession and of bar-

---

* Hence the increased difficulty of forgiving an offence repeated after
(apparent) repentance; because we lose our confidence in the assumption, that such repentance promises a different future.

Observe also, that though he who punishes *finds his justification in the
Past*, yet he has no means of fixing the *sufficient* amount of punishment
but by looking on to the Future; for (in spite of the remark in Note to
p. 65) we have no true common measure of Guilt and Punishment.
Hence when Punishment is not wanted either for Prevention or for Reformation, it vanishes of itself.

gaining for forgiveness. Does the anxious moralist insist that suffering for our sins is essential to permanent amendment? does he demand Self-Condemnation and Self-Abhorrence as a pledge of sincerity? Let him so do it, as to awaken Contrition with hope, not Remorse with despair. To hate the past self is good, to hate the present self is a deadly thing. Whoever hates himself hates God also. The great, the imminent danger is, that the soul which begins to turn once more towards God, should exaggerate the difficulties in the way of its restoration: and often, nothing can be happier, than if in a fit of unreasoning enthusiasm it suddenly conceive itself to be the special object of the divine favour. Let the man but once come really under a sense of God's unchangeable complacency, and he will then soon mourn bitterly enough for his sins, and profitably to himself. " Thou shalt be loathsome in thine own eyes, *when I am pacified with thee* for all that thou hast done."

Indeed, we may add, that as human guilt is not determined by the character of outward acts, but by the hardness of heart which accompanies them; so this hardness is by nothing so truly measured, as by the mode in which Mercy affects the soul. When violent or vicious men are melted into apparent sorrow for their sins by the thought that there is mercy even for them, we discern that they are not hopelessly hardened, even if the depth of their repentance is still doubtful; and in proportion as our opinion of their hardness of heart is lightened, so is our opinion of the intensity of guilt which their actual state implies. But the most dreadful consequence of wilful sin,—sin against moral and spiritual light,—is this very thing, that it palsies the heart against believing and accepting Mercy. Apathy and callousness are the fatal symptoms, in comparison with which a too great readiness to appropriate divine forgiveness to oneself must be judged a smaller evil. There always indeed have been, and there always will be, those who want to be made comfortable in their sins. No severity of doctrine will certainly thwart the self-complacency of such; for their deficiency is in depth of conscience and self-knowledge. But it need not on that account be feared that the doctrine of Free Grace to sinners may make sin appear a light matter to one whose conscience is really affected: he will not indeed measure his sin by the outward acts, and may condemn himself *less*, for those which the world condemns beyond comparison *more*. But for wilful sin,—committed against moral light, after tasting mercy,—though it seem small to others, no true penitent (I conceive) ever forgives himself; but always carries a sore spot on his soul, and is secretly humbled in mature or

declining age even for sins of youth.   Eternally does he cry to
God against himself, "*I deserve* thy wrath;" and this is a bitterness, which probably no sense of pardon and reconciliation
entirely removes.

The principles which have been here laid down, serve to explain the recovery of men from deplorable hardness or remorse,
under the influence of doctrine commonly esteemed fanatical, but
practically proved to be far more powerful to convert and rescue
than any wisdom of the mere moralist.   The preacher anxiously
warns the sinner not to think that he must make himself good
and righteous *before* he comes to Christ: but let him "come as
he is, ragged, wretched, filthy, with all his sins about him:" let
him believe that he is accepted, and he shall instantly be made
whole; he shall be received with joy, as the prodigal son return-
ing: a ring shall be placed on his hand and shoes on his feet:
the angels shall be glad because of him: he shall be justified in
the midst of all his ungodliness, and his Faith shall be counted
as Righteousness.—Undoubtedly if the hearer imagines that this
is some process for *enabling him to continue* in sin without evil
consequences, it is a ghastly delusion; but if he accepts it as a
method of *freeing him from the power* of inward sin, as well as
from all farther spiritual consequences, it is precisely the thing
needed for his case.   His faith or his credulity or his enthusiasm
(whichever men may choose to call it) grasps at the idea, that, in
spite of all that has passed, he may yet live a purer and a better
life under the smile of God; and the fact of his grasping at it
attests the birth of higher desires, which forthwith become
cultivated by exercise and (in happy instances) are ultimately
triumphant.

There is no single thing which more strikes me as indicating a
defective philosophy current concerning the Soul, than the incredulity and contempt which is cast upon *sudden* conversions.
Sudden political revolutions are never treated as incredible or
marvellous.   It is readily understood that in a State two or three
different powers are struggling together with independent force;
and often with alternate success.   At last a party which was depressed rises in sudden might, deposes that which held the chief
power, and assumes the helm.

Many moralizers seem not to be aware, that, similarly, in the
narrow compass of one man's bosom two or three powers are
often striving together for mastery.   Rather they know of nothing
but "Reason and Passion;" and as Reason acts gently and
very steadily, and only Passion by violent impulse, they can
understand indeed that a man may fall into dire sin all in a

moment, but not how he can rise out of it all in a moment. This is because they know nothing of the forces of the Soul, which are in fact true Passions themselves. Nor only so; but just as in Political, so too in Spiritual conflict, any great abuse of power by one party is apt to damage its cause, and irritate the opponents into vehement exertion : hence many a tyrant and many a dynasty has been ejected in consequence of some wanton and atrocious deed. Exactly in the same way is the paradox to be explained, (which is a fact, whether people choose to be scandalized at it or not,) that the commission of some unusually great sin has been known to lead to a change of the whole character for the better; in fact, to a marked spiritual conversion. It needs no great insight into the soul to understand the principle of such things. A man of impulsive passion and moderately strong will, is perhaps ordinarily correct enough to satisfy his conscience; and if now and then carried a little beyond bounds, he yet manages to keep up a good opinion of himself. But if his passions on some day run out to fearful riot, his self-complacency is mortified, his conscience is deeply stirred, his soul (for the first time perhaps) is called into activity : a general insurrection of the whole man takes place against the tyrannous usurpers; and, though beforehand the issue of such a struggle cannot be foreseen, no one who has even a feeble knowledge of God's power in the soul will be incredulous about its ever ending victoriously. Moralists perhaps think, that even if true, such a thing is dangerous to tell, lest any should trust to what he calls his "good luck," and sin boldly in the hope that he will be saved from sin at last. One however who argues thus with himself, does *not* hope (for he does not wish) to be saved from sin, but only from its consequences. No system of doctrine, true or false, will in itself avail to give to such a person a new heart, and make him feel that there is evil in the sin itself, even if the usual consequences be thwarted. The profligate will never want *excuses* for sin; but they are not the persons to be most considered, even if to hide facts would do them any good. Our business is, if possible, to understand aright both the weakness and the power of the soul; and what throws light on it, must not be suppressed for prudery and decorum and fancied expediency.

But perhaps there is another illusion. It is alledged that *every* evil deed goes to establish a Habit, and thereby weakens the moral principle : hence that a sin should be the antecedent of a conversion, is thought to be self-contradictory. But though a series of deeds committed *not* under strong passion make a habit, it is not true of a single deed of passion.   A child that slaps its nurse with little or no provocation and is not checked, will probably gain a habit of ill using her : but a boy who in sudden passion should strike his mother violently, having never done anything of the sort before, would probably be horror-smitten at his own deed, be melted into tears, and become far more affectionate and dutiful than previously.   Exactly so, in the ups and downs of an early struggling spiritual life, when powerful passions sway the man both ways, it is certain that a wilful sin, by the agony which it causes to the soul, may act like an arrow shot in a sleeping lion, who springs at once furiously on his enemy, and dashes him to the ground, though sore wounded himself.   For it is not more true that the flesh lusteth against the spirit, than that the spirit lusteth against the flesh; and when awakened to danger and its mettle roused, the spirit is by far the mightier, as that needs must be, which is in contact with God. Hence also man is ennobled, not by weakening his lower nature, but by unfolding and strengthening his higher.*   It is absolutely impossible to turn the above, by any legitimate argument, to an immoral purpose.   For if a person deliberately said, " I will sin, *in order* so to move my soul," he would manifest a state of soul which *could not* be so moved.   Only full life can suffer keenly ; and this man has no life.

In the farther progress of the soul, Habit becomes of increasing value ; but if in the early stage the views of mere moralists were true, its prospects would be sad indeed : nor could it possibly contend against the passions.   On the contrary, its great forces are all impulsive, and capable of being very intense.   St. Paul, who knew something of them, scruples not to call them (*in* the soul) the same mighty power of God, as raised Christ from the grave to the highest heaven.   And certainly, when he was inviting men to sacrifice all earthly prospects for a heavenly hope, nothing short of an energetic inward spirit which they felt to be of God, could possibly animate them to accept such proposals. Hence too he calls the Spirit within them " the earnest" of their future inheritance.

But indeed the remark may be made on all *intuitive* impressions,—that they are at first sudden and impulsive.   The beauty of a scene, of a statue, of a human face, strikes us with impetus.

---

* This is only one point of the absurdity involved in *Fasting* in order to weaken the passions.   But in fact I believe it does *not* weaken them, even temporarily, to any spiritual purpose ; for sin is in the mind, not in the body.   Irritability, with other pettishness, is confessedly increased by this Babylonish practice.

Not that we discern it always at first sight : we may have needed some familiarity with it before we see it in the right position and gather up into a single whole that on which the effect depends ; but at last we catch it all in a moment, and perhaps wonder why it never so affected us before.   In modern England indeed the most powerful love which man feels for woman is founded, not on mere beauty, but on the internal character ; and as this is not brought out and discerned in a moment, Englishmen do not in general fall in love very suddenly.   But in countries where women are secluded, where in consequence beauty is rarely seen and free courtship is impossible;—all the accounts which we read, of men falling in love with beautiful maidens, represent it as so sudden and violent, as to strike us with incredulity and laughter.   We justly regard this as a less advanced, a more puerile stage of human nature ; yet it is not a less instructive illustration of the mode in which intuition affects the soul.

The thing to be *desired* undoubtedly is, such a constant presence of God's Spirit with our spirit, that there may be no more " variableness or shadow of turning" in us than in Him; that our hearts may be altars, whence the smoke of incense perpetually rises to heaven; that our Wills may be animated by a power uniformly equal to their task, so that Duty may be nothing but healthy exercise, without labouring or groaning.   But if this is not yet attained, if we get into a stagnant lethargic atmosphere, which threatens to benumb us, we must be thankful for an occasional healthful typhoon, and not cavil that it is not a trade-wind. Individual character and circumstances of temptation differ so much, and false theories so derange the proper progress of things, that it is delusive to assert any result to be *generally* true ; but it seems impossible to doubt that *in a healthy* state, the internal life of spiritual men tends to become more and more tranquil, until the observer can detect no disturbances.   Happy are those, to whom Habit gives that steadiness which the moralist admires, without that languor which the spiritualist dreads.

If it appear that Selfishness is the most unmanageable disease in spirituals, (since it is a virtual death of the Soul, when complete,) and that a pure Enthusiasm is its proper antagonist, a *cold* nature would seem to be the least hopeful soil for spiritual growth.   The *passionate* temperament (which is however not to be judged of by superficial display) generally gives greater depth and power of life, with more capacity of sorrow and joy, though also, especially if the original moral training has been neglected, far greater danger of sudden sin and public scandal.   And here I am led to avow, that the Churches of England, and that

decorous part of society to which they set the tone, appear to
take a less true and less Christian view of the relative enormity
of sins, than the common heart of the world takes.   The world
broadly distinguishes sins of selfishness and malignity as unbearable, and imposes on them many opprobrious epithets,—mean,
sneaking, rascally, &c.: and these are precisely the sins which
of all indicate that a man has no stamp of the Infinite Spirit
upon him.   But sins of passion,—not *so* indulged as to injure
or betray others,—the world treats very mildly : and these,
though of course implying the temporary conquest of the soul by
baser impulses, yet by no means denote the total absence of
God's Spirit, if the sins have been unpremeditated or the passion
violent.   Mean and griping conduct, especially if habitual, is a
far worse spiritual sin than a bout of drunkenness ; yet a Church
will animadvert on the latter and dares not touch the former :
—probably because it is forced, like the Law of the land, to act
by rules capable of strict definition.   Thus we get the astonishing result, that while the Church (in its treatment of transgressors)
typifies the Law, the World comes nearer to the Gospel !   As
the Publicans and harlots were nearer to the kingdom of God
than the Pharisees, so were Byron and Shelley than many a
punctual reciter of creeds : and this, the world well knows, but
the Churches have no mouth to declare.   Out of the above
grow moral difficulties concerning all church discipline whatever,
which, I confess, now seem to me of a most unmanageable kind.

   It is time to sum up this Chapter.   Its subject has been, the
struggle of the soul to get and keep peace with God, and to
conquer sin.   Peace is no mere matter of *comfort*, but essential
for sanctification : hence it is impossible to overrate its importance.   If it is obtained and kept, there is indeed grief, pain,
mortification, humiliation, in finding that our Affections do not
keep pace with our Will ; yet a copious dash of this sort of
humiliation seems to be beneficial, implying, as it generally does,
high aspirations rather than very low performances.   The man
who, after being crushed under a sense of sin, has been healed
by God, is sore no longer, yet permanently tender ;—a tenderness felt through his whole spiritual and moral nature : hence he
is mild in his judgments of others, while severe on himself.   He
has also probably much contentment and balance of soul, not
only infused by a cheerful sense of the mild light of God, under
which he lives, but also as he feels himself unworthy of all his
enjoyments : thus he tastes a new sweetness in the common goods
of life.   To be honoured by men pains him ; to be disesteemed
by those who are not spiritual, does not trouble him,—except in

regard to that outward innocence, of which common men are excellent judges. And while he has thus learned to be abased, he has in some degree learned also how to abound. If new earthly wealth and grandeur were to flow in upon him, they would no doubt be a temptation; yet his previous discipline would above all things aid him to bear them. To endure affliction and sorrow, such sorrow especially as wrings the tender affections, he is perhaps not yet armed;—indeed, who is?—still, should such trials come, they will probably tend to the perfecting of his spirit, by opening new doors of access to God. Meanwhile, if such mellow fruits of righteousness as have been named, are borne by his having been painfully exercised, he will not think that the time of conflict was thrown away. God does not expose all to the very same trials, and let not *us* cramp all men to one form; but He leads us through ways that we know not, dark and various, until by his mercy, having become guileless before Him, we dwell with Him, and are satisfied by the sight of Him. Whoso has gained the harbour, needs not care about the course. To have had to undergo spiritual conflict through ignorance or through perversity, is certainly not in itself matter of congratulation : yet it may be a process not without positive advantages for us, if we are called on to comfort men in spiritual sorrow " by the comfort wherewith we ourselves were comforted of God." But, conflict or no conflict, matters not, if the heart has learnt to hate sin and rejoice in mercy. Then faithful resolute energetic souls do not stay in simple peace and moral tranquillity; they soar into a higher blessedness, and mingle in some upper part of the heaven-streaming current with those who are about to be described in the next Chapter.

NOTE 1, *referred to in page* 45.

At the request of some readers of my earlier editions, I here annex a literal translation of Cleanthes's Hymn to Jupiter.

> Almighty alway! many-nam'd!
> most glorious of the deathless!
> Jove, primal spring of nature, who
> with Law directest all things!
> Hail! for to bow salute to Thee,
> to every man is holy.
> For we from Thee an offspring are,
> to whom, alone of mortals
> That live and move along the Earth,
> the Mimic Voice is granted:
> Therefore to Thee I hymns will sing,
> and alway chant thy greatness.

E

Subject to Thee is yonder Sky,
    which round the Earth for ever
Majestic rolls at Thy command,
    and gladly feels Thy guidance.
So mighty is the weapon, clench'd
    within Thy hands unconquer'd,
The double-edg'd and fiery bolt
    of ever living lightning.
For Nature through her every part
    beneath its impulse shudders,
Whereby the universal Scheme *
    Thou guidest, which, through all things
Proceeding, intermingles deep
    with greater lights and smaller.
When Thou so vast in essence art,
    A king supreme for ever,

      *   *   *

Nor upon Earth is any work
    done without Thee, O Spirit!
Nor at the æther's utmost height
    divine, nor in the Ocean,
Save whatsoe'er the infatuate
    work out from hearts of evil.
But Thou by wisdom knowest well
    to render Odd things even ;
Thou orderest Disorder, and
    th' Unlovely lovely makest.
For *so* hast Thou in one combin'd
    the noble with the baser,
That of the Whole a single Scheme*
    arises, everlasting,
Which men neglect and overlook,
    as many as are evil :
Unhappy! who good things to get
    are evermore desiring,
While to the common Law of God
    Nor eyes nor ears they open ;
Obedient to which, they might
    good life enjoy with wisdom.
But they, in guise unseemly, rush
    this way and that, at random ;
One part, in glory's chase engag'd
    with ill-contending passion,
Some, searching every path of gain,
    of comeliness forgetful,
Others on soft indulgence bent
    and on the body's pleasure,
While things right contrary to these
    their proper action hastens.

But, Jove all-bounteous! who, in clouds
    enwrapt, the lightning wieldest ;

---

* The word is *Logos*,—reason ? system ?

Mayst thou from baneful Ignorance
　　the race of men deliver !
This, Father ! scatter from the soul,
　　and grant that we the wisdom
May reach, in confidence of which
　　thou justly guidest all things ;
That we, by Thee in honour set,
　　with honour may repay Thee,
Raising to all thy works a hymn
　　perpetual ; as beseemeth
A mortal soul : since neither man
　　nor god has higher glory,
Than rightfully to celebrate
　　Eternal Law all-ruling.

Cleanthes was born about B.C. 300, and lived 80 years.

NOTE 2, *referred to in page* 53.

No apology is needed for assuming that the advocates of what is called Orthodoxy decline to reconcile their doctrines with one another, according to the common principles of Logic. They generally say that the truths hinted at (and not fully stated) in their propositions, transcend Logic, and must not be submitted to that ordeal. This, it seems to me, would be *primâ facie* admissible, if these propositions were arrived at not by logical processes, but by direct discernment.

In the present argument, I am not concerned to censure the self-contradictoriness of any creeds, *except so far as it hurts spirituality*. But it appears insane to deny, that it *is* self-contradictory to call Jesus simultaneously omniscient and advancing in wisdom, omnipotent and needing support, infinite and finite : and when people say that they believe he is *at once* God and Man, they deceive themselves. What they really believe is this ; that he was *once* Man, and is *now* God.

The use and abuse of Logic in religious inquiry is a topic large enough to fill a treatise. As long as religious teachers have to establish by *argument* the Infallibility of the Scriptures or of something which they call "the Church," it is a ludicrous absurdity in them to affect that their results are invulnerable to logical attack. If one result contradicts another, it is evident that in the course of their long arguments they have made some mistake. It is for them, not for us, to find out *where* : and if they declaim against Logic, they do but declaim against themselves.

Widely different is it, when the internal faculties discern separately each of two truths, which, when stated in words, seem to be logically inconsistent. If they are really so, it will merely show that we have not successfully interpreted into words the impressions made on our inward sense, and that some modification of one or other statement is needed. But I confess that this is with me an imaginary case. I know no instances of such apparent collision, except between the Soul (or Conscience) and *the Understanding*.

The most startling, because the newest, extravagance in England, is the phenomenon of educated and acute men,—professors of Tri-unitarian and even of *Romish* orthodoxy,—who refuse to allow their own creed to be subjected to the test of logical self-consistency, and yet assail all other

E 2

creeds with this weapon. *I* forsooth, if I discern with about equal dis-
tinctness two truths which my critic thinks inconsistent, *I* must choose
between them, and repudiate one of the two, or he will brand me as
illogical! Let him make (or at least believe) his own creed logical,
before he throws this stone at others.

All absolute truth is self-consistent: hence it is unquestionable that
we are *somewhere* in error, if we are entangled in real inconsistency.
Human truth however is not Absolute, but only Approximate; too
valuable to throw away, though not perfect: and to detect inconsistency
does not in itself warn us where the error lies, and what sort of correction our propositions need. Much and patient inquiry is often essential
to find this out; and meanwhile we are right in holding (though with
diffidence and charity) to a system of propositions, which, we are conscious,
involve some inconsistency. To throw away one of them *at random*, in
order to secure agreement in those that remain, would be doltish. Yet
this is what those virtually advise, who preach up internal Consistency as
the grand virtue of a religious system. Consistent Truth is perfection;
but Consistent Error would be far worse than Inconsistency. For a
believer in Transubstantiation and in the pseudo-Athanasian Creed to
enforce upon others, as at any rate essential, a logical coherence in their
intellectual faith, shows either dense self-ignorance or gross untruthfulness.

CHAPTER IV.

SENSE OF PERSONAL RELATION TO GOD.

§ 1. REPLY TO AN OBJECTION.

BEFORE proceeding to the real subject of this Chapter, it may be well to notice an objection. Some will say, that in all spiritual action, the Soul itself is the only agent, and that the idea of God acting upon it, is a mere dream : that it has, no doubt, its own feelings ; but these feelings do not point to anything that goes on in the mind of God, which is essentially unchangeable towards us.

My general reply is, that I do not write as a metaphysician, or pretend to any but a popular phraseology. Time may disclose Laws in the actings of God towards the Soul; nay, none imagine that he acts capriciously, except a remnant of a school which veils caprice under the word *sovereignty*. There can be no objection to Science exploring spiritual action with purely scientific ends, provided that it ascertain the popular facts correctly on which it is to refine. But this proviso includes, first, that the men of science shall treat with tender thoughtfulness the facts alledged by the unscientific men who have felt them ; and shall cease to shower on them vague phrases of contempt, as mysticism, fanaticism, &c.; secondly, that the would-be scientific classifier of facts *shall not strangle the facts in their birth.* Now this is what those are trying to do, who lay down, that a man is to pray for spiritual benefit, not expecting that God will deign to notice him,—only because it is a mode of influencing his own heart. This would turn us into feeble hypocrites. What! can a man go, as if before God, and say,—"O God, I ask Thee to subdue this or that evil desire, knowing that Thou hearest not, but hoping that by this conscious fiction I shall call my own soul into action" ? This certainly is foolishness. No spiritual facts at all will be left for the man of science, if we commence thus.

It is to me axiomatic, that man can no more fully comprehend the mind of God, than a dog that of his master. Our
clearest notions must be rude outlines : our vocabulary is all one
of transference, and of course enormously vague : yet he who, in
anxiety for scientific accuracy, refuses to become experimentally
acquainted with the facts, is the last man to succeed in heightening our conceptions or perfecting our phraseology. Meanwhile,
as a dog lives on his master's smile, and rejoices, so is it fit that
we should live on the smile of God, though knowing only the
outer edge of His heart and mind.

"But," (will the man of science say?) "it is all well and
happy for *you* to believe that God hears your prayer : perhaps I
wish I could believe it too ; but unfortunately I cannot : you
offer me no proof." But what sort of proof could satisfy him ?
If he say—"None;" this would imply that there is an essential
absurdity in the case ; but we must then call on him to point out
the absurdity ; since *we* do not see it. But if he admit that the
thing is not in itself absurd and self-contradictory, then, it seems
to me, he cannot ask any other proof, than exactly that which
abounds : viz. the unanimous testimony of spiritual persons to the
efficacy of prayer. He may reply : "Yes, that is the heart
acting on itself;" but he might deal exactly in the same way
with the evidence of sense. *Perhaps* there is no outer world, and
our internal sensations are the universe ! Syllogistic proof of an
outer world will never be gained, nor yet syllogistic proof that a
God exists or listens to prayer.

We well know that there are persons, who say that *substance*
and *matter* are illusive terms ; and that a substance is nothing but
a congeries of forces, coherent and repulsive. It may be so ; but
we should not attain greater accuracy by expunging the two
words from our vocabulary. Indeed, the philosopher who so cor-
rects us, has, after all, no more definite idea of the reality than the
vulgar have. He cannot conceive of one centre of immaterial
forces pushing away another centre of immaterial forces. The
imagination wants something material for a force to push against.
The vulgar mode of conception and speech may be inaccurate ;
but, as also in spiritual matters, it is the best we can get. Not
by subtlety of thought, *but by specific sense*, do we gain any
acquaintance with the realities of things : and the Soul is the
specific sense in which we come into contact with God. Let us
not deal more slightingly with its testimony, than with that of
the Touch or the Taste.

The active part of man consists of powerful instincts. Some
are gentle and continuous, others violent and short ; some baser,

some nobler; all necessary. A moral control over them all is desirable; and by all means let any vagaries of the Soul (as in all fanatical religion) be severely checked by our moral principle. With this limitation, the instincts have an inherent right to exist and to act; and the perfection of man depends on their harmonious energy. As operating alike on all ages, perhaps the instinct which seeks after God and the Infinite is the most powerful in man. Let us follow out this great and glorious tendency. Let us give free play to our nature, without fear of the critics : we shall get holiness, peace and joy ; and may haply bequeath facts for some future man of science. If we drink the heavenly nectar ourselves, others may analyze our juices when we are dead.

The objection here considered, comes ill from a moralist who believes the originating power of the human Will : for *he* can no more *prove* that Will is not a mere necessary result of circumstances unknown or uncontrollable to us, than I can prove that it is God's influence and not my own which I feel within. But we refuse to surrender to the Necessarian our instinctive belief in a self-determining Will, because we cannot act wisely and well except by adopting the belief : for if there be no such Will in us, it is still useful for practice to believe that there is ; and the man who most knows the Truth, is then most likely to act foolishly !* This is so intense a paradox, as to confirm most people in their conviction that the hypothesis is false, or that there *is* a self-moving Will in each of us.—Now every word of this argument equally applies to the belief that God acts upon the soul, when the soul approaches Him. The objector then ought in consistency to become a Necessarian,—to deny the propriety of praising or blaming, to treat self-reproof as ridiculous, and cut away the springs of moral as well as spiritual life. Perhaps, if he will be logical, he ought farther to be an Atheist ; for, as insisted in the First Chapter, if we know nothing of Will in ourselves, it does not appear how we know anything of it in the Universe. Thus, the objection treated is frivolous, unless it means to destroy both Morals and Religion entirely.

If it be admitted that in the Infinite One there dwell (what we may approximately call) Designs, Desires, Affections ; then surely all his creatures who also have affections and minds capable of discerning Him, may both love and be loved by Him. That we *ought* to revere Him, is as trustworthy a moral judgment as any other, as soon as His existence is discerned. That he perceives and approves our revering Him, is a judgment

* See the Introductory Remarks, No. 9, for farther elucidation.

equally inevitable. But *the man who at the same moment that he adores, perceives that his adoration is perceived and is acceptable, has already begun an intercourse with God.* Two moral beings cannot come into such intercourse, without the commencement of a new moral relation; not though the inequality between them be infinite. Nor does it avail to dwell on our littleness as any objection: the chasm is still infinite, between the *highest* creature and the Creator. But in fact, this infinite disparity is just the thing essential to the relation and characteristic of it.

§ 2. LOVES OF THE SOUL.

Human characters have often been distributed into two great classes, which may be called *masculine* and *feminine*. In the masculine, are stronger and coarser passions, self-confidence somewhat overbearing, more promptitude to act and more versatile energy, deeper conscience and more prominence of the idea of Duty, high ambition to achieve Right; warm and rich love, of gushing impetuosity. In the feminine, are pure and gentle instincts; strength more passive than active; slowness to act, except when affection moves; a heart that guides to Duty and to Right, but thinking of it not as Duty and as Right but as that which is lovely; finally, a love which is tender, transparent, and steady. Of course there may be intermediate characters. Yet if we contrast the two more concisely, thus: the *former*, (partly from Ambition and partly from the activity of the Conscience,) is impelled to action before the affections are fully ready for it: the *latter* is little moved by a sense of Duty, and is satisfied not to act until impelled by Affection: then the two characters exclude one another. And this is perhaps a view suitable to our present purpose.

Where Conscience predominates, the struggles described in the preceding Chapter may be apprehended; especially if to this be added an ardent ambitious nature. Exactly in such natures other passions also are apt to be strong: hence the man is a bundle of forces not yet in harmony: and the harmonizing of them is generally attempted by direct conflict, before Love comes in to reconcile them. The more feminine character probably avoids struggle, not by any strength of love, but by the unformed state of the conscience and delicacy of the passions: for powerful love to God can in very rare instances be developed so early as to anticipate conflict. Many persons of masculine soul, nevertheless, by severe sorrows, especially from the deaths of those whom they love, are in great measure moulded into the feminine type;

and possibly this is the most perfect character. But at present I confine myself to the other.

There are those of amiable natures and soft affections, perhaps also very susceptible to natural beauty, who appear to approach religion altogether on its sunny side. They see God, not as a strict Judge, not as a Glorious Potentate ; but as the animating Spirit of a beautiful harmonious world, Beneficent and Kind, Merciful as well as Pure. The same characters generally have no metaphysical tendencies : they do not look back into themselves. Hence they are not distressed by their own imperfections : yet it would be absurd to call them self-righteous ; for they hardly think of themselves *at all*. This childlike quality of their nature makes the opening of religion very happy to them : for they no more shrink from God, than a child from an emperor, before whom the parent trembles : in fact, they have no vivid conception of *any* of the qualities in which the severer Majesty of God consists. He is to them the impersonation of Kindness and Beauty. They read his character, not in the disordered moral world of man, but in romantic and harmonious nature. Of human sin they know perhaps little in their own hearts and not very much in the world; and human suffering does but melt them to tenderness. Thus, when they approach God, no inward disturbance ensues ; and without being as yet spiritual, they have a certain complacency and perhaps romantic sense of excitement in their simple worship.

It is not by a lucky accident that their early course is so tranquil. It arises out of the fact that their crude views of God are really more true than those of the opposite character. He is *not* a stern Judge, exacting every tittle of some law from us. There is *nothing* in Him to terrify the simple-minded. He does *not* act towards us (spiritually) by generalizations which may omit our individual case, but his perfection consists in dealing with each case by itself as if there were no others. In short, only the primitive ruder notion concerning Him is the stern one ; that of the riper spirituality testifies to his infinite Love. Now it deserves remark, that, quite in accordance with this, women come more easily to pure religion than men. In fact, men are accustomed to deal with affairs of life on a great scale, where (by reason of *our* mental infirmity) fixed general rules are essential : hence come men's notions of abstract Justice, in which the Judge is forced to sacrifice his personal feelings to some law *external to himself*; an idea which they erroneously transfer to God. But women act in detail, and judge of each case for itself and by their own feelings. So again ; all moral rules

E 5

are a generalization ; hence Conscience, which bids us observe
such rules, implies generalization : but women do not generalize
much; they rather seize on particulars.   Therefore they are
less liable to be tormented by a Conscience, which (on some
abstract principle) lays more on them than their affections
can bear.   But chiefly, it is important, that men deal much
with their equals, and have to stand out for their rights;
hence the sharpness with which the idea of Justice and Right is
stamped upon them.   But women are chiefly concerned with un-
equals ; with a husband above them and children beneath them ;
and in younger age of course equally so.   Thus affectionate
obedience and tender mercy are prominent with them ; and they
carry these sentiments into their religious relations.   Moreover as
young women are not subject to passion in the same coarse forms
as young men, their temptations are probably weaker, they wound
their own consciences less, and their religious course is far
smoother.   On the whole, we may well admire the instinct, which
made the old Germans regard Woman as penetrating nearer to
the mind of God than Man does.

That none can enter the kingdom of heaven without becoming
a *little Child*,—guileless and simple-minded, is a sentiment long
well known.   But behind and after this there is a mystery, revealed to but few, which thou, oh Reader, must take to heart.
Namely, if thy Soul is to go on into higher spiritual blessedness,
it must become a *Woman* ; yes, however manly thou be among
men.   It must learn to love being dependent ; and must lean on
God not solely from distress or alarm, but because it does not
like independence or loneliness.   It must not have recourse to
Him merely as to a friend in need, under the strain of duty, the
hattering of affliction and the failure of human sympathy ; but
it must press towards Him when there is *no* need.   It must
love to pour out its thoughts to Him, for the pleasure of pour-
ing them out.   It must utterly abandon the idea of having
either Rights *or Liberty* as against God, and will then instinctively know that God claims no Rights against it, but in all his
direct dealings with it is thinking solely of its individual welfare, as much as if it were· the only creature in the universe.
Though all the Scribes and Pharisees of Christendom should
assert it, believe not, oh Reader, that God keeps any spiritual
scores against thee.   It was a strong-minded man, deeply versed
in human nature, but as painfully dark concerning the Divine,
who said : *The gods care to avenge, but care not to save.**
Those were Pagan and external gods.   But our inward and

* Tacitus, Histor. i. 3.

spiritual God *cares not to avenge, and cares only to save*: and to err concerning this, would make us less holy, as well as less happy.   Farther, the soul must learn to follow her own instincts more; to deal with every case for itself, and enact no artificial generalizations; to think, not what she *may* do without sin, but what best harmonizes with her own delicacies; so that the law of the Spirit within her may set her free from, by raising her above, the law of sin and of death. Lastly, she must change that Jewish precept, "Thou *shalt* love the Lord" into another: "Thou *mayst* love thy Lord."

But those gentle souls which are drawn so quietly towards God, by no means go without their share of sorrow, only it seems to take a different form.   It is not that an evil conscience stings them, that Duty works them hard, and their Affections fail: but they doubt whether they may suppose that there is *any definite relation at all* between them and the Infinite God.   God is hitherto to the Soul as a pleasing poetical dream: He has not (as in the case described in the Third Chapter) been felt in the Conscience, first as one painfully judging the heart, and then as subduing it; and He is in fact still a mere external God to the worshipper. While this is the case, there is Sentiment, but not as yet Spirituality; and though the religion is not formal and stiff, but poetical and free, still the soul can have no active life. But from this very circumstance a sense of *vacuity* arises.   One who begins to realize God's majestic beauty and eternity, and feels in contrast how little and transitory man is, how dependent and feeble,—longs to lean upon him for support.   But He is *outside* of the heart, like a beautiful sunset, and seems to have nothing to do with it; there is no getting into contact with Him, to press against Him.—Yet where rather should the weak rest than on the Strong, the creature of a day than on the Eternal, the imperfect than on the centre of perfection? And where else should God dwell than *in* the human heart? for if God is in the universe, among things inanimate and unmoral, how much more ought He to dwell with our souls! and they too seem to be infinite in their cravings: who but He can satisfy them? Thus a restless instinct agitates the soul, guiding it dimly to feel, that it was made for some definite but unknown relation towards God. The sense of emptiness increases to positive uneasiness, until there is an inward yearning, if not shaped in words, yet in substance not alien from that ancient strain,—"As the hart panteth after the water-brooks, so panteth my soul after Thee, Oh God: my soul is athirst for God, even for the living God."—"I wait for the Lord; my soul doth wait; as those that watch for the morning." But, by the continuance of such exercises, the fervency of desire gradually ripens into love, and love goes on heightening till at last the soul becomes conscious of it ; and then the crisis is reached. *I believe* at least that the transition depends on the following principle :—no soul can possibly know that it loves God, and not at once infer (whether aware or not of the mental process) that God loved it first :* so powerful and clear is the direct perception that all our highest and best feelings are shadows of His : if therefore *we*, imperfect and puny, in truth love *Him* who is unseen and dimly known, how much more does *He*, who cannot overlook us, assuredly love *us* ;—not indeed because we deserve it, but because it is part of his own nature's perfection.

In claiming a *personal* relation with God, nothing *exclusive* is intended : nay, he who thus learns that he is loved by God, learns simultaneously that all other men and creatures are also loved : (though a hateful dogma may here mar his soul's instinct.) That is an important lesson for the man's external action ; indeed, is a foundation of universal love in the soul ; but its inward movements towards God proceed exactly as if there were no other creature beside itself in the universe. Thus the discovery that *it loves* and *is loved in turn* produces sensible Joy ; in some natures very powerful, in all imparting cheerfulness, hope, vivacity. The personal relation sought, is discerned and felt. The Soul understands and knows that God is *her* God ; dwelling with her more closely than any creature can ; yea, neither Stars, nor Sea, nor smiling Nature hold God so intimately as the bosom of the Soul. What is He to it? what, but the Soul of the soul? It no longer seems profane to say, " God is my bosom-friend : God is for me, and I am for Him." So Joy bursts out into Praise, and all things look brilliant ; and hardship seems easy, and duty becomes delight, and contempt is not felt, and every morsel of bread is sweet. Then, though we know that the physical Universe has fixed unaltering laws, we *cannot help* seeing God's hand in events. Whatever happens, we think of as his Mercies, his Kindnesses ; or his Visitations and his Chastisements ; everything comes to us from his love :—and this may be very illogical, (and *possibly* may be a mere illusion,) yet we should do such violence to the soul's instinct in *not* thus thinking that we follow it unreasoningly, and leave others to reconcile the paradox. Thus the whole world is fresh to us with

---

* In Creeds, this practical and blessed truth assumes the vexatious form of a logical, or rather illogical, doctrine, called **Preventive Grace**.

sweetness before untasted. All things are ours, whether affliction or pleasure, health or pain. Old things are passed away;
behold! all things are become new: and the soul wonders, and
admires, and gives thanks, and exults like the child on a summer's
day;—and understands that she *is* as a new-born child: she has
undergone a New Birth! It is not birth after the flesh, but a
birth of the Spirit, birth into a heavenly union, birth into the
family of God. Why need she scruple to say, that she is "par-
taker of the divine nature," if God loves her and dwells in her
bosom?

Reader, accept these mystical metaphors as such. Behold in
them the soul labouring to express her feelings; but freeze
them not into logical terms, or they will become *the letter that
killeth*.

Is all this to the philosopher a vain dream? can he explain it
all? does he scorn it all? Whatever *theory* he may form concerning it, it is not the less a fact of human nature: one of some
age too: for David thirsted after God and exceedingly rejoiced in
Him, and so did Paul; and the feelings which they describe are
reproduced in the present day. To despise wide-spread enduring facts is *not* philosophic; and when they conduce to power
of goodness and inward happiness, it might be wise to learn the
phenomena by personal experience, *before* theorizing about them.
It was not a proud thing of Paul to say, but a simple truth, that
the spiritual cannot be judged by the unspiritual.

The single thought, "God is for my soul, and my soul is for
Him," suffices to fill a universe of feeling, and gives rise to a
hundred metaphors. Spiritual persons have exhausted human
relationships in the vain attempt to express their full sense of
what God (or Christ) is to them. Father, Brother, Friend,
King, Master, Shepherd, Guide, are common titles. In other
figures, God is their Tower, their Glory, their Rock, their Shield,
their Sun, their Star, their Joy, their Portion, their Hope, their
Trust, their Life. But what has been said, will show why a still
tenderer tie has ordinarily presented itself to the Christian imagination as a very appropriate metaphor,—that of Marriage. The
habit of breathing to God our most secret hopes, sorrows, complaints, and wishes, in unheard whisper, with the consciousness
that He is always inseparable from our being, perhaps pressed
this comparison forward.* Yet there are other still more marked
phenomena, acting in the same direction, which will need to be
presently analyzed.

Thus an important beginning is made of that process, by

* See Note 1 at the end of this Chapter.

which all the passions of human nature are to be harmonized and glorified. Indeed, where the phenomena are marked, for the time it might seem as if the secondary principles were swallowed up and lost: for even Conscience fails to operate as such; the words Duty and Virtue become distasteful, and Merit exceedingly odious. Now this is angelic, so long as all duties are notwithstanding performed; for to act from love to God and from the new instincts of the Soul is far better than to act from a sense of Duty, which is apt to be a dry and external thing. Yet there is here a danger, in regard to that class of duties which are *ordinarily* performed by affection, and are no mere external thing,—chiefly those among blood relations: for the domestic affections are sometimes absorbed and starved, not ennobled, by the new affection; and this is a great calamity. Young persons especially are put *out of relation* to their parents, brothers and sisters by their change: for they find a new prompter to action, which supersedes former conventional rules; and they do not conceal that they feel themselves wiser than their elders. Or if they do, still it is hard for them to behave with the same sort of deference as before. In many old ways the new life is cramped and uneasy, and demands enlargement; and slight breaches of the delicacy of domestic relation are made, which are difficult to repair. While thus Habit and Domestic Affection, the two most strengthening and purifying springs of common virtue, receive some little shock, many smaller duties are apt to suffer, unless the new principle is wonderfully energetic and the Soul follows its own instincts most faithfully, without derangement from men's false theories which meet it. But this is seldom possible; and in many cases one part of the moral conduct becomes less amiable than before, for reasons which are now to be detailed.

Allusion was made towards the end of the Second Chapter, to rudimentary but honest worshippers, who feel sincere reverence towards God, and are kept by that reverence at a certain distance from moral evil, although religion is to them rather a negative than a positive thing. The religion of such having no powerful inward spring, is very much influenced by external circumstances; as, first of all, by the national morality; and this again, by political institutions. Nor only so, but it is affected by the quality of the spiritual (or it may be poetical or fanatical) tendencies, which are in contact with it, but do not pervade it. Perhaps it becomes worst, when it has no such external antagonist at all: which was the case in Judæa, after Prophecy and Poetry had sunk, while no culture of Fine Art existed, where Enthusiasm was shut up in rustic brotherhoods, and Priests possessed the political government. Hence the religion became a dead, formal and often hypocritical routine, more offensive than Paganism, for the very reason that Paganism makes no professions of a holy God and a moral worship.—But that which thus appeared as Pharisaism in Judæa, became in Greece Stoicism, where Imaginative Culture relieved the deadness of the atmosphere: and the noble Hymn to Jupiter, composed by the Stoic Cleanthes, shows us that there was a true heart in Stoicism. In Rome, side by side with rising Christianity, Stoicism improved still more: and that excellent Emperor Marcus Antoninus exhibits it to us in the height of gentleness as well as of self-sacrificing conscientiousness.—In modern England, the political institutions and the diffusion of considerable spiritual light, have in the same way acted from without upon the Stoics of our day; and unless we resolve to blind our own eyes, we shall see around us persons of great worth, whose character I may sketch as follows.

Conscience in them takes the lead of the conduct, and they are capable of the greatest sacrifices at the call of Duty. They discern intellectually all the moral perfections of God, and sincerely revere Him. The thought of his All-seeing eye braces them against temptation, nor are any more trustworthy persons to be found for all the ordinary outward duties of life. Yet their religion is not a very inward nor productive one: it sanctions and confirms, but does not animate and elevate their morality. They rather know with the mind, than feel with the soul, that God searches their hearts: as may be inferred from their not understanding inward conflicts. They are, probably, generally persons of a strong Will, moderate Passions, or very well trained from childhood. While they are mild towards the unselfishly irreligious, and show towards penitent offenders a feeling which, though not tender, is considerate, they are exceedingly keen critics of all professors of spirituality, and cannot make allowance for errors of impulse and neglect in such. They have apparently a good conscience before God, derived perhaps from a benevolent and healthy mind, which acts too vigorously upon that which is without, ever to feed upon itself. To do their duty is their sufficient satisfaction, without reflecting on their own doings: but their standard of duty is principally an external one. They lean upon God in times of trial, but probably do not seek to Him for pleasure at other times. They do not press passionately after Him, but rather suspect all such things as delusion. That there is no vivid and satisfying sense of His presence, is known by the liking which they show for outward distinctions, and many artificial pleasures, as also by their regard for fashion and for the world's opinion in trifles ; yet they have strength of mind to rise above these things, whenever clear duty calls. They act " upon principle," that is, upon rules capable of being defined in words ; and seldom think it wise to follow the instinct of the soul, even so far as to hear *this* instead of *that* preacher. In short, the Will is strong in them, the Moral Faculties are sound, Reverence is unfeigned, yet the Soul is weak and inactive ; there is no painful want of Peace, for there is no keen sensitiveness as to inward Sin and no fervent aspiration ; but Joy cannot exist, because there is no passionateness in the soul.

Now, between such a character and a soul which has suddenly come into new and vehement life, there is some natural repulsion : and they may often be actually members of the same domestic circle. Each sees the other's defects. The one appears to be stiff, dry, pharisaic, and certainly unregenerate ; the other to be self-pleasing, uncontrolled, incapable of conscientious sacrifice, one-sided in moral conduct, self-confident and very presumptuous. The former, having little or no consciousness of spiritual *instinct*, gathers, with mingled indignation and concern, that the latter believes himself guided by the Spirit of God within his heart.* The discovery of this excites alarm, similar to that which a hen feels, whose ducklings are venturing on an element which would be fatal to *her* ; and gloomy presages occur, on remembering all the sins and inconsistencies which are real or reported concerning professors of spirituality. But self-confidence, as a universal imputation against them, though plausible, is untrue ; for the young and new-born soul is so conscious of ignorance, as to lean even unduly on the judgments and advice of the more experienced, in whom it discerns congeniality. Yet what do these teachers do, to aid it in avoiding injurious collision and unjust sentiment ? They steep it in bigotry and superciliousness. They identify the *unregenerate* with the *ungodly*, and teach that these are under the wrath of God, and on their way to everlasting misery. So the young soul, which confidingly drinks in their instruction, learns to look on conscientious and

---

* A consciousness of this *new* instinct has in every age led spiritual men (Jews or Christians) to speak of it as God in them, Christ in them, the Spirit in them. It is felt as something *superadded* to their old nature, and to contest whether their phraseology is logically accurate, appears to be useless, unless we can first know what is the essence of God and what the essence of Instinct. Perhaps it is not quite superfluous to add, that no man can without absurdity adduce the inward movements of his own Spirit as an argument to another, or as any justification *of conduct which needs to be justified*.

devout worshippers as under God's anger and condemnation!
This is to poison spiritual sentiment in its opening life; and
words will not adequately express the amount of evil caused by
it.—There is indeed an opposite school who see this, but are
very unhappy in their remedy; namely, they sanction the dogma,
that "the unregenerate are ungodly," but proceed to ignore the
whole momentous reality of the New Birth, by identifying it with
a magical process effected by sprinkling water on an infant! and
then, forsooth, justify this by quoting certain figures of bold
rhetoric from the New Testament. Between such immoral
bigotry on the one hand, and such dead mechanism on the other,
it may seem difficult to choose; but nothing in God's real world
confines us to the alternative.

God has two families of children on this earth; *the once born*
and *the twice born*; both obedient, both reverential, both imperfect, each essential to the other. Let neither despise the other,
but let each learn his own weakness, and the other's strength.
To those who were religious, but not spiritual, we above applied
the words: "We have a little sister, and she has no breasts:"
but, behold, the little sister is grown up, and she still has no
breasts, for she is a Man! And this opens to us the relation of
the two classes, in their present development. We see in them
the Man-soul and the Woman-soul, that which thinks and that
which feels, the negative and the positive, the formal and the instinctive, the critical and the creative, the principle of conser-
vatism and the principle of progress: in the one the Conscience,
in the other the Affection, takes the lead; yet one without the
other could never be made perfect. How the more formal and
rigid has been mellowed by contact with the more poetical and
affectionate, has been already noticed; but conversely, it is equally
certain that wild fanaticism has resulted and may result again,
where the passions of the men of Soul are not controlled by the
moral influences of the men of Conscience. It is by their mutual
action that God has provided for the growing up of human
nature into a capacity or predisposition for true religion. Hence
the schism between the two characters is far less in modern
Europe than it was in antiquity; and each individual of us must
look to combine more and more the excellences of both. Not
that it seems for a moment doubtful, which of the two has the
higher order of religion; in fact, they are fundamentally related
as Law and Gospel, and in some respects as Priest and Prophet; but a novice in the latter may be less trustworthy, though
of greater promise, than a veteran in the former; and although
it is inevitable that one of the new born, while the feelings are

all fresh, will discover who *are* and who *are not* congenial, he needs not to despise the latter. The two forms of character are as parallel streams, neither of which can stop,—nor their distinctions be wholly obliterated,—until, blending gradually, they become one in the bosom of God; who is neither male nor female, but feminine in soul and masculine in action; so that the old Orphic hymn was not far wrong in saying,

Ζεὺς ἄρσην γένετο, Ζεὺς ἄμβροτος ἔπλετο νύμφη,

Jove was a male, and Jove was an immortal damsel.

So also should we translate the old heathen maxim, *suaviter in modo, fortiter in re*, into, *tender in heart and firm in action*. Moreover, it is to be calculated that if the new life proceed happily, it will as a thing of course at length take up into itself all the steadiness of the opposite character. On the contrary, it is not easy for the developed *Legal* religionist to superadd the *Gospel* qualities, except either by domestic afflictions and other sufferings which deeply probe the heart, or by conflicts such as were described in the Third Chapter: yet no one can say what might be effected, if a deeper and wiser teaching on these topics abounded among us.—After this digression, we return to the case of the new-born soul.

If such evils as have been alluded to,—presumption and superciliousness, and their unlovely despiritualizing results,—be avoided, nevertheless the lapse of no long time brings to light certain defects in this state of inexperience. Perhaps, indeed, the soul has not as yet at all learned to look on God as *the source* whence its life is to come, and is simply living on its own affections. So long as its addresses to Him abound with unforced outpouring of love and joy, all seems to go well; but when the affections become exhausted, the sense of His love seems to vanish with them, and discomfort ensues. This circumstance alone must ensure a new set of actions in the soul, directed to give stability to the affections: but several causes may combine in setting it to the difficult practical problem,— how to keep the affections lively, and how to recover them when lost. Let us think for a moment how this problem is related to the other,—of winning and keeping Peace.

It appeared that the Will and the Affections are the two parts of man which have to be perfected according to the will of God. As soon as the Will is conformed to God, Peace comes of itself, unless intellectual error pervert the proper actings of the Soul. If the Will have gone astray, there is only one cure, but that is a sure and speedy one,—an immediate laying bare of the heart to

God, by which the evil Will is expelled; then Peace is regained, as soon as the path of duty can be recovered. But farther; the utility (so to say) of Peace, is, to enable us to come into so close contact with God's Spirit, as to have our Affections acted on by Him. Now if there has been no marked flagging in them, no difficulty may be incurred. But nothing is more common than for persons not to know that worldly occupations, especially mental distraction, must needs unstring the spiritual affections; and then they are apt to be severe on themselves, when they find it out. Most have to learn by their own errors and sufferings, and at last discover with some surprise what was meant by *the prayer of Faith.** He whose faith is well rooted, if he detects himself to be dull, unthankful and cold, instead of losing his energies in self-reproach, can at once cry in self-despair and con- fidence: " My flesh, O Lord, is weak, but my spirit is willing: my heart is barren and dry, but Thine is an ever-flowing fountain: I am cold and starved, but Thou art an eternal Sun: *Thou wilt melt me into new love, and kindle me into holier life than before.*" One who in very earnest so calls to God, recovers in one half minute all that had been lost: but the power of so doing is one of the things most to be coveted, and, I imagine, hardest to at- tain; because it presupposes a confidence, *settled in the intel- lect, and yet a practical one*, of God's unchangeable and active love to us. At any rate, it is a "Faith that worketh by Love"; for no one can exercise it without a *true* love to God, though that love may be so *weak*, that the person is unconscious of it. Our sense of his love (we said) was primitively excited by our own affections to Him, and therefore it is apt to vanish when they wear out: thus we might seem to run round in a circle, when we are to get back our Affections by the exercise of Faith, when Faith presupposes his Love, and His Love is only known to us through our own Affections. But this is not quite correct. Faith does not imply any *sensible feeling* of God's Love, such as

* Mark xi. 22. "Have faith in God: for whosoever shall say to this mountain, Be thou removed, and be thou cast into the sea; *and shall not doubt in his heart, but shall believe that those things which he saith shall come to pass:*—he shall have whatsoever he saith. Therefore I say unto you, *What thing soever ye desire when ye pray, believe that ye receive them, and ye shall have them.*"
Does it not appear almost a moral certainty, that Jesus alluded solely to spiritual desires, and to mountains internal to the soul; although, in the very imperfect report which we have of his words, he is made to refer to physical miracles such as the blasting of a fig-tree? I know an excel- lent man, who, resolving to subjugate his understanding to the obedience of faith, attempted on the authority of this text, to heal a blind person. What Bibliolater can blame him?

would produce present joy; but the remembrances of the past suffice to stimulate it; hence it strengthens with time and experience.

In many cases there is a new crisis in the religious life brought about by the pressure of temptation. It is not here requisite to insist anew on the mortal antagonism between immoral will and spiritual aspiration, or to suggest the numerous causes which may lead to severe assaults of temptation, when the "First Love" of the soul has drooped. The forms of trial must differ exceedingly in every two persons. If the old habits were bad, but were swept away by the new flood of life, the soul perhaps thought they were gone for ever; but as soon as the tide ebbs, they seek to return. Not to consider the melancholy, but perhaps common case with such persons, where relapses into wilful sin have deeply wounded the spirit; no sooner have the affections towards God decayed, than a man finds himself as it were on the brink of a precipice, where his head swims and his soul turns sick. Or again, the conscience has become more sensitive, during the period in which the affections were powerfully excited; and inward evils begin to be discovered to an amount before unsuspected. The man *has become self-reflecting*; and may be plunged into a struggle similar to that of the preceding Chapter, though modified by his remembrances of the past. Or thirdly, totally new dangers may have grown up by lapse of time, change of circumstances, the development of new passions, nay, and even by the action of the new life itself, in conjunction with erroneous theories. Whatever the series of causes, a horror oppresses him, lest, after tasting the sweetness and glories of a higher, he should fall back into a baser, life: and it is probable that some conflict of this kind, *more* or *less* severe, is essential to give tenderness of Conscience to one who at first was drawn only by Sentiment. However pure and sound this sentiment may seem, it is likely to be unequable in its action and too unmixed with religious fear. In a soul of this character, as was observed, the Majesty of God and all his more overwhelming attributes are kept exceedingly in the back ground: He is loved only as the impersonation of Beauty and Purity, Kindness and Mercy, and is felt to be as it were the Soul of the soul. Too little sense of the infinite inequality of God and his creature, perhaps here operates: and it is wholesome for such a one *now* to be made to tremble for fear of forfeiting his favour. The alarm and anxiety however have nothing slavish in them: sin is dreaded, not because of apprehended punishment, but because it will grieve the Spirit of God, and shut out the light of His countenance: and by such conflicts the soul is to learn to shun sensitively any near approach of sin, and never to trifle with it, or think any thing light. In some cases the distress becomes very lively ; and half-instructed persons are apt to fancy that they have committed " the unpardonable sin ;" or that they are those into whom Seven devils have come, for the One which was cast out. Out of all these agitations grows a new form of desire, viz. to secure *the permanence* of that union with God which has already commenced : that is to say, the soul is no longer satisfied with *present* good, but is solicitous also for the *future.* This implies a growing up of thoughtfulness and self-distrust; with a sense that it cannot depend upon its own affections, but must look to God as the great source whence life and power are to originate : now then probably Prayer commences with an intensity before unknown, while the songs of Praise and Joy are dumb. By such exercises, what was defective in the former view of God gets corrected, and a habit is formed of prayer against temptation the moment it approaches : a habit which could hardly exist, while the soul was deficient in self-reflection and self-knowledge.

How long this crisis may last and in what way the result may be evolved, may vary greatly, and in part it may be affected by doctrinal theories ; nay, the mind may be led off into critical discussions about the "Final Perseverance of the Saints." But no proposition that needs to be authoritatively guaranteed ever supplies a spiritual want ; and it does not appear in practice that that doctrine is by any means essential to comfort. That eminent saint, Fletcher of Madeley, was as well without it, as his Whitfieldian opponents with it. Although traditional theories greatly obscure this part of the subject, it appears to me that the following statement is fundamentally accurate.—A person who vehemently desires and prays for a particular object, is in the intervals necessarily much engaged in asking himself, whether he is praying for that which God can properly give. When therefore what had at first been cries of distress, perhaps from a faithless and double mind, become genuine and fixed desires ; when crude yearnings for—he hardly knew what, clear up into distinct petitions which can be afterwards meditated on ; the soul wakes at length into a full self-consciousness that *it is wanting nothing, except exactly that, which of all things it is certain that God must rejoice to grant* ; viz. that it may never break away from His love. As soon as this is intellectually discerned, if earnest desire is at the same time acting, anxiety and fear fall away of themselves. The man is, in fact, hungering and thirsting for righteousness, and he has now found out that he is : it is then not to be wondered at, (much less to be derided as vain,) if he unhesitatingly believes that God will supply all his need, will keep him from falling, and will preserve him faithful to the end.   He now may, or he may not, frame out of his experience a general proposition about the "Final Perseverance of the Saints;" but no such proposition is wanted, while his heart is in harmony with God ; none does him good while he is perverse or double-minded.

Those in whom these phenomena have been sharply marked, so as to make a new crisis of the life, seem instinctively to compare the process which they thus undergo to a Spiritual Marriage. We have seen the longings of the soul to convert God's transitory visits into an abiding and indissoluble union.   On getting a clear perception that it is asking that which He delights to bestow, it believes that its prayer is answered : so it makes a covenant with God and pledges itself to him, well-assured that He accepts the pledge.   " Not now only, Oh my Lord," it exclaims, " but henceforth and always, Thou art mine and I am thine.   I have known somewhat of Thy gloriousness and loveliness : I have loved Thee a little : this heart has been Thy dwelling-place : now do I claim that my Lord shall never go away, but dwell here inseparably, eternally."—It is therefore very far indeed from a gratuitous phantasy, to speak of this as a marriage of the soul to God : no other metaphor in fact will express the thing ; and it is hard to think that any can have experienced it and not feel the suitability of the phrase, though (for fear of casting pearls before swine) one must ordinarily avoid every allusion to what is not only a sacred but a momentous transaction.   Momentous : for even the intellectual remembrance of such vows, such claims, such joys, such hopes,—gives to the soul immense power of recovering its affections, when lost as they must be continually lost, if only by the wear and tear of the world.   At the same time I am not defending the language of human loves, in the extent to which grave and pure-minded persons have often here applied it. .

Yet the strongly-marked analogy between the Soul's love to God, and that borne by a woman to her husband, is in several ways instructive and even suggestive.   It gives the solution to various anomalies.   Many utterances of passion are right, healthy and amiable in secret, which, when exhibited before the cold-minded, seem only ridiculous ; not but that, if one could condescend to the task, rapturous love might be defended even to a utilitarian.   And this is the reply to those, who sneer at what they think (in religion) to be moping fancies, self-invented sorrows and empty joys.   When spiritual life gushes out fresh and powerful, it may possibly be turbulent and irregular, like the mountain torrent or like the early affection of lovers; but in its later course its tendency (when happily guided) is to become tranquil and even-flowing, fertilizing to those who know not its source. Who would get rid of the noisy brook, if with it he must lose the noble river? Who that knows the ever-fresh delights of long wedded love, thinks them dearly bought by the alarms and sorrows and palpitations and jealousies and undue absorption of the mind in courtship?

So deeply impressed in Jewish and Christian religion have been the exercises of soul just described, that out of them has arisen the perception of a new attribute in God, before unknown; namely, his *Faithfulness*. It is difficult, or perhaps impossible, to silence the objections of philosophers to the idea, that the Most High has entered into a private stipulation with this or that soul; and we may admit, that such a statement does but crudely express the real truth at which it hints, and which the intellect imperfectly embraces. Yet nothing will convince the Soul which has passed through such processes, that it does not discern a spiritual reality, when it dwells on the Faithfulness of God. Hence it has been said: "The *Secret* of the Lord is with them that fear Him, and He will show them his *Covenant*:" and indeed, the conception of a definite Covenant between God and the Soul, as it is ascribed to the very birth of Judaism,—to Abraham, Isaac, and Jacob; and again, as renewed with Moses and with David,—so it lasts to the end among those who trace their spiritual lineage through these progenitors. That the fallible human intellect may here attach error to its truth, is freely conceded. Men may pray for external things, as for the possession of a strip of land, or the continuation of an earthly dynasty; and may imagine that they have gained assent to their prayer,* so that its accomplishment is guaranteed to them by a divine Covenant. It is even possible, that as Prayer began in petitions for outward things, and only in a later stage ripens into a spiritual form, so also the idea of God's Promises and Covenant has necessarily in its origin something of error mingled with it. Nevertheless, if the soul's assurance that God attends to spiritual prayer is not a mere delusion,—(to assert which is to make Theism and Atheism equivalent, as far as internal and spiritual life are concerned,)—then neither is it delusive to believe that we may call God's Strength in to aid our weakness, and may rest upon His *faithful* performance of that to which we have pledged Him.

* See Note 2 at the end of this Chapter.

A distinction must be here made, not only between outward *events* and inward phenomena, but perhaps also between the moral and the spiritual within us. All spiritual men confess their utter impotency to be as spiritual as they wish; but they do not by any means so entirely confess to moral impotency. Sharply to mark where the moral ends and the spiritual begins, is perhaps impossible, or at least need not be here attempted. It is enough to say, that where we feel that God has given us abiding and inherent strength, we of course have to stir up that strength, but cannot seek to cast ourselves on his faithfulness. Such reliance on Him belongs exclusively to that class of actions in which we know we are weak:—that is, in contending against our besetting moral sin, (if by nature or by old bad habits we have any in particular,)—and, in all purely spiritual affection. Of the latter emphatically God is the source; and here that the soul is practically correct in relying on God's faithfulness as a reality exterior to itself, appears from the result :—namely; thus, and thus alone, is its inward love, strength, joy, peace, renewed and developed.

The feeling of this contrast between our inherent strength and our fitful weakness, has farther led to the phraseology which contrasts "Nature" and "Grace." All Nature indeed is from God. Nature is divine if any thing in this world is: why should any one think to honour God, by undervaluing Nature? —There is truth and weight in that objection; and many religious people lay themselves open to just reproof on this head. Nevertheless, they have a meaning, and a correct one, in the contrast above denoted. Thus when it is said, that "Nature, without Grace, will not enable us to serve God acceptably; they mean,—that the strength which the Soul regards as its own, and *natural* to it, because always at its command, is found not to suffice for the exigencies of spiritual life. It needs, over and above, a strength *out* of itself, obtained only by self-despairing faith in God; and this strength from God is called *Grace*.

Herein we farther see, that the Soul's Covenant or Marriage with God is something more than a simple act of Self-Consecration. For it is possible to devote ourselves to God in a self-relying spirit; and many a man, with the best intentions, has brought himself into deep spiritual unhappiness by resolving and vowing to God that which (experience soon shows) is beyond his ability to perform. Probably such disappointing and humiliating attempts are with many preliminary to that better Covenant, which is made without self-reliance, and in which an eternal support is found: which *is* indeed a self-consecration, yet one in which we look to receive, not to bestow; to drink of God's water of life, and only of His own to render to Him. To enter however into such covenant with God is a blessedness not to be attained by means of *book-faith*; which at best only brings men to believe some general proposition,—perhaps an important one, yet inadequate without special application. *How* inadequate, is clearly seen, when any carry Bibliolatry out to its legitimate conclusion, by maintaining that "it is no want of faith for an individual A B to suspect that God means to leave him in his sins for ever; *inasmuch as nowhere in the Bible is it asserted that God intends to save A B.*" The extravagance of this result, which deprives Faith of all practical value, has always led a majority of spiritual men to modify the theory, generally perhaps by alledging that "the Spirit," as something separable from and higher than the Word, "*applies* God's general promises to the particular case." Indeed very opposite schools of spiritual doctrine have agreed that the saint learns "by the Spirit" to say *My* God, *My* Father, and (in short) to take *to himself personally* all that God has to bestow. This not only cannot be communicated by book-faith, but moreover has nothing to do with any historical faith at all. It was possessed, in a high degree and earlier than Christian times, by many of the Hebrew Psalmists; and it obviously depends on the absolute trust of the soul in God as in one with whom it has actual intercourse. If it has a real perception and consciousness of such intercourse, its insight and its trust are personal and direct, and do not depend on any historical opinions: if it has no such perception, it cannot possibly get that appropriation which is confessedly essential to a living and happy faith. The evidence of this obtrudes itself on the mind in so many forms, that the admission of it is perpetually slipping out from spiritual persons, even though their intellect has been from childhood pre-occupied by a baseless Bibliolatry, and by a carnal* homage to outward miracles.

In reply to those who despise all inward experiences as simple delusion, it would be a sufficient defensive argument to say, that love to God is as respectable a passion as love for the Fine Arts: but the surpassing magnitude of the moral consequences justifies us *theoretically* in assuming a much higher tone; and the only

---

* *So* carnal are the prevalent notions, that a man who does not believe that God reveals himself to *eye* or *ear* is at once called *an unbeliever in Revelation!* As justly were men called Atheists by the Pagans, for holding God to be invisible. Revelation was differently understood by Paul, Ephes. i. 17; Rom. i. 19: so Matt. xi. 25. On the Christian idea of Revelation, see farther in J. D. Morell's Philosophy of Religion.

F

thing that *practically* is apt to put to shame and stop the mouth
of its advocate, is, the deplorable bigotry (of word, if not of feeling,) in which none indulge so much, as those who speak earnestly concerning the love of God. When it appears, that they
not only regard themselves as Heaven's sole concern, but count a
doctrine to be *good news*, which simultaneously proclaims everlasting Glory to them, and everlasting, ever-torturing Sin to the
vast majority of the human race,—the common heart of the
world boils up with horror at the apparent intensity of selfishness in those, in whom Self ought to be swallowed up by divine
Love. When upon this comes an anathema against all who
differ from them on intellectual questions, men turn away in
despair superadded to disgust. Such bigotry is the real cause
why the heathen have cast down the walls of God's vineyard, and
the boar out of the wood lays it waste; bigotry, inexcusable by
the plea of "submitting the understanding to the Scripture."
For *if this be* Scripture doctrine, (—I waive the question of interpretation—,) then it is a wicked thing to submit their understandings to it : the moral sense and conscience ought to revolt
against it, as against any other heathenism. It ought to show
them that the book is not immaculate, and to drive them to the
teachings of God's Spirit. In fact however I believe, this evil
side of their doctrine is brought out only now and then, to do
mischief in controversy; but commonly lies buried in dust in a
corner of the intellect; it would therefore be unjust to impute to
individuals the selfishness inherent in their theoretic creed.

Let the philosophical moralist farther be assured, that the
more enlightened minds among spiritual Christians disbelieve the
most outrageous part of this traditional doctrine; though laymen
have no voice to say so, and priests are generally too timid. It
is not just in him to be thus repelled; and by it he maims his
own science. Morals can seldom gain living energy, without the
impulsive force derived from Spirituals. We do not indeed
doubt that a man's own *self-respect* may make him choose to die,
rather than live degraded in his own eyes by deviating from his
ideal of right conduct: let earnest Stoicism be confessed to be
noble and honourable; though it makes the mind too exclusively
reflexive, and endangers pride and self-confidence. But however
much Plato and Cicero may talk of the surpassing beauty of
Virtue, still Virtue is an abstraction, a set of wise rules, not a
person; and cannot call out affection, as an existence exterior to
the soul does. On the contrary, God is a *Person*; and the love
of Him is of all affections by far the most energetic in exciting
us to make good our highest ideal of moral excellence, and in

clearing the moral sight, so that that ideal may keep rising. Other things being equal, (a condition not to be forgotten,) a spiritual man will hold a higher and purer morality than a mere moralist.   Not only does Duty manifest itself to him as an ever-expanding principle, but,—since a larger and larger part of duty becomes pleasant and easy, when performed under the stimulus of Love,—the Will is enabled to concentrate itself more on that which remains difficult, and greater power of performance is attained.   Hence, "what the Law could not do, in that it was weak through the flesh," is "fulfilled in those, who walk not after the flesh, but after the Spirit."   In nothing perhaps is this more intelligibly exhibited, than in the sweet spirit of loving re-signation, with which hundreds and thousands of obscure Christians have endured long sickness and excruciating pain; while mere Stoicism with difficulty obtains from the strongest minds more than the suppression of unmanly lamentations, and is forced, alas! to leave suffering unsoftened by a sense of superior Love.

But is it to be hoped, that one who has attained the happy be-lief of his permanent spiritual union with the Father of Spirits, will retain his happiness and his strength unabated? that his conflicts are passed once for all, and that it is constantly a heaven on earth, which he will thenceforth live?   No one has a right to say of his brother that it may not be thus; but we see very many causes which make it hard to be thus.   All probably are summed up in Frailty and in Ignorance; and of these two the latter at least seems to be at present inevitable.   For now no concord is discernible in those who ought to advise or direct; and inexperience generally has to learn by its own failures, if exposed to circumstances which require wisdom.   Let us suppose that there is no Frailty to be blamed : that the heart remains brave to duty and ever faithful to God; still, in the complicated affairs of life, it is often most difficult to ascertain *what* is our duty.   So many principles of action are established in the world as abso-lutely right which are not wholly right; so often does acqui-escence in that which society demands or expects, clash or seem to clash with that which the spiritual instinct suggests; espe-cially, in dealings with others, so hard is it to know where obedience and deference must end, and resistance begin; where mercy will be weakness, and severity is essential; where we must yield up our rights, and where we must contend for them;—that even the coolest mind, and the best furnished with information and experience, must often doubt.   But, in fact, men frequently have not time for cool and full deliberation.   In the press and

hurry of life they are forced to act first and think afterwards.
Moreover we do not foresee the after-results of innocent and well-
meant actions, but first get entangled in perplexing positions.
Now, since to act without a clear conscience involves us in a
sense of sin, what can happen, if we are forced to act, and yet
are unable to decide which of several paths is the right? In
theory it may be replied, that a man who does what on the
whole seems to him best, or least bad, ought not to reproach
himself: but in reality when the conscience is dim and doubtful,
men are apt not to know whether or not they have been faithful
to their light. For these reasons, increasing wisdom is probably
always as essential to permanent peace of conscience, as it manifestly is to profitable action.

But we are far too favourable to human nature, in excluding
the hypothesis of Frailty. However powerful may have been the
convictions of spiritual truth, however vivid the impressions, yet
it is hard for new impulses to wage war against old habits or
against the insensible tendencies of the common nature; and
every special temperament has its own weak side. If no strong
blasts of passion carry the soul away, or if no cankering worldliness undermine its powers, yet perhaps a time and place comes,
where it cannot follow its convictions of duty without a sacrifice
which it has not strength to incur. Sophistry is then brought
in, to prove that no such sacrifice is really demanded. The heart
thus loses its simplicity, and languor and self-justification go
hand in hand. Many are the possibilities of this sort;—God
only knows them;—so many, that it may seem to be almost
superhuman happiness to avoid them all.

In the Third Chapter some notice was taken of the daily
shortcomings which often cloud the heart of spiritual men: but
the subject is not easily exhausted; and there is a peculiarity in
the case which was better reserved for this Chapter. One who
has not only recognized God's personal relation to him, but by
his own act (so far as human acts can avail), has entered into a
permanent bond, and believes the Most High to have accepted
his self-consecration; such a one, when made uneasy in conscience, is not at all in the same position as he was originally. A
small sin is in him great, because it is committed against mercy,
love and daily vows; yet it is to be compared rather with the
naughtiness of a child, than with the defiance of a stranger or of
an enemy. He still feels the sacred ties which unite him to
God, while he mourns that the face of God is hidden from him
because of his transgression. A child, who, when called to receive the parent's commands or caress, is attracted by some other

object, and refuses to come, knows that he has done wrong and has incurred displeasure, yet does not apprehend abiding or fatal consequences from the parent's anger : he is self-displeased and unhappy, until he has thoroughly confessed his fault, and has purged away the self-will and undutifulness which caused it by drinking more deeply into filial love.   Just so the child of God is affected, suffering self-reproach and grief (greater or less according to the case) but no fear ; and no other anxiety except as to how long it will be ere he shall again see his Father's countenance shine bright upon him. It has become an axiom of feeling to him, that he belongs to God: a feeling which is not lost, even by conscious wilfulness and perversity.

Herein we discern the root of the evangelical and prophetic (as opposed to the Levitical) idea of a peculiar and chosen people of God, who continue to be his people even when they are disobedient.   The notion has appeared frightfully immoral to those who do not know practically whence it arises and how it acts ; nor can it be denied, that if imbibed by the intellect as a mere verbal formula, the belief of an arbitrary divine Election is as purely mischievous, as it is shocking when coupled with that of the arbitrary damnation of the non-elect.   Yet it is certain, that a singularly large fraction of the most spiritual and faultless Christians have been deeply impressed with the idea of their Election by God, not as a mere dogma, but as a truth for daily life.   Their intellectual processes were probably erroneous; yet it is instructive to disentangle, if possible, their spiritual perceptions.—So long as they are consciously obedient, they may know themselves to be God's true people, but the idea of an arbitrary election, irrespective of their own obedience, is not likely to arise, or at least to take deep hold.   But when in the midst of conscious *dis*obedience the soul cannot help crying out, "Though I have sinned, yet surely I am Thine," and experiences that this sense of appropriation to God goads and scourges the heart into sorrow, making sin a thousand times more bitter, until the wanderer is brought back to the bosom of Divine Forgiveness ;— then he regards himself as freely and undeservedly chosen by God, "predestinated unto good works," "to be holy and without blame before Him."   Thus the spiritual facts which underlie the speculation, are, *first*, that the man who has once been consecrated to a divine union, ordinarily retains an assurance that that union is undissolved and indissoluble, even when he falls into an evil conscience and loses all happiness in his God; and, *secondly*, that this assurance is like a chain of love, by which God gently draws back to Himself His perverse but self-re-

proaching child, until shame and sorrow are swallowed up in the
outflowings of faith and gratitude.

There *are* however far more grievous cases,—though it is
always hard to judge whether a man exaggerates his own vileness,—in which, after " tasting the heavenly gift," a very awful
hardness of heart has been incurred.   In the retrospect of such
matters, every one so loathes his past self, as to lose calmness of
judgment and the power of measuring his language; hence,
where no specific facts are alledged, great deductions should be
made from all that a man states against himself.   Paul calls
himself the chief of sinners; he wrote it sincerely; but who of
us takes him at his word ?   It is difficult and dangerous to make
any comment on secrets known fully to one soul only, if even to
one ; yet there is much to give us deep confidence in the intense
vitality of spiritual desire, when it has once assumed its highest
evangelical form.   I cannot hesitate to feel, that though hurri-
canes of passion should have blown off the buds of religion's
early spring, yet if no selfish injustice has sapped the vital sus-
ceptibilities of the soul, it is never too late to hope for a restoration both sudden and final.   The "backslider" (as many scrip-
turalists call him) is inwardly self-condemned; self-despising
and self-hating, he probably continues in his sinful state through
despair only.   But on some favoured day he all at once remembers "the joy of his espousals;" and the thought gushes into
his heart that God once loved him, although foreknowing all his
vileness.   He meets the eye of the Almighty, and knows that it
is an eye of Love:—let no pen seek to tell what bitterness in
him its glance causes.   But it is as an electric stroke rending
open his inmost nature, fusing all its dross, burning out the
heart of sin, transforming the spirit into a living magnet which
obeys the heavenly attraction, until the prodigal son is brought
back with honour and blessing, though elder brothers frown with
incredulity.   Still he is like one who is recovered by severe
remedies from an acute disease; his frame is sore, his strength
shattered, his soul struck with shame, his finger is as it were on
his lips, and he dares not speak; but, like the leper, conscious
of uncleanness, he shrinks into solitude, and there makes complaint to Him who freely forgives.   Time however will, by God's
mercy, restore the prostrate soul; and it may be, that in this
way lessons have been learnt and defects extirpated, for which
no more lenient process would have been successful.   To the
milder forms of such humiliations all are liable, from the constant gravitating of the heart towards negligence and sluggish-
ness and its old world;—(a dear old world, far too much re-

viled by spiritual men, yet not able to satisfy the Soul;)—and grievous as it is that they should be needed, it is certainly instructive to have some insight into them.   In vain is the moralist sceptical concerning the intensity of spiritual forces, when he carefully keeps out of their region:—what knows the mere mechanician of electricity?   In fact, perhaps, the great transformations of the will *must* be sudden.   Between living for Sin and living for God, there is a yawning chasm; which must be passed *per saltum*, if at all.

The Scriptures of both Old and New Testaments are as emphatic in asserting, as moralizers are timid in admitting, the unlimited mercy and long-suffering of God : but surely it is one of the first elements spiritually discerned, that the impediments to acceptance with Him lie solely *in us*, and that there is no time or state conceivable, in which a man shall turn towards Him, and He refuse to hear.   We cannot expect too much readiness in Him to save, too much tender compassion, for the plain reason that these qualities in Him are infinite.   We are not straitened in Him, but we are straitened in our own bowels : our great danger, folly and even sin, lies in Unbelief of His inexhaustible long-suffering.   As soon as we do believe it, the thought of it kindles all our generous affections, and puts life into us.   Nor is it possible for one who believes *the right thing*, to abuse it to evil ends : for it is not, that God will never leave a perverse and faithless heart to its own ruin and misery, or that if we harden our hearts to-day, He will soften them to-morrow ; no : but that if *now* we turn to Him with all the heart, nothing that is past (however black it seem to us) is any obstacle with Him.   I repeat it, from a deep sense of its importance; as long as we are desiring *the right thing* of God,—that is, immediate spiritual recovery and renewed vigour,—we cannot expect it too enthusiastically.   All the danger is the other way : we are double-hearted, we wish not, we expect not, and therefore we receive not.   When we have become cold and uninterested in all spiritual things, we often cannot exactly tell *why*: perhaps it is through sinful negligence; or perhaps it is through the worry and distraction of business, and not wholly without physical causes.   If we set about self-analysis to find out how far we are personally guilty, we may get into insoluble questions, and be more and more discouraged, the more we look within; for there is assuredly nothing there to strengthen us.   But if we *can* exercise the energies of Faith, the fact is our sufficient warrant; for it proves that we are true-hearted: and thus we suddenly become strong out of the midst of our weakness.   After we are in

peace and power, self-analysis is most valuable and indeed necessary ; it is instructive, humbling and bracing: but while we are
cold and weak, it is a poisonous thing, like a draught of quinine
while the ague-fit is upon one.

While it is needful to know the ways by which the Soul, when
fundamentally upright, can always regain her lost love, it would
be discouraging indeed, if we might not look earnestly forward
to attain, even on this earth, a state in which the affections
should be recovered as fast as lost,—at intervals so short, that
the heart should never reproach itself for sin, but only sigh over
its inherent weakness.   This seems to be the state, which the
Wesleyans (to the scandal of other Christians) have denominated
Perfection or Full Redemption, and after which they breathe in
many plaintive or glowing hymns.   Surely we may expect, and
ought to strive, that moral light may be so superadded to fervency of soul, that divine love may at length become in us, not
as a torch blazing and smoky at intervals, but as a pure serene
ever-burning flame, pervading all our nature, animating all our
acts, consuming our evil principles, and kindling us to everything good, great and useful.   This will lead us to inquire, whether the mind can form any more definite ideal of that to which
it is to aspire, and whether there are any outward helps towards
it.   To these subjects the next Chapter will be devoted.

Note 1, *referred to at page* 85.

The Hebrew prophets, especially of the later school, habitually represent the relation of the Israelitish *Church* collectively to Jehovah, as that
of a wife to a husband; but this does not seem to be applied to *individuals.*

The metaphor was adopted by Paul, who makes the *Church* the bride of
Christ: (so the Apocalypse:) yet he first set the example of concen-
trating the similitude on parts of the Church: " I am jealous over you
with a godly jealousy, that I may present you as a pure virgin to Christ."
When the visible Church became a huge mass of Paganism, clearer
room was left for the individual to claim the metaphor.   Indeed in one
text (1 Cor. vi. 17) Paul himself had been led on to apply it to individuals in rather too physical an aspect.

Note 2, *referred to at page* 95.

I knew intimately an eminently devout and in many ways remarkable
man, who, when pronounced by physicians to be in hopeless consumption,

was entirely convinced, though in the full possession of his ordinary faculties, that God had promised and covenanted with him that he should not die, at least without being raised up to preach *once more* to his people. He died without so doing. Here some intellectual hallucination had so entwined itself with his devotional exercises, that they could not be separated. There are doubtless thousands of such cases still; and where the theory of religion is in that lower stage which admits of a confident expectation that prayer for external things will be granted, (as, the praying that it may or it may not rain,) it is perhaps impossible for the highest and purest saints wholly to avoid painful mistake on such matters. The present generation of the world simply calls such things *Fanatical*, and avoids the error by discrediting *all* Trust in God.

CHAPTER V.

ON SPIRITUAL PROGRESS.

It has been seen, how the Soul, weak and wandering, like a storm-driven bird, learns to nestle in the bosom of the Infinite One, seeking peace or strength, until at length love towards Him is born within it: how then out of love springs insight,—insight of His prior and greater love to it; whence the opening of a purifying, strengthening and happy intercourse of the secret heart with Him. But what is it desiring? In word, it is easy to say,—it wants holiness and goodness like His own, that being perfectly like Him, it may be indissolubly united to Him : but, in fact, it sees no true image of His holiness, and often scarcely knows what it wants. Moreover, when outward and moral evils have been triumphed over, when the best known spiritual sins have been beaten down, it has strength to spare for action ; and the question then arises, How is that strength to be employed?

It is a great error to imagine that high excellence can ever consist in a mere suppressing of some worse and lower tendency ; the better part which we choose, may be itself not very elevated. The soul may be freed from struggle and the conscience be at peace, because its highest convictions have triumphed ; and yet its highest may be far from high. Nay, the triumph may be due, as much to the weakness of the inferior passions, as to any energy of the spiritual nature ; so that a comfortable mediocrity is all that will result, unless the moral perceptions keep rising ;—which is indeed the only healthful state. To this, however, it is probable that increasing mental culture is in certain stages essential. The subject is too wide to be here discussed, and can only be glanced at : but it is easy to see how pure intellectual error, depending on causes wholly unmoral, *may* and *does* perpetuate moral illusions, which are of the deepest injury to spiritual life, and keep it down to a very unsatisfactory level. In such case, the advance of that knowledge which is purely intellectual and *negative*, (which on that account religious men are apt to dread,) is absolutely requisite for farther spiritual progress. To destroy superstition does not in itself impart religion; yet the destruction is necessary, if religion is to flourish.

But again: while the soul desires a higher holiness, it inquires, what are the peculiar aids (if any) towards attaining this object; and especially, what is the value of those which are offered by the practices of social religion or by others which are esteemed as "means of grace." And although it is hard to give unity to these two discussions, it is not convenient to keep them far separate.

§ 1. ON THE IDEAL OF EXCELLENCE.

From childhood we hear it repeated, until it seems an axiom, that the human life of Christ is the pattern which we are practically to imitate: yet the moment we in good earnest attempt such imitation, we are beset by the most embarrassing difficulties. We find that his vestments will not fit us; his shape cannot be ours. The figure of him sketched out before us is, in part, fully painted up, but evidently inapplicable to our case; far more of it is left blank, so that we have to fill it out by our own imaginations. On this whole matter men willingly delude themselves: there is a great fiction which they dread to have unveiled: and it may be impossible to allude to broad matters of fact, without giving very grave offence. However intense one's conviction, common sense or humility forbids (for example) to stir the bad passions of men invested with power by publicly denouncing them as hypocrites, blind guides, whited sepulchres; to speak at men's hearts, instead of answering their words; to use enigmatical and paradoxical expressions, which offend and confuse the hearers, and then withhold public explanation of them; purposely to encounter the malice of the unjust, and lay down one's life by self-chosen martyrdom. Grant that these things were all right in *Jesus*; still we discern and feel that they would be all wrong in *us*. And if in none of them we can follow him, it is equally doubtful whether we should wisely imitate him by spending whole nights on the mountains in prayer, or forty days in fasting. In short, the more every detail is pursued, the more absurd it appears to propose his *conduct* (in deed, in word, or in its inward plan) as a pattern for ourselves. As to the *spirit* of his conduct, in contrast to the *letter*, no book can tell it to us, if our own hearts do not ; and even as to outward things, numberless points will day by day present themselves, on which we are left to guess how he acted or would have acted. For instance, is it really true that he never laughed ? This question goes deeper than at first appears. Let the image of Puritanical constrained gravity be duly considered, and we shall see how pernicious it is to imitate one to whom laughing may not be ascribed. Nay, but in our whole conception of revered names an illusion floats over our minds. Those who ad-mire Paul in Raffael's cartoon, might perhaps despise him in a mean unpicturesque garb, especially if they found him short in stature, stammering, or sore-eyed,* with nothing romantic about him. Exactly as we refuse to imagine him of vulgar appearance, so do we shrink from the idea of his hearty sympathy with a jocose expression or act : yet it would be rash and gratuitous to maintain that Paul could not laugh with the same geniality as Luther. These are not matters which we could expect to find recorded ; yet whatever may be said concerning their dignity, to conceive rightly of them is very important. A sober view of human life shows that to proscribe the jocose side of our nature would be a blunder as grievous in its way as to proscribe love between men and women ; though in this last point again we see, that neither Christ nor Paul is an example to men in general. True religion wages no abstract war against any part of man, but gives to each part its due subordination or supremacy, and breathes sweetness and purity through all. There are times and places when we *can* not, as well as *may* not, laugh ; but it is by no means the highest state always to stifle laughter. That rather belongs to the stiff precisian, who fears to betray something false within him, and habitually wears a mask, lest his heart be too deeply exposed ; while the true-hearted fearlessly yields to his impulse, and no more wishes to hide it from the All-seeing eye, than a child would hide his childish sports from the eye of a father.

There is no question which has more vexed spiritual persons, than the propriety of occasionally gratifying others by joining them in some of the gaieties of life, by abstinence from which they often cause great offence : yet no authoritative solution can be gained by appeal to any scriptural pattern. *One* reasons : "Jesus went to a wedding ; therefore I may go to a ball :

---

* His enemies said of him that " his bodily presence was weak, and his speech contemptible." The " thorn in the flesh" of which he complains, has been plausibly explained both of stammering and of sore eyes. The present Bishop of Winchester supposes him to have been afflicted with extreme short-sightedness, and so accounts for many smaller curious facts.

especially since at an Oriental wedding there was often dancing and music." *Another* retorts: "A wedding is a serious and religious transaction, consequently it cannot be here adduced: but we are commanded not to be conformed to this world: a precept which forbids us from gay parties, from the theatre, the opera, and public concerts, as well as from horse-races and country sports."—No analysis of the letter will ever decide such controversies. He who is under the Law, is satisfied with re-marking that "conformity to this world" means nothing but con-formity to *its sins*, and that the text does not help to decide whether this particular case involves sin. He who desires to live to God, tries to feel with his soul whether sin (to him) *is* or *is not* here implicated; so the Spirit within is the real guide, and not the text, any more than the scriptural example. Only a madman could reason: "Christ and his apostles are not recorded to have attended Plays or Oratorios; therefore I am prohibited." In short, whatever practical question may be started, we always alight on the same result, that *authoritative* examples and precepts (as such) can do us no good in the region of spirituality. LAW can forbid definite acts of sin and command definite acts of duty; but when an action is not in itself sinful, nor in itself obligatory, no book-rules can forbid or command it. This is precisely the class of things with which *spiritual* (as transcending *moral*) life is concerned; and the conclusion is plain, that a book-revelation on such subjects is impossible. A person who converts the history of Christ or Paul into a new authoritative *Law*, will often be driven to violate his own right feelings and sober judgment. Manifestly all sound-minded persons use these histories only by way of *suggestion*, and not as prescribing anything authoritatively. Thus the recorded life of Jesus is to us, in principle, only what the life of Melancthon or Pascal may be; for it sometimes does, but far oftener does not, call us to imitation; and we have not and cannot have external guidance, when to follow it and when not; or external information as to the spirit in which each re-corded action was performed. Indeed, when we read the exhor-tations of Paul or Peter "to imitate Christ," it ought not to be forgotten, that, *on the one hand*, these were addressed to persons who had no written narratives to call out the ingenuities of ex-pounders; *on the other*, the end sought was always to recommend by his (vaguely reported) example such virtues as heathen moral-ists often denied to be virtues: such, namely, as humility, resig-nation, long-suffering, condescension. So important was it to propose to the converts something in a concrete form that would make the meaning of such words more vivid to the mind, that

Paul does not hesitate to refer to *his own* conduct, as a model which they would do well to imitate.

The case of conscience just now touched on is an instructive illustration of a general principle. The world at large is nearly divided between surprize and contempt at the repugnance shown by spiritual persons to certain artificial pleasures; and undoubtedly the disposition of many to enact a new ceremonial law, which proclaims, "Thou shalt not dance: Thou shalt not play cards," &c., &c., will excuse, if it cannot justify, a great deal of ignorant raillery. Yet it cannot be by accident, that in different ages and countries, without any definite scriptural prohibition, spiritual persons coincide so markedly in apathy or dislike for pleasures of this description. I see not how to doubt that an instinct of the soul guides them, which is without law, and really higher than all law. A man who drinks within his own heart from a hidden well of joy, cannot run to fill his pitcher from an artificial tank: and if by any means that well is closed, his soul is widowed, and dreads to be comforted: then less than ever can he enjoy even the most innocent gratifications. Else, there are many pleasures which, if they come of themselves, he will accept, but which he cannot go to fetch. The simple glee of children, or the unstudied sallies of wit, may have a great zest for him in their measure; and yet he may feel an invincible repugnance to go out of his way for mirth or wit: if they are to be pleasant, they must be unsought and unpremeditated.* So in regard to the gratification derived from those Public Amusements which profess to address the sense of Beauty, a discomfort might depend on the amount of effort required by them; but this probably is rather secondary. A feeling of Vanity in *the circumstantials* is that which is painful and wearisome to the religious soul, though the feeling is often smothered through kindness and good breeding and from a belief that it will do harm to show it. What is meant by giving to outward glitter and manufactured mirth the offensive name "Vanity," is more than some can comprehend, who, having no notion of any higher rule than Law, think that they settle the matter by asking, "what harm there is in a pretty sight." Perhaps there is none to them: they are in a puerile state: it may sometimes be right to humour them: at least this appears the best way of showing that no morosity mingles with distaste for such things. But it cannot be doubted, that a person who *against the instincts of his soul* should become

---

* Is not all relaxation and amusement most effective, when there has been the least previous forethought spent on it?

(for instance) a constant opera-goer or play-goer, merely to please others,—although it is most true that he is free from Law in such matters,—will incur great spiritual mischief: for he will overbear and beat down the inward law of his heart.

And this leads farther to a distinct enunciation, that as we can neither wish nor have a better rule, concerning the things which a common moralist calls "indifferent," than the Law of the Spirit within us, so real spiritual progress will be attended by the clearing and strengthening of this inward instinct; in short, therefore, by the overspreading growth *of a healthy enthusiasm.* This is the greatest charm of character, even where it is partial and independent of spiritual influences : but the highest idea of human perfection, is, that this should pervade the whole man, and, in consistency with the truest wisdom, should animate every set of actions, while the instinct guides through all delicate questions of right and wrong. The upright and faithful soul knows and feels what things do, and what do not, impair communion of heart with its God; this is its great clue to its wrong and right; so it is alternately scrupulous where a moralist would be bold, and bold where a moralizer might be prudish. Again, by the nourishment of its generous affections it gains a power of impulse, by which it is enabled to carry into effect its right conceptions. All know that in the practical world enthusiasm is the chief moving power; and is very effective, even when joined with narrow and distorted judgment. Our misery has been, that the men of thought have no religious enthusiasm, and the enthusiastically religious shrink from continuous and searching thought; and this must go on until our Theology is shifted away from its present basis. That the instincts of the soul, if there are any, are of first-rate importance, ought to be confessed even by those who know nothing of them : for if the instinct of brutes be the guidance of God within them, (*Deus anima brutorum,*) what else is the Soul's instinct but the Spirit of God? But, be it granted, such analogies are deceptive : still, by what else but this instinct was Divine existence ever discovered at all ? what, but the Soul, groping after Him, taught all nations of men to be familiar with these high ideas? And if the unenlightened Heathen soul achieved so great a revelation, what ought that soul to do, all whose powers are stimulated by the love of God, and by constant intercourse with him?

This is not a doctrine much talked of nowadays; but time was, when it was believed by prophets and apostles. They did not tell of *two* Spirits of God, one extraordinary, and one ordinary;

one, which by them dictated propositions, and another which in-
clined the hearers to "submit their corrupt understanding" to
the propositions.   Every living member of Christ's body, the
Church, was (in *their* belief) animated by "the Selfsame Spirit,"
who "divided to each severally as He would;" and the Gospel
was preached, in order that those who believed it might *all* receive
that life-giving and enlightening power, and be themselves able
to listen to the voice of God directing them.   Thus of Zion it
was to be said, "All thy children shall be taught of the Lord,
and great shall be the peace of thy children :" out of each man's
heart were to flow rivers of living water: and their teachers professed not to usurp "dominion over their faith, but only to be
helpers of their joy :" nor did they give them a new law of the
letter, written with ink, but a law written on the fleshy tablets
of the heart; bidding them not to quench the Spirit, and to
prove what was the perfect will of God.   But now, by idolizing
the letter, men do quench the Spirit within them ; and then, are
unable to understand that very letter, which they blazon forth in
purple and gold.

If we would be holy and enlightened as Paul, we must do as
Paul did; not by slavishly copying the outside of his conduct,
but by nourishing our inward spirit as he nourished his.   He
refused to learn his religion of men, but listened to the voice of
God : and so have all the great and good men done, whose religious action can be thankfully remembered.   Undoubtedly they
have all been liable to the grievous inconsistency of being unwilling to leave other souls as free as they claim that their own
shall be.   They feel to the very bottom of their nature, that
they cannot serve two masters ; and that if they are to be
subject to God in earnest, they must be free from the yoke of
men : and yet, alas ! no sooner do they find themselves at the
head of admiring and obedient multitudes, than they proceed to
impose their own yoke on others, and, if possible, on their successors for ever.   In early times, the intense evils of this had
not been historically unfolded, and the apparent practical advantages of it overbore the abstract remonstrances of conscience ;
but in the present ripeness of experience all cultivated minds
have before them the full means of freeing themselves from such
illusions.   The immense progress of pure intellect must show
every thoughtful man the impossibility (not to say the wickedness) of sacrificing the Intellect to the Soul ; and wherever there
is true Faith, there is an unhesitating conviction that there cannot possibly be any real collision between these two parts of
human nature.   It is now no common guilt, when a man uses

his spiritual influence to frown down any honest intellectual research: but more of this afterwards.

The pure and pervading enthusiasm to which the soul should tend, is a very different thing from eccentricity, and would not show itself in superficial excitement, much less in wayward and fickle conduct. It is a deep inward fire, slowly fusing the opake mass of nature, and bidding it to crystallize into new shapes and refract God's light into a thousand hues, so that the whole man is about to be transparent, only that the eye of the observer is dazzled. Under this influence, each soul will assume *its own character*; no one aping another, all being unlike, yet the likeness of God being on all: for God has myriads of forms, but one essence. In the commencement of this action the instincts of the Soul are hardly self-conscious; and long after, no intellectual idea of that at which they aim, is as yet presented to the mind: but unless this is a mere dream of theory, it would seem that in all higher types of spiritual life each must at length shape to himself *his own Ideal,* and know what is his service. So Paul conceived of one as an Eye, one as a Hand; no two members alike, but each fitted for his own work. The work, described positively, may be called God's work; but if we ask what work deserves to be so named, the easiest reply is the negative one, that it is *not* that of the world or of the flesh;—which means, not that of selfishness and self-indulgence or self-glorifying. *He* works the work of God (even if he knows not God,) who works unselfishly for a good end: thus also Faith in God is justly said to "overcome the *world,*" or, to mortify all the *selfish* principles which are collectively so denoted. Now nothing is more unworldly than enthusiasm in every form: in Art, in Science, in Politics, in Trade, it is (even when isolated from religion) an inveterate antagonist of selfishness: nor is there any character for whom the worldly (or selfish) man feels so much contemptuous pity, as for an enthusiast, until some undeniably great result forces him to confess that enthusiasm is a powerful reality. The enthusiasm however, of which we speak, is not, like these, a partial and one-sided impulse, but implies a warm love of everything Good and True, with as warm indignation against their opposites; both feelings rising out of the sympathy of the soul with the centre of all Goodness, and its forgetfulness of self in the midst of the great interests all round at stake.

In the Third Chapter of this essay, it was shown, how Self-consciousness becomes intenser, as we advance towards a deeper spirituality; and evidently without this, there can be no spiritual self-control and responsible action. Yet unless *an opposite* principle were simultaneously unfolded, Self-consciousness would painfully embarrass and weaken us, by constantly directing the thoughts within, and magnifying the image of self. That opposite principle is this Enthusiasm; which fills the affections with thoughts wholly foreign to self, and lifts us above vulgar criticism. If this is defective even in statesmen, acuteness and experience make them overcautious, inactive, and wise too late. For the practical man, Impulse is as essential as Guidance: there is serious instruction in the witty saying of a satirical poet, that we must not " fear the flames, required to boil our kettle."

While in all "indifferent" matters (that is, those which Law cannot command or forbid) the inward instinct is the rightful guide, its powers are stimulated by discerning the instincts of others; and this is God's provision for the progress of moral sentiment. Even brute animals have taught men most valuable lessons, and act as daily monitors to us. Their patience and docility, their gratitude and faithfulness, their bravery and self-devotion, are delightful to see: and the same may be said of a hundred virtues, which, like wild flowers, bloom all round us in simple half-instructed natures. Let not the spiritual man despise the world of common men; for if he is wise, that world is his best outward moral teacher, at least until there shall be more of nature in the church. From time to time indeed a young enthusiasm arises, and displays on the border of the church some new virtue, as zeal against* war and against slavery in the Society of Friends, reverence for intellectual freedom in the Unitarians, and others which cannot be mentioned without moving controversy as to fact. Against all new virtues a false church fights long and hard, alledging that they "are not in the bond" of her Law; though, when they have conquered men's consciences, she comes in to claim the victory, as won by her energies. Christianity itself in its origin was nothing but a new enthusiasm, born in men's souls by the working of God's Spirit; so, believers " challenged one another to love and good works." This mutual rivalry still continues, with benefit, I suppose; although our increased knowledge of the complicated framework of society shows us how much political and intellectual wisdom is often needed for judging what *kindly meant* works are really *good* works.

But are there antiquated virtues, as well as new ones? Was it

* I do not intend to express admiration of the unqualified mode in which this is pressed. *Defensive* War is generally a sacred duty, when one's soil is invaded.

a folly in the first apostles to abandon their boats and nets, in order to become fishers of men? or was it a virtue which is now wholly out of date? and is no lesson whatever now to be learned from that apparently fanatical saying,—If a man forsake not all that he hath, he cannot be my disciple? Consider, Reader, whether the following is not true. Many persons, and peculiarly teachers of religion, are liable to find themselves in a position, where rules from without forbid them to follow freely the Spirit of God within them. A man who discerns this to be his own case, is called by God (more clearly than if it were spoken by thunder from a cloud) to give up all his worldly interests, as Paul did; and until he gains strength for this sacrifice, he stunts his own spiritual growth, and loses living energy. The same thing applies to all, who find the routine of their worldly business or profession to involve practices, which the Spirit within them condemns : if they are faithful to God, they will at all risks of worldly loss refuse consent to such practices. No greater trials of principle can in these days (when bodily martyrdom is unknown) befal men who have wives and children depending on them, and whose sphere in life seemed to be fixed. To condemn those who shrink from the sacrifice, could not occur to any one who duly knows his own weakness : yet he would not the less sorrowfully feel, that such persons will not be counted worthy of promoting the kingdom of God.

Nevertheless, there is no excellence in mere outward self-denial, when it surpasses what morality may claim : nor can anything but self-righteousness or morbid consciences be generated by enjoining *in the abstract* such sacrifices. Indeed, this may seem to be only part of a wider doctrine ; namely, that the great and universal *spiritual* duty is to Be, not to Act, nor to Suffer: a truth, the abuse of which may be reproved as Quietism, but which is nevertheless of much importance. *Moral* Actions have a value in themselves, and at any rate require no more in the actor than general sincerity of good intention : but the value of (what is intended for) outward *Spiritual* Action is often indefinitely small, even when very rightly meant. Transcendental acts of Duty, performed without Insight,—as, to give one's goods to the Poor or to the Church,—are of very doubtful value. Again, consider the attempt to improve the spiritual state of our neighbour by profitable and holy words : an attempt, which may result in pure mischief, not only if done unseasonably or indiscreetly, but if it is not a manifest overflowing of heart which speaks. The weight of words is not in themselves, but in the speaker ; and the lessons which are not intended as lessons are often the most forcible.

If then we give our whole effort *to be* what God would have us,
He will provide the ways by which our life shall redound upon
others. The restless desire to attain "spiritual usefulness," is
very often a mere carnal ambition which imposes upon us. If
we are entangled in this, it will too often happen, not only that
we address ourselves to a divine work with earthly minds, but,
what is worse, frame for ourselves a code of action to which we
are spiritually unequal, and then, incur self-reproach as languid and cowardly for shrinking from a task which we cannot
profitably undertake. Not to harm our neighbours' souls is indeed a primary duty; but a majority of us will ordinarily best
promote the edification of others as well as our own by concen-
trating effort on our personal improvement. Much latitude is
conceded by all to professed religious teachers, and a decorous
respect is paid to their words; yet it is notorious that the very
same sentiment coming instead from a layman is often more
effective: for the clergyman is suspected of speaking for his
office' sake only. There is probably more knowledge in the professional man; but love, not knowledge, is that which edifies:
and to justify our concerning ourselves with the soul of another,
a real and deep love is felt to be requisite.

And this connects itself with the subject of Intercession.
Concerning the actings both of Intercession and of Hope, valuable hints may be gleaned from the history of a soul so full-grown
as that of Paul, presented to us in the outpourings of authentic
epistles. The topic of Hope is reserved for the next Chapter.
As for Intercession: when the divine Spirit has so conquered the
old or common nature, that though there may still be occasional
conflict, there is no anxiety, but (under all ordinary trials) a calm
foresight of victory as soon as any collision of desires is felt;
the soul, I suppose, overflows self, and commences cares or
anxieties for others: which are impossible, and their pretence
hypocritical, while the self is still consciously but half subdued.
Hence there came upon Paul daily the care of all the churches.
Hence his fervent and continual prayers for the spiritual advance
of his beloved children in the faith, and for the progress of divine
truth. Nay, to judge by his letters, prayer for his own soul
might seem to have been swallowed up in prayer for others. That
this is the highest or *limiting* state, we appear as it were to
divine. Accordingly Paul himself, while seeking reverentially to
shadow forth the occupation of Messiah in the heavenly world,
could imagine no loftier ideal of excellence, than that he was
engaged in Intercession: a view, which at a very early date recommended itself to the whole church.

A philosophical difficulty may nevertheless be here started. The soul (it may be said) not absurdly hopes that God will aid its own desires to be obedient to Him: but He does not give it a *carte-blanche*, to ask for things which do not concern its own perfection. How can we possibly know, that He will fulfil our prayers for the bodily or even spiritual health of one dear to us, to say nothing of distant matters? The reply does not seem difficult: We do *not* know that he will fulfil them. Then why do we pray? Why, neither do we know that he will *not* fulfil them; hence, when the soul is deeply moved, it *cannot help* praying for what it wants. Not to do so, would be an unnatural constraint: the full heart *must* vent itself to the Lord of Mercy and Love, who surely cannot disapprove of this. Nay, we know and are certain, that even though His inscrutable wisdom should see that the prayer cannot be granted, He would accept it, and we should be blessed in uttering it.

It may still be asked, Why do we pray for things, about which we do not feel much concern? This however I may leave others to answer: it certainly appears a mere dreary hypocrisy, like Fasting and Prayer at the word of command: yet something will be said on the point in the next Section under the head of Liturgies. It here suffices to remark, that "to pray because we think we ought to pray," is not really prayer, but at best is meditation or reverential homage. If a man has no heart for prayer, yet knows that he ought to desire certain things, let him muse until the fire kindles, and at last let him speak with his tongue. But when no fire is kindled, it is heathenish credulity to imagine that God will care for a verbally offered petition.

It may also appear that after the earlier and most necessary steps of spiritual advance, the soul can profitably bear stronger views of the grander attributes of God, and takes more pleasure in contemplating them; whence is derived a tranquil dignity to itself. Its joys also have less of excitement, but greater depth, continuity and evenness: nay their current is uninterrupted, though manifold sorrows may ripple on the surface, by impulses from without. At least this is that which *à priori* may be expected, as agreeing with all analogy. So also it is in this stage that the magnificent researches of modern Science, which strengthen our powers of imagination concerning the extent of Existence, in time and space, and the pervading uniformity of Law, become peculiarly beneficial; because there is no longer danger lest the personality of God, and his proper relation to the individual soul, should be lost in the dim Infinity which is spread out before the intellect. Then we can admire and wonder at Him, as the Blessed and Only Potentate, dwelling in light which no man can approach unto; and not at all lose the fixed assurance, that he dwells also in every contrite heart, and opens His ear to every cry of the hungering and thirsting soul. Thus also a reconciliation is finally brought about between Faith and Science, the Soul and the Understanding. God is recognized both *without* us, and *within* us. Man is seen to be essentially free, yet is felt both in right and in fact to be God's servant and friend. All that he has, is from God, and is to be cultivated for God: powers of mind are not to be left unused, any more than riches.

There is certainly something wanting to the Ideal of the perfect man, prevalent in religious circles: nor is this to be wondered at. As long as it was supposed that Christ would in a few years return, to close this earthly scene: while the fields were ripe to the harvest, and the labourers were few;—while a messenger to tell the truth, seemed of all things most urgently needed; no course was judged so serviceable, or so noble, as that the rich and cultivated man should abandon his wealth and his worldly calling, forswear his learning and his tastes, and become a preacher of the gospel. The total change of circumstances, and no small amount of experience, now give warning that this can only in exceptive cases be desirable. If such a person has dedicated his soul to its rightful owner, he will find some way of bestowing his energies in great measure for unselfish objects; either for external and immediate Utility, or for the attainment of abstract, or for the diffusion of practical, Truth; for the establishment of Right and Justice, or in works of Love and Mercy, or in the unselfish cultivation of the Beautiful. Yet with many (unless I mistake) it is a sort of enigma, how Art and Politics and Science are to blend with the highest religious character; and that, because our notions are unduly based upon those Scriptural heroes, whose position was too different from ours to make them any adequate pattern. I do not think it an exaggeration to say, that among ourselves the most spiritually-minded persons (if we speak of them in the mass) are apt to be more or less scandalized at zeal for Science or Fine Art in one whom they hope to be spiritual. They sigh over a good man, who lavishes his talents on such objects instead of devoting them to (what they call) the glory of God; a phrase which would seem to mean,—direct attempts to teach spiritual truth. They condescendingly patronize an astronomer or scholar, who is reported to have some religious tendencies and to be orthodox; and if he be very enthusiastic in his own pursuits, they still hope, that *in spite* of this, he has "the root of the matter in him," and will gain some low seat among the redeemed. Such notions are only another development of the same error, which once sent men into deserts or convents, and misnamed long prayers "divine service." To sacrifice Imagination or Intellect, and to sacrifice Domestic Affection, are about on a par. That the human mind was meant to labour for the Useful, to contemplate the Beautiful, to possess itself of the True, and contend for the Right, as well as to worship the Holy, or imitate the Bountiful One, seems to be quite an axiom of thought; and wisely to blend all, as circumstances allow, must be the highest human perfection. A true Faith believes without proof that all these things shall work together for good; and that God, who is at once Productiveness, Beauty, Truth, Right, Mercy, Bounty, and Holiness, is in them all.

May we not here gain some instruction from that which is told of celebrated Italian painters?—how they have, from mere love of their art, spent on a picture labour tenfold of what the set price required, and have preferred to live in extreme self-denial, rather than not execute it in their highest style? This seems to typify the unworldly spirit, in which, when we are more perfect, we shall follow our trades or our professions, of whatever kind. There is a prevalent opinion,—I fear not destitute of foundation, that *as a body* the more religious part of our nation is more sordid in its business-tone than the world. Possibly this may be interpreted, that there are among the former fewer instances of unselfish devotion to their worldly calling; which they are accustomed to regard as not deserving their affections, but only fit to be pursued for its gains. It is principally in men who have no ostensible religious character that we see the self-devoting pursuit of some honourable profession: and these are now in England only too rare. For alas, there is such eagerness to get rich, that enthusiasm, for one's work, *in and for itself*, is scarcely credited by the majority; and there are many necessary employments, which may seem almost incapable of calling out enthusiasm, and yet, most distressingly over-occupy both time and mind. I do not at all mean to say that every man's profession *ought to be* his absorbing passion: only, it *may be*, and that, on a religious ground.* It is certainly a narrow belief,

---

* The germ of this sentiment is seen in Paul, who bids slaves "to do service with good will, *as to the Lord, and not unto men.*" The precept shows how entirely he felt the meanest occupation to be sanctified by and to a religious heart; and that if he were exhorting us moderns, he would enlarge it to embrace our several professions. Indeed this is not at all

taken up on too slavish a principle of imitation, that when there
is the deepest and soundest spirituality, the actions will proclaim
this on their surface. Where the deed is lawful, so that the
moralist is satisfied, the question for the spiritualist is not, what
it is, but in what spirit it is done. An enthusiastic geologist or
chemist or astronomer or sculptor, whose whole life seems to be
absorbed in what many religious people would erroneously call
the World, not only may be eminently unworldly, but may be
serving God, and man too, more effectually than he could in any
other way : for the evolving of Truth and culture of Imagination
tend to elevate and perfect Man, side by side with the influences
of direct Devotion. For nearly two centuries, men of Science
have been our only school of Prophets. There is no war between
the parts of the human mind ; and (other things being equal)
he who best loves God will with most untiring energy and single-
ness of purpose pursue whatever good work his genius has fitted
him for. No one needs so little relaxation as he, in whose heart
dwells the Lord of strength and of peace.

§ 2. ON THE "MEANS OF GRACE."

It cannot be doubted that we in this day are the spiritual pro-
geny of Patriarchs and Prophets, derived by a genuine *Apostolic
Succession*. As in Science, so in Religion ; we have borrowed the
light of our predecessors, and it has kindled light in us. We
see and believe by means of Prophets and Apostles, and yet not because of them ; for though our life has come through them, it would
not be life, if it were not now independent of theirs. The Mathematician enjoys the fruit of high intellects such as Archimedes,
Newton, Euler, La Place ; and had not these men, and hundreds
of congenial spirits, laboured before him, he would not now know
what he knows : yet by their aid he so sees the whole truth from
it simplest elements, that their names and their authority never
enter the premisses of the argument which convinces him. Just
so is it with the modern worshipper. Although he sees for himself, he gratefully acknowledges the essential aid derived from
great predecessors, and feels the golden chain which binds him
to the past. . Consequently, neither can he overlook the last link
of that chain,—the instrumentality by which his heart was first
brought into sympathy with Psalmists and Apostles. And if so,
he cannot despise or under-value those external media of spiritual

a strained interpretation of his words in Rom. xii. "Not slothful in
business, fervent in spirit serving the Lord :" that is :—serving the Lord
by being not slothful, &c.

improvement, which, as transmitting feeling from soul to soul, might be briefly denoted as "means of Fellowship."

But Fellowship, like everything else that is good in spiritual things, has been turned into *formality*; and we are beset with a variety of competing "ordinances," which claim to be "means of grace." The most prominent are Fasting, Sacraments, Attendance at Liturgies, Prayer Meetings, and Sermons. With a view to most of these, many will press the close observance of Sunday.

1. It is truly vexatious, eighteen hundred years after Paul's career, to have to fight Paul's battles against those who profess themselves not only his grateful children, but his unreasoning obedient disciples. It is indeed superfluous here to prove, what is on the face of the New Testament, that Sundays are not Sabbaths, that Sabbaths are no part of Gentile Christianity, and that Sundays have in the Scripture nothing to do with abstinence from worldly business. The Puritan School of England and Scotland shuts its eyes to the plainest facts, because it believes it to be *useful* to hold that Sunday is Sabbath, and Sabbath binding upon us. In vain shall we point to Paul's contemptuous disavowal of Sabbaths, and to his declaration that he who disregards sacred days is justified, so that he only disregard them to the Lord. In vain may it be proved from the Christian history, that until Constantine, Sunday was a working day with Christians. In vain will it be shown that all the great Reformers held the ancient and Catholic doctrine, that the observance of Sunday is a mere ordinance of the Church, not a command of God; and that until the English and Scotch Sabbatarians (late in the 16th century) invented the Puritanical doctrine on this subject, it was unknown to the Christian Church. As long as Englishmen care more for supposed Expediency than for Truth, they will, through thick and thin, stickle for a divinely obligatory Sabbath, unless one show them that this falsehood has its evil and dangerous side.

Our ears are dinned with the false cry: "The Sabbath, the *boon* of the working man." In many cases, say rather, his *bane*. He rests from labour: true: but he labours only so much the harder on the other six days. Physically, he would be better for labouring six hours on Sunday, and one hour less on every other day. Spiritually also this would be far better:—first, for the irreligious man. For the irreligious are tempted to make Sunday a day of carousing and sensuality; and the more its sanctity is preached, the greater is this danger; because it makes their conscience bad, and generally hinders them from getting any but bad companions. More sin of every kind in England and Scotland is committed on Sunday than on any other day of the week; and of this, the (so-called) Sabbatical Institution is in great measure guilty.—Then as for the less religious, yet conscientious man. The Sunday hangs heavy upon him: it is a stupid sleepy day : superstition forbids his even improving his mind during its hours ; and with one seventh part of time left free, he still (strange to think !) has no leisure for mental cultivation. Puritanical notions about the Sabbath are thus at present the greatest of all impediments to the effectual education of the industrious classes. Thirdly, even for the sincerely religious poor, Sunday is far too long a day for continued spiritual thought. They have not inward energy enough to fill up the time with it, and they covet to be in church as much as possible : very generally *three* " services" do not seem to them too much ; but this very fact proves that their souls are passive under it all, and get no more good than they might have from *one*. Far better would it be, to have on Sunday six hours of work, say from 6 to 9 in the morning, and from 5 to 8 in the evening ; with *one* meeting in church to last from 11 to 12. The working man might then have a pleasant relaxation on Sunday, with no time heavy on his hands. There would be hours enough for religious meditation and for the greetings of kinsmen, and there might also be an hour's more rest on every day of the week. Surely this would be both spiritually and physically better.

It is thus pure fiction, that a Puritanical Sabbath is better *for a working man* than a Christian Sunday, such nearly as Christianity in its second century was glad to observe. But the modern Sabbath tends a great deal more to the *grandeur of a sacerdotal body*; and this was felt by the instinct of those bishops who first moved Constantine to enact it. On an English Sunday the clergyman and the " minister" are in their glory. They are not conscious that this impels them so urgently to enforce the day ; but when we see the trumpery nature of the arguments, both from the New Testament and from expediency, on which they rest its positive moral obligation, it appears certain that there is *some* sinister bias ; and if so, I see not how to avoid the opinion that—I do not say the *individual*, but the strong *public*, opinion on this subject, is generated out of the merely professional zeal of religious ministers. As military officers want larger armies and great wars, so does a professional clergy cry out for long Sabbaths, more churches, and crowded seats. These things are, with the few, means to a higher end ; but with the majority the end most felt is, the increased dignity of the profession.

Sundays are now a political institution : no one can propose to abolish them : but let every one try to make the best of them.

FIRST, by abandoning the false pretence of their observance being a divine command:—itself an intrinsic incredible absurdity, as well as without a shadow of New Testament proof. SECONDLY, by encouraging mental cultivation of the largest and most liberal kind on that day, and greatly shortening the prayers.: —but of this, more will be said. THIRDLY, by facilitating and inviting attendance at church, wherever masses of people are disposed to flock for the recreation of country air ; as at Richmond and Greenwich near London, and many other places near to great cities. FOURTHLY, by solemnly urging, that religion demands the whole heart for God on *every* day, and that no compromise can be made by looking grave or dressing clean for one day.

The truly spiritual, who turn many hours of the Sunday to the best purpose, generally value the institution; for they, not unnaturally, neglect to inquire whether it does not take away from them on six days the time which it seems to give so liberally on the seventh. A few may possibly use the whole day profitably for purely spiritual action, but I suspect that they are *very* few ; and the more acute their sense of the sacredness of the hours, the greater the danger of misery from it. Personally I can testify, that for several years of my life, when a youth and very young man, Sunday was of all days to me the most painful ; because, with all my efforts to consecrate it, I could not practically reach up to my abstract idea of its sanctity. It also threw me into collision with my elders, and caused me to refuse obedience to them, under the idea that the Law of God constrained me. Justly then do I hate the Sabbatical fiction, as a cause of real sin to the anxious and well-intentioned, as well as to the careless and uncontrolled.

2. And is it requisite here to speak of Fasting? If any one after trial thinks that he himself finds spiritual benefit from such a practice, no one can blame him for continuing it. Yet it may justly make others watch more sharply, whether it developes in him Pharisaic and other Sacerdotal vices : and if they see him disposed to uphold hierarchical dominion and asceticism generally, they will have a right to say, that he has gone back from spirituality into a system of carnal ordinances. On the other hand, a more offensive piece of impertinent domineering, in spiritual matters, is scarcely conceivable, than for a number of " divines" to meet and pass a law as to the days and hours at which other people, and indeed generations unborn, shall fast for an imagined spiritual end. Those who call themselves successors of the Apostles and defend such things, should at least point out in the

authentic writings of the Apostles some instances in which they thus dictated to their converts.

But what says Paul? "If ye be dead with Christ from the elements of the world," [such outward ceremonies as he has just named,—meat and drink, holy days, new moons, and sabbath days,] "why, as though living in the world, do ye subject yourselves to dogmas,—Touch not! Taste not! Handle not!—all which [dogmas?] tend to corruption in the using; after the commandments and doctrines of men? Which things have indeed a show of wisdom in will-worship and humility and neglecting of the body; but are not of any value in comparison* to the satisfying of the flesh." The sense of some words in the Greek is contested; and I do not pretend certainty that he means in the last clause;—" adequate nourishment to the body *is of some value*; while fasting is of no use at all, either to body or soul." But it is quite certain that the entire passage was intended to throw contempt upon *the ordinance of* Fasting, as upon other Asceticism, and exhort his converts to refuse subjection to those who tried to impose such things. Against the *practice*, as such, he evidently no more made war than against the ceremonial law, and he speaks of it without reproof, 1 Cor. vii. 5; but there is not† evidence that he himself looked on it as of any value. Of meats and drinks in general we may say with him,—Let every one be persuaded in his own mind: if he eat, let him eat to the Lord and give thanks: if he eat not, let it be to the Lord that he eats not; and let him give thanks. It may be added, that according to Christ's precepts, whoever fasts must conceal the fact of his fasting. This entirely condemns *Public* fasts.

3. Sacraments and Liturgies may be embraced in one thought; for it is superfluous to argue against the pretended magical force of a Sacrament, until some tangible proof of it is adduced. Men's feelings towards Liturgies appear liable to go through several stages. The original rude and unspiritual feeling is that of those who do not attempt to pray with the heart, though they may devoutly repeat the words, but receive them all as a sort of *bidding to pray*. Such is clearly the case with children, and with great numbers of grown people. Thus the Liturgy is to them, not a prayer, but an aid to meditation, and an instruction, by example, *how* to pray: as such, its use appears to be very great. They more or less intelligently think over parts of it;

---

* Οὐκ ἐν τιμῇ τινι πρὸς πλησμονὴν σαρκός. Coloss. ii. 20-22.

† The fastings of Paul, 2 Cor. vi. 5, xi. 27, are both times enumerated by him among *involuntary hardships* endured for preaching the Gospel.

and now and then really join in some prayer, especially in those for temporal mercies and for forgiveness of sins. Thus a Liturgy, like the old Law, is admirably adapted to those whom Paul calls "the children of the bond-woman," who have not yet received the Spirit of adoption ; and therefore fitly belongs to any very extensive or hereditary Church.

But secondly, there are many who rise above this puerile state ; who reverentially essay to pray all the prayers, and believe that they succeed in it. These are those whom I have called *the once-born* children of God : who, having a sound conscience and sincere mind, have yet no strong development of the soul. Their hearts do not prompt prayer actively, and it is rather pleasant to them to have petitions suggested to their intellect from without : and as they have no depth of spiritual sorrow or joy, they can without conscious hypocrisy play rapidly one after another all the modulations of an ample Liturgy. The most varied tones find in them an equal response : " Have mercy upon us, miserable sinners ! Oh come let us sing unto the Lord ! Sing we merrily with a loud noise ! Lord have mercy upon us ! Christ have mercy upon us ! We are tied and bound with the chain of our sins ! We thank thee for the hope of glory !" The doleful repetitions of a Litany do not pall upon their spirit, but seem to soothe it. Their hearts are as wax to be moulded by the recitation ; and though it is difficult to call this *prayer*, it cannot be denied that they have been *in a devotional posture of soul*. Whether they listen reverently to the sounds of a voluntary, under the " dim religious light" of a stained window, or respond to the low chant of the cathedral " service,"—seems to be nearly the same thing. They pray feebly for five hundred different things, taking no absorbing or strong interest in any. They do not pray because they want a thing, but because it is a duty : and certainly the process reminds them of God, enlivens their conscience, soothes their mind and refreshes it after the worry of life, tranquillizes all rude passions, and altogether, brings much moral benefit. It is an error to undervalue this ; the persons are engaged in an act of Reverence, if neither in Prayer nor Praise. They wonder how any can disparage the excellent institutions of " our Church," and attribute it to an unreasonable presumption, bordering on impiety. And long habits of attachment to the same cling to them very frequently, even when they pass into the number of *the twice-born*, if the transition has been gradual, slow and ill marked.

Thirdly, those in whom the phenomena of the new birth have been powerfully brought out, are often (and I should suspect, generally) thrown into uncomfortable collision with a Liturgy, at least such a one as that of the English Church. Their spirit rushes in one direction, when the Liturgy would call them in another. They vehemently want one thing, and are hereby made conscious how little they care for the rest of the five hundred things : then they feel ashamed and guilty for the lukewarmness of their prayers, and their hearts are made heavy by attendance. They have plenty of narrow but energetic prayer in themselves, and cannot bear this miscellaneous profusion from without : and when their minds deviate into meditations of their own, (far more profitable *to them* than such languid prayer could be,) they often have an unquiet conscience, and scourge their wanderings as a grievous sin. Besides, many things are probably felt as a positive offence, through some want of harmony between the joyful or hopeful state of the worshipper and the depressed and often depressing tone of the Liturgy ; which seems made for persons strong and copious in orthodoxy, but weak in spiritual life. I forbear to illustrate this, lest I needlessly give pain : for the remark is not directed against Liturgies *as such* : nevertheless, it tends to show how delicate is the problem of constructing a formulary which shall neither impede high devotion nor involve anything too peculiar.*

A woman of fervent and transparent soul informed me, that she always, *on principle*, allowed her heart to carry her in prayer wherever it pleased, in spite of the Liturgy ; in which way she could always enjoy it *more or less*, by dropping all that was uncongenial. And this appears to be the transition to the fourth state ; in which the person who has long struggled in vain to adjust his soul to the Liturgy, at length discerns that it cannot be ; that it is an unwise attempt ; that God does not ask it of him : and if still he sees a general benefit in the institution to others, and that there ought to be some such thing, then in conscious uprightness before God he boldly assumes a freedom which he once would have thought profane : leaves off scolding his mind for wandering, translates words into others more suitable to him, and cares only for one thing,—that his heart shall rise to God, or brood over holy thoughts, whether in connexion with the public prayer or otherwise. And the same nearly applies to the prayers of Scotch and Dissenting Churches, whenever they are intellectually constructed. But, it will be perceived, that a

* The Lord's Prayer appears to be a perfect formula, as *dictating the topics* of fixed Public Prayer. But one party among us has made it a formality, by merely adopting its letter without the spirit, another dislikes the Prayer for its meagreness. For a Liturgy, its imagined meagreness is its excellence.

person who attends public prayer in this spirit, is really "going to Church *for example's sake:*" he would get more benefit in private. Hence he does this out of the superabundance of his spiritual strength, as a charity to others : which, however possible now and then, is likely to become an unbearable tax for a continuity.

Be it however admitted; there is possibly, beyond all these, a fifth state, in which the Spirit of Intercession has developed itself and a serene atmosphere has been reached; the Soul retains all its earnestness, and yet is so harmoniously blended with the moral Will, that the man can to a great extent determine the direction and force of his own spiritual affections. The Catholicity of his internal experience enables him to accommodate himself to words either of confession and complaint, or of hope and joy, or of entreaty for others ; in the spirit of one, who is raised above the painful pressure of any one want, and who can calmly say, "Father, I know that thou hearest me always." A character thus perfect, would be able, if only the petitions of a Liturgy are right ones, to pray them all in turn. Such persons, it is to be feared, are very rare : (for where that holy spirit of Intercession lives, the whole man must be wonderfully perfect, nor would this be an unappreciable fact :) and if there are such, they must have gone through lower states in attaining their elevation, and will not represent it to be an easy thing to carry the heart and soul along with a various Liturgy. For these reasons it appears to me that fixed Forms of Prayer may with much truth be called useful, in the inverse proportion to the development of spiritual life. To the ignorant and to young persons they are of extreme importance, as instructing them how to pray; but for these likewise, they ought not to be tedious. To the religious who are elevated the first step above these, they afford *a time* for vague and perhaps dreamy reverence, like the sensuous worship by music; but are profitable, chiefly because little attempt is made to use them as genuine prayer and praise. To the young spiritualist they are a painful burden ; by the advanced spiritualist they may be borne perhaps, by reason of his strength, but they are often or always a trial to that strength and in no respect a help to him. He may nevertheless find blessing : for when all the heartstrings are tuned to the chants of heaven, the soul will often respond sweet melody even to the discords of heathenism.

If however this is not all true, if there be some other side of the question, which is here overlooked,—still I am justified in protesting against that tyranny of public opinion, which stigmatizes as irreligious all who are indisposed to "come to Church," and hinders each from following the indications of his inward monitor.   Under Church, I include Chapel; for there is much in common.   The Prayer of the Dissenting minister is less various in its topics and much shorter than the public Liturgy : these are advantages : but there is no better security that it shall stand in any relation to the existing state of the hearer.   There are ministers perhaps, who, before prayer, try to bring the hearer's mind to the right tone, and then pray in the suitable key : and this appears to me the only plausible way.   The Sermon or Address ought (I think) to *precede* the prayer, which should on no account seek to be comprehensive.   Where the minister can follow his own judgment, much may be done for the better :—but then also, much may be for the worse; all depends on the individual. Consequently, there is no justification of the new ceremonial law, which orders all to Church or Chapel, whether benefit be experienced or no.   Nay, the old phrase "divine service," (in Greek, "Liturgy" or public service,) expresses the prevalent idea.   It is imagined that we are to go to Church *to do some service to God*, not, to get some good from Him : and this superstition stands firm, equally among Dissenters, unawares.

It would be wrong here to deny that there may be persons, whose hearts are such gushing fountains of spiritual affection, that their private prayer is uniformly a full stream, as is in fact supposed in following a public Liturgy.   But (as far as I am able to learn) this is with the majority of devout persons rather an exceptive case.   Ordinarily the contrast is great between the private and the ostensible worship.   For, except when the heart is peculiarly full, the prayer of earnest solitary devotion may be compared to a bird of short flight : it mounts up with sudden impulse, but before long stagnates or falls again.   Moments of meditation seem necessarily interposed, before a new effort is possible ; so that it consists of many disjoined irregular breathings of the heart, not always momentary, yet seldom long, even though it be based upon the words of a book open before the worshipper.   Hence, in a continuous system of public prayers, a very frequent wandering of the mind appears (to me, I confess) quite inevitable, a thing to be calculated on, because of the prevailing weakness of the worshippers.   Even to keep up with the simplest and best known of formulas,—the Lord's Prayer,—is to some an unmanageable task, unless the reader were to occupy threefold of the time which is generally allowed, with pauses between the versicles.

But after all, how much of *Fellowship* is there in public

prayer? It is difficult to say how little. Each worshipper is isolated: there is little or no mutual consciousness. When indeed a whole congregation is sensibly animated by one Spirit, then no doubt there is Fellowship: but that, it is to be feared, is so rare, as scarcely to deserve mention here. Nor can I at all admit the notion, that (as an ordinary thing) *long* prayers in *private* are that which the new nature dictates, in proportion to the energy which it displays. Indeed if we ask for what moral purposes the Soul is imbued with the love of God;—the reply will be: first and chiefly, for its own sake, that it may attain its own best condition: but secondly, *that it may work, in and for the world*; "with good heart, doing service, as unto the Lord, and not unto men." Most erroneous, and as I sincerely believe, most unscriptural, is the notion, that much continuous time is then to be occupied by what are called "religious exercises,"— long prayers, long public services, or any of those things which experience proves rather to generate Pharisaism. Paul recommends to his converts to pray *always*, rejoice *without ceasing*, and *in everything* give thanks, but we find in him no exhortations to church-services, sacraments, fastings, or any formal processes. I cannot but think, that these things, as practically conducted, need to be reckoned with "the cares of this world, the deceitfulness of riches, and the lusts of other things," which blight the young gospel-blade: and the matrimonial analogy might here give a clue to the real position of things. Young lovers are so absorbed in long earnest talk, so anxious to win or sound one another's hearts, that they are drawn off from other business: but when their new relation is ascertained and their mutual affection is a fixed fact, they become the more energetic in their respective tasks because of their love; which love would languish, if they were idle and tried to live upon it. Thus too the soul, when so conscious of its fixed union with God, as to be strung to a new and unusual pitch of spirituality, (if not drawn aside by artificial doctrine,) runs with fresh alacrity to *its common duties*: and should they be such as thoroughly to engage the intellect, still in every interval it breathes forth desire, complaint, if not rather love and praise and hope: it remembers its Lord and its true home, and gains new strength to do and receive all in His name. Rule, habit, or lingering superstition, chiefly or alone, seem then to send a man to formal and set prayer: for he has a more continuous and involuntary worship. His Sun goes not down, be his day serene or stormy. As he walks the streets, as he enters company, as he changes his occupation, his inward spirit gazes upon his

Eternal Friend, and is glad, even if his lips frame no word, nor his intellect any clear proposition. The Spirit itself pleadeth within him, perhaps in inarticulate utterances, until some new and deep want explains itself in his soul, and a fresh series of prayer begins. One thing only is essential to his heavenly intercourse,—that he shall be quite unobserved: and this very thing is sometimes not easy to secure in his own church and his well-known seat: to make up for which disadvantage (as regards Prayer at least) some signal benefit ought to be enjoyed there. As to private devotions, it certainly is not to be denied that there are cases (known to each man) when he extremely covets to prolong them. By all means let him freely follow his own spiritual instinct: "Is any afflicted? let him pray: is any merry? let him sing psalms." But when *long* Devotions are *not* cried out for by the soul itself, they are deadening and tend to hypocrisy. In fact, some men's worst temptations rise out of such times: action and company is the healthiest state for them, except when the soul is carried into prayer as by a vehement flood. For church-rulers to prescribe long Prayer, (as many would now wish,) when they cannot give the Spirit of Prayer, would be tyrannizing in the dark.

4. In regard to Special Prayer Meetings, little need be here said. It is obvious that their value must depend upon the harmony of soul with soul. In theory and in the abstract I regard them as blessed companies: but they demand mutual trust, perfect unsuspicion, a common and a pure enthusiasm. There is in them a revelation of soul, by which holiness may become as it were contagious, but which *may* make them intensely painful or very mischievous. *Corruptio optimi est pessimum.* The time may be in store, when social worship shall ordinarily be a real outpouring of soul: but an immense revolution of opinion, and yet more of heart, must take place first.

5. But the Sermon! Can any one say a word against this? Is not this at length the "means of grace?"—Reader, must I ask whether thou hast ever heard a bad sermon? one so dull and drowsy, that it was impossible to maintain attention: one so empty, that no food for heart or mind could be found in it: one so logical, that the soul was never addressed at all, but only the critical faculty called out: one so illogical, that the hearer's Understanding violently resents it and will not leave his Soul free to feed on the good food which is intermixed: one so uncharitable, as to turn the heart sick: one so full of gross carnal superstition, as to excite indignation, that Paganism and Formalism still live to vex us: one so vulgar, coarse and profane in

the manner of address, as to spoil good matter: one which makes Atheism seem preferable to Theism, by painting the Holy and All Merciful as an omnipotent devil who insists on being complimented? Under all these things, I, oh Reader, have groaned a hundred times: perhaps thou hast not. They are to me no small counterweight to the benefit of hearing sermons, because, unfortunately, I cannot make the preacher say or leave out what I choose; and practically that is what we all want (*more* or *less*) to do. But let this pass, and suppose we have got a perfect preacher,—one of a thousand; and what then?

Obviously and clearly, the preaching of such men is, more than all other causes together, a means of spiritual awakening,— of conversion from sin and of stimulating to an independent active life in the spirit. God forbid that I write one word to depreciate the exertions of our truest aids and champions. The great pity is, that they are so few, and that the same man is often so unequal to himself. However, not every pious and wise person makes a good preacher, profitable to hearers in every stage; and it is absurd to treat it as a personal slight, if one does not get benefit from somebody's sermons. No doubt there are those who will retort; "It is your own fault: go on *until* you find advantage from it,"—as the quack puffs off his pills. The fact is that sermon-hearing is regarded as an end and not merely as a means; it is to the modern Protestant, what the Sacraments were to the old Church. Was the minister eager for his own honour and not for my welfare, when he was not satisfied by my assurance that I found private meditation, with an occasional book or a walk in the fields, so profitable, that I had no longings after his discourse? No: but there was at the bottom of his mind the assumption, that there is some abstract *duty* in hearing sermons, as if they were an end in themselves. On the contrary it would seem that we *ought* all to grow up towards a state, in which we care less and less for human teaching; or rather, come to select our own aids in the form of books. In the first stage of spiritual life, we are as infants, fed by the nurse's hand: but gradually, we ought to learn to feed ourselves. And so indeed of common education. The teacher is essential to children and desirable for youths; but to keep the full-grown man under tuition would blight all intellectual fruit; indeed, the whole use of higher teaching is, to call forth and stimulate personal energies, in order that the hearer may very shortly need teaching no more. Occasional listening to a preacher will always be more or less coveted; but it is very hurtful to imagine that we *all always* want a "regular ministry" to teach us. Nothing

is more desirable for those who are already fully fledged, than
that each should be driven out from the nest to seek his own
food by soaring through God's wide heaven, instead of huddling
together, as now, with closed wings, on the flat earth, gaping for
morsels of meat, killed and cooked by another.   When that other,
who is the sole teacher, is, over and above, younger than many
who are to be taught,—younger too in spiritual age,—the absurdity becomes so manifest, that people betake themselves to the
plea, that we ought to attend "for example's sake."   But this,
however well occasionally, degenerates into a very hollow system
when it becomes habitual.

Are there then *no* aids to higher spiritual progress, to be obtained from other men?   Undoubtedly there are.   It is not requisite to speak of intercourse by word of mouth with good men ;
which, by reason of our shyness and dread of hypocrisy or its
appearance, is perhaps ordinarily less profitable even between
friends than it admits of being made.   But the two inexhaustible sources of spiritual supply and stimulus, are Hymns for private recitation and Books : both having this in common, that the
Soul is *active, and selects from them what it pleases*, in which
they differ from all the preceding.   The peculiarity of Hymns
consists in their being adapted to rest in the memory.   Hence
they are available for those who cannot read ; moreover, even for
one who can, they are of first-rate importance, because they
accompany him everywhere, in darkness or light, at home or
abroad.   Historians judge the sentiments of a nation from its
Ballads : much more is the devotion of a Church cognizable
from its favourite Hymns.   Well might Paul advise the Ephe-
sians and Colossians to "teach and admonish one another in
psalms and hymns and spiritual songs, singing and making melody in their hearts to the Lord."   The traveller in his idle
hours, the loiterer whom an unpunctual friend disappoints, the
invalid who wakes in the night, every man in his odd minutes,
who does not find holy thought to come unbidden,—yet if the
memory be stored with hymns selected by the soul's own preference, gets in them a soothing or elevating stimulus, as his
case may require.   Hymns are in fact the truest links that bind
ancient and modern souls in one.   Many of the Hebrew Psalms,
or parts of Prophecies, have inspired pure hearts in every age.
In modern times, great numbers of sweet and touching hymns
have been composed by unlettered persons, whose tasks were
solitary and silent.   Our own language is rich in them, but in
German (I understand) they abound still more, and are in versi-
fication far from despicable.   Not that elegance of form is essen-

tial to a hymn : the use of the metre is to facilitate memory, and if there be nothing in its composition to give positive offence, this is literary merit sufficient.—Hymns seldom become logical and dry; hence they have a *primâ facie* superiority for nourishing the soul, to prose books ; and on the whole, there is nothing to compare to them in this department.

But inasmuch as some cultivation of the moral intellect is essential for spiritual progress, and some general cultivation of the mind is extremely desirable, Prose Works have their own place, as eminent spiritual aids. But it is needless to say a word more on a subject which everybody so well appreciates.

What then is the sum of this argument? That our first want is, the expansion of *individual* life. We need to see and know something for ourselves, and to learn to feed ourselves spiritually. To be dependent, is hardly to live. What would it avail, to believe *on the authority* of some person, corporation or book, that my nature is weak, or that I myself have sinned? that there is a God, or that he desires my moral perfection? Such second-hand conviction is not Faith, and would produce none of the energetic results of Faith: the ancients* would have compared it to a drunken man gabbling the moral verses of Empedocles. We need more of *Nature* in the soul ; that is, a reverting to first principles, a development of primitive instincts, and some increased confidence that there still lives a God to hear and teach us. Never shall we by mere herding together, or by leaning on authority old or new, make up for intrinsic weakness in each separate soul. Moreover, it is only by insight into the Present, that we can understand the Past. In political history and in all physical science this is acknowledged : one who knows nothing of the existing forces, in States or in unorganized Nature, cannot rightly discuss past events. So, if *a chasm* be gratuitously assumed between the spiritual action which we know and experience, and that which animated apostles and prophets,—or, what comes to the same thing, if we know nothing of any spiritual forces at all within ourselves,—we shall for ever be in the dark concerning their minds and souls. But with more Individuality, more Independence of man, there will be more capacity to learn of God. Then we shall not aim (in theory, any more than in practice) to become little Christs or little Pauls; we shall as freely disclaim it, as in literature the becoming little Homers. Such imitation does not tend to excellence but to stupidity. Men of little faith fix their eyes on the Past, as did the Scribes and

* Aristot. Nic. Eth., lib. vii. 3, 13.

Pharisees : Faith gratefully and reverently acknowledges *and uses* the Past, but sets her face towards the Future. Those who build the tombs of the prophets, but alledge that all inspiration is now closed, would in former days probably have aided to persecute them: those, on the other hand, who use individual prophets only as aids towards the Eternal Source of Prophecy, are the true imitators of those holy men. When we sympathize with God, and with the inmost yearnings of His devout servants, we can afford to smile, though mournfully, at the invectives of misguided zeal, if it blindly regard us as enemies of God. But let the songs of praise or of sacred complaint, which the pious of past ages have bequeathed to us, nourish our spirits and link us to them: let us hope and seek that the life of God may be in us, as it was in them, a guide into truth and an energy for action; then shall our daily work be daily joy, and we shall eat angels' food.

CHAPTER VI.

HOPES CONCERNING FUTURE LIFE.

ONE of the earliest speculations forced on the Soul during its infancy, related to a state after Death. The mysterious question, *Whence came we?* necessarily suggests that other, *Whither go we?* but the attempt to give an intelligent reply does not in the first instance come from the Soul, but from the inventive and superficial Fancy. Owing to the constant association of Body and Soul during life, the Soul is supposed to go with the Body beneath the earth, and the idea of a Hades or Tartarus is generated. When either the Understanding or the Moral Faculties begin to be more unfolded, a great change soon takes place in the views held on that whole subject.

The most celebrated attempts to establish by means of argument a doctrine concerning the Soul's immortality, come down from the school of Plato; which, with various modifications, have been reproduced in modern days. There is no agreement among minds capable of appreciating these arguments, as to their validity. Metaphysical philosophers on the whole maintain them; a majority of physiologists, and nearly all unphilosophical but not unintelligent Christians, reject them. To me the discussion loses all interest, from the fact that it is not addressed to the Soul, but to the pure Intellect, and is consequently unintelligible to the vulgar. But this remark needs to be expanded.

Not Plato's celebrated discourse merely, but every modern attempt in the same direction (as far as I know) appeals only to facts of which the spiritual and unspiritual have equal cognizance, and uses arguments of (good or bad) logic, in estimating which the Soul is at liberty to be asleep or non-existent. We are told of the contrast of Mind and Matter, and that Mind *cannot* perish by reason of the dissolution of the body: and much more of the same kind. That such doctrines have ever seemed to me unmeaning words backed by very fallacious reasoning, may arise from my own obtuseness; however that may be, they are (if correct) truths of pure Science and in no respect doctrines of Religion. To judge of their accuracy, requires, not a pure Conscience and a loving Soul, but a clear and calm Head; hence to go wrong about them does not indicate a religiously defective state, but a weak or ill-informed understanding. Now it is self-refuting to treat the doctrine as one of high religious importance, and yet to confess that those in whom the religious faculties are most developed may be far more liable to err concerning it than those who have no religious faculty in action at all.* On the contrary, concerning truths which are really spiritual it is an obvious axiom that " he who is spiritual judgeth all things, and he himself is judged of no man." This objection is so decisive, and apparently so obvious to the feelings of the soul, that one might have fancied no spiritual man could for an instant have felt religious interest in such arguments.

Very different was the history of thought among the Hebrew people, although it started with a primitive conception of the Underworld, not sensibly different from the Greek Hades. But when prophecy had arisen, and pure moral reverence had supplanted crude imagination, all hard ideas concerning a ghostly or rather material soul seem to have vanished, and the Underworld remained only as poetical imagery. Thus one Royal Psalmist pointedly avows that the dead can neither praise nor hope in God; and other unknown yet powerful writers harp on the same sad note.† Modern divines might seem to be incarnations of selfishness, if they were judged of by their fatuous doctrine, that all religion (perhaps all morality) is wrecked, if immortality be lost. According to this, Conscience is presumed to be non-existent, and Prudence to be the sole stimulus to action. The generous feelings of man, the love of Virtue for its own sake, and much more the love of God, are forgotten; and it is sagely remarked, that such romantic principles will never take effect on the vulgar, who, if they are to be religious, must have a *quid pro quo*. And thus men who call themselves spiritual teachers—(all happily are not such)—degrade religion into a prudential regard for our interests after death. The mischief done by this selfish

---

* Christians have added an argument of their own for a Future State, but unfortunately one that cannot bring personal comfort or assurance. A future State (it seems) is requisite *to redress the inequalities of this life.* And can I go to the Supreme Judge, and tell him that I deserve more happiness than he has granted me in this life ?

† Isaiah xxxviii. 18, 19. Psalm cxv. 17 ; lxxxviii. 10-12. Eccles. iii. 19.

view in all its ramifications, would need a treatise to set forth.
If the Christian belief of immortality, *as a pure intellectual dogma*,
has had any beneficial effect, it is in a very different way.
Namely, by ascribing *One* element of infinity to individual man,
it gives him a contact, appreciable to the pure intellect, with Him
who is all infinite; and thus allures the human soul to seek
fellowship and friendship with that Eternal Spirit. But to return to the Hebrews. We do not find all their Psalmists equally
desponding concerning the soul's futurity; and if it were possible
to ascertain the dates of the 16th, 17th, and 49th Psalms, it
might have some historical interest. In these we read, not
indeed any abstract dogmas, but personal aspirations in a tone of
confidence, based upon the soul's own love to God and knowledge of Him.

Ps. xvi. 8. 11 : "I have set the Lord always before me: because he is at my right hand, I shall not be moved. Therefore
my heart is glad, and my vitals rejoice : my flesh also shall rest
in hope. For thou wilt not leave my soul in the underworld,
nor suffer thy saint to see corruption. Thou wilt show me the
path of life : in thy presence is fulness of joy, and at thy right
hand are pleasures for evermore."

Ps. xvii. 15. "As for me, I shall* behold thy face in righteousness; I shall be satisfied, when I awake, with thy likeness."

Ps. xlix. 14, 15. "Like sheep they are laid in the grave ;
Death shall feed upon them ; . . . . . . but God will redeem
my soul from the power of the grave ; for he will receive me."

There may be some other passages of the same tendency, but
none that rest on any different basis. The soul, conscious of a
certain union with God, is thereby excited to the hope (more or
less confident) that that union shall never terminate : and the
peculiarity of such a view is, that the *argument* (if one may use
the phrase) is utterly inappreciable to the mere acute logician :
it is foolishness to him, "because it is spiritually discerned."
This is as it should be. Can a Mathematician understand Physiology, or a Physiologist questions of Law ? A true love of
God in the soul itself, an insight into Him depending on that
love, and a hope rising out of that insight, are pre-requisite for
contemplating this spiritual doctrine, which is a spontaneous impression on the gazing soul, powerful (perhaps) in proportion to
its Faith; whereas all the grounds of belief proposed to the mere
understanding, have nothing to do with Faith at all.

When we turn to the New Testament,—(where the doctrine of

---

* I observe that Ewald translates it *Möge*—! Oh might I behold!

the saints' immortality, *as a fact,* is unquestionable,)—to ask
for the ground and root of the belief, we find Paul, as usual, the
fullest source of knowledge, because of the various unfolding of
his mind in his numerous authentic epistles. Yet this doctrine
has two sides with him,—one connected with the Resurrection of
Christ, and one more obviously based on the older Hebrew view.
Each will need some notice here.

The 15th chapter of the 1st epistle to the Corinthians, is the
well-known passage in which he elaborately developes the idea,
elsewhere familiar to him, that Christian hope of immortality
essentially depends on the Resurrection and Ascension of Christ.
In modern days it has been understood as follows : "The resurrection of Jesus was an external miracle designed to prove both
the *power* of God to raise the dead, and his fixed *intention* so to
do :" Paul however can hardly have meant this. If he had
looked on the resurrection of Christ as Paley or Priestley did, as a
miracle to be proved only by testimony, he would have anxiously
gathered up and collated that testimony in an authentic form ; he
would have given the names of the 500 brethren who witnessed it ;
in short, his first business must have been to fix, at their earliest
source, the fluctuating testimonies, before they became diluted and
worthless. This he must have done, if his notions of logic had
anything in common with the school of Paley. On the contrary,
he cared nothing for Christ "*after the flesh,*" but sought acquaintance with Him as a living ascended Lord : he tells the
Galatians (among the proofs of his independent apostleship) that
he carefully kept clear of the eleven at his first conversion, and
received his gospel of God alone. For when it pleased God to
call Paul by His grace and reveal His Son *in him,* immediately
he conferred not with flesh and blood, neither went he up to
Jerusalem to those which were apostles before him ; but went
into Arabia ; and preached Christ three years before he met any
of the Apostles.* It is clear that Paul regarded himself to have
adequate grounds for believing the resurrection of Christ, quite
independent of human witness, and that he (in a certain sense)
prided himself on that independency. It seems evident that to
doubt the resurrection of Messiah was to him an intrinsic
absurdity : he believed in it from Prophecy, and from its own
propriety, or from personal revelations. Messiah was to be
Judge of Living and Dead ; and how *could* such a one be holden
by death ? Here then came in the Pauline doctrine of Head and
Members : if Christ lives, his people shall live also.—Now this
is an appeal, not to the logician, but to the spiritual heart. He

* Galat. i. 11. 19.

does not argue for something which a jury of physicians and surgeons might be summoned to decide, as Paley might seem to think : but it is really the old Hebrew view under a new phraseology, only the name of Christ standing in the place of God. While an Asaph or a Heman would have said : "Jehovah lives for ever, and I am his servant : He is my God and my portion : therefore I shall live in Him :" and where Jesus says : "God was the God of Abraham ; but He is not the God of the dead, but of the living ; for all live to Him :" Paul puts it thus : "Messiah was to triumph over the grave, and to say, O Death, where is thy sting ? Since then Messiah could not be holden of death, but is risen, I, who am a member of his mystical body, must rise also." And this may suffice as introduction to the other side of his view.

That a purely *historical* is as unsatisfactory as a *metaphysical* basis for a spiritual doctrine, is obvious ; indeed, Paul gives us clearly to understand that the future hopes of the soul were to be discerned by the soul itself, for itself, and did not depend upon man's wisdom, as a question of history does and must. "Eye hath not seen, (says he, 1 Cor. ii. 9, &c.,) nor ear heard the things which God hath prepared for them that love Him ; *but God hath revealed them to us by his Spirit*; for the Spirit searcheth all things, yea, even the deep things of God. *Now we have received not the spirit of the world, but the spirit which is of God ; that we may know those things which are freely given to us of God."* It is evident that under the word *we* he includes more than his single self ; at least all whom he had above called *adults,* as opposed to *babes* in Christ : in fact he never claims an inspiration differing in kind from other faithful Christians. Thus in his judgment, those in whom the Spirit of God becomes vigorous and casts out the spirit of the world, gain an eye to see the unseen joys which God has prepared for those who love Him.

There is another interesting passage which throws light on the processes of Paul's mind. "The Spirit itself (says he, Rom. viii. 16, 17) beareth witness with our spirit that we are children of God." So far, we have a fact, resting on the direct knowledge of the soul itself : but he proceeds to draw intellectual inferences :—"And *if* children, *then* heirs ; heirs of God, and joint heirs with Christ ; if so be that [or, seeing that ?] we suffer with him, that we may also be glorified together." All seems now clear. He had (as far as he here tells us) no direct perception of anything farther than that he was a "child" of God, and from this he *inferred* that he was to be "an heir" of God, that is, was to be a member of the future kingdom of Messiah of which all the prophets had spoken.

Paul indeed may have had more of direct insight into this deepest of subjects than the passage last quoted denotes: God forbid that I should presumptuously limit the insight enjoyed by his most favoured servants. Yet his light does us little or no good, while it is a light outside of us: so long, we are depending on the soundness of Paul's faculties. If he in any way confused the conclusions of his logic (which is often extremely inconsequent and mistaken) with the perceptions of his divinely-illuminated soul, our belief might prove baseless. Faith by proxy is really no Faith at all, and certainly is not what Paul would deliberately have recommended. Our real question then is not, what he believed; but how far he gives us either aid or materials for exerting a Faith of our own.

When a divine voice is said to have declared, "Because I live, ye shall live also;"—the mind which is conscious of Union with the Divine, feels weight and plausibility in the argument. But modern Reason considers those arguments alone to be cogent, which are appreciable by the unspiritual consciousness; and has accordingly endeavoured to build up out of the *fact* of the resurrection of Jesus, a logical demonstration of human immortality. Yet if we take the whole case as Scriptural orthodoxy represents it, the fact in itself proves nothing of the sort. For Jesus was no specimen of common humanity, but a supernatural being, whose mother indeed was a woman, but his physical father the Supreme God. No one could expect such a one to pass out of life like other men, or even to die at all: and if after an incomplete death, which stopt short of corruption, he was reanimated, with the scars of his wounds still seen in his palpable body of common flesh; what is there in this exceptive phenomenon, that can avail even as a presumptive proof that common men, born of human fathers and not demigods in origin—whose death has been complete, whose bodies have been dissolved—will rise again in heavenly forms, unscarred by the past, and incorruptible in the future? What is there in this resurrection of a perfectly sinless man, every way singular in relations, character, and destiny, that can in itself imply that sinful men also, and indeed unrepenting sinners, will rise as he? If death was the penalty of sin, the wonder is, not that a sinless man could not permanently be holden of it, but that he could be holden for thirty-six hours. The immortality of the sinful, certainly cannot be deduced from that of the sinless; and how much less, if he was not merely a demigod, but a Divine Eternal Person in disguise!

I have called this a modern argument : I believe it is at least unknown to the New Testament; where it is only *the people of Christ* that are said to rise because he rose, and live because he lives. As far as this is concerned, (which seems to be the only Scriptural *argument* on the subject,) John and Paul have added nothing to the means of conviction and assurance attainable by a pious Jew. For no one will say that we more certainly know that Christ lives, than that God lives; or that a union with God is less efficacious for immortality, than a union with Christ. The only possible question is, whether it is easier to ascertain our spiritual union with Christ than with God. Clearly it is not. Christ is not accessible to the bodily senses : granting all concerning him which any school of orthodoxy can wish, an invisible Christ, like God, can only be approached by the soul : and to ascertain our union with *Him*, or with *God*, is a problem of exactly the same order.

I may indeed be told by Christians of one school, that Paul did not believe the miraculous conception of Jesus, nor his pre-existence before the worlds : nor yet do they. I know not whether they will proceed to deny his sinlessness, and thus aim to fill up the breach of analogy between the sinless immortal, and the sinful mortal : certainly it would seem to me gratuitous credulity, to admit a thing so unproveable and improbable, as the sinlessness of one who has nothing superhuman in his physical origin. But it is needless here to pursue the argument : for if any one supposes Jesus to be, however eminent as a man, still a sinful man—and therefore, neither our Lord, our Saviour, nor our Judge—he is forced to believe (at the least) such delusion and misrepresentation to pervade the gospel narratives, as leave him no ostensible right to receive the resurrection of Jesus as a fact, if the fact would ever so well serve his argument.

Such remarks, I fear, may be felt as exceedingly painful by those who are accustomed to imagine a fixed logical dogma on this subject to be of first-rate importance, and even of necessity : but a little reflection as to the high tone of spiritual elevation maintained by the Hebrew bards, ought to suffice to show that that "necessity" is extremely exaggerated. But this is not all. Need we ask what sort of influence the current views exert over the irreligious ? Are they less profane, for the dreadful doctrine of the Eternal Hell ? Are not men also driven into a self-righteous belief, that they in some sense deserve heavenly glory, merely because they cannot feel that they deserve the awful alternative which alone is treated as possible ? Again, if it be said that the fixed doctrine comforts us on the loss of pious relatives,

is it forgotten what distress it inflicts on those whose near kins-
folk die without clear marks of piety? This proves nothing as
to truth or falsehood : but when people appeal to the *expediency*
and *desirableness* of the prevailing creed, it is not fair to take a
partial view of the case.

Some, however, will say :—"We discard the idea of Judgment and Punishment : but we still desire to retain the immortality of the righteous, as an external dogma, because of the extreme importance of this as consolation and support in the prospect of death and in other times of trial."—That a firm belief
of immortality, *rising out of insight*, must have very energetic
force, I regard as an axiom ; but *as an external dogma* I cannot
but think that its efficacy is prodigiously overrated. In this
connection it is not egotistical to speak of myself. Seventeen
or eighteen years ago,* I was to all appearance dying of fever.
I firmly believed (if belief at second hand can be firm) that a
blessed immortality, guaranteed by the resurrection and word of
Christ, was about to open upon me ; yet so feeble was the effect
of this belief, that it gave me not one throb of joy : calm re-
signation to an inevitable but unwelcome event, and thankfulness to that merciful Love which had revealed itself to my spirit,
were my highest emotions.—But I will refer to another : a pure
and passionate soul ; living, breathing and moving in divine
things ; ever rejoicing in union with God in Christ, in theory
anticipating eternal Glory ; and yet to my certain knowledge,
most thoroughly unwilling to die prematurely. This is only
what may be expected from a faith on hearsay, however much the
person would be shocked at being thought not truly to believe.

It is not obscure, why the well-conducted part of society so
desires a proof of a future life *addressed to the unspiritual part of
our nature.* The doctrine is valued, less by each for his own
soul, than as an engine of government. Yet Bibliolaters have
ostensibly the least right to press for this : since, if it is desirable anywhere, it was eminently wanted in the Mosaic law, to
restrain offenders, and to comfort good men who were in an
embryo spirituality : yet it was not there given. Guilt was
restrained only by temporal inflictions : and among ourselves
also, beyond a doubt, crime is repressed in bold and wicked men,
only by fear of the visible and present judge. Whether hell be
in theory believed or disbelieved,† it has no practical power,
except over the less hardened. But the attempt to turn Religion

---

* Written in Feb. 1849.

† That a vague fear of *possible retribution from God, we know not how or
when,* is a wholesome restraint to crime and sin, I do not doubt : but this

into a system of State Police, is an impiety, which inevitably defeats its own end. Nor less does it desecrate divine Hope, to apply it as a means of softening the sorrows of the unspiritual. Natural sympathy is far more effective for consolation, than any of those conventional topics, poured forth professionally on an uncongenial mind. If Hope is to comfort men in their darker, it must live with them in their brighter hours; it must gush up out of an inward fountain. I know it is said, that the poor are made more patient by the notion so current among them, that in another life they will get compensation for the hardships which they endure in the present: but this is to buy patience, by propagating delusion.

But do I then deny a future life, or seek to undermine a belief of it? Most assuredly not: but I would put the belief (whether it is to be weaker or firmer) on a spiritual basis, and on none other. It seems to me a sort of first principle, that such a belief cannot justly rise out of anything but insight into God's mind, gained by a full sympathy of our spirit with God's Spirit. What we *see* at one time, we may *remember* at another, and such intellectual remembrance is of importance; yet it is not the same thing, and is exceedingly inferior in energy, being intellectual only, not spiritual. The same applies to the report brought to us of what others have discerned: it serves to animate us to open our eyes and gaze after the same sight, but does not supersede our personal vision. Nevertheless, I never knew* any one who professed to have attained (by spiritual insight) certain or confident expectations in this matter. There is indeed a dubious passage in Paul, which perhaps will express prevalent feelings: "We are saved by *hope*: but *hope which is seen, is not hope*; for what a man seeth, why doth he yet hope for? But if we hope for that we see not, then do we with patience wait for it." Rom.

is quite different from the defined dogma which alone is valued by some. It would be instructive to learn, what sort of persons fear the torments of hell. I have known several instances of morbidly disposed and apparently good persons, who have been made unhappy by alarm; but all *bad* people seem to me to think that they are not quite wicked enough for so dreadful a place. I cannot remember, as a boy, (when I read a great deal about it and believed everything that I read,) that I so much as once dreaded it for myself. One might almost doubt whether wicked people ever dread it for themselves.—A very few perhaps, after committing a great crime, are really oppressed with this horror; whether for better or worse, it is hard to judge.

* I now find Mr. Maccall, in an eloquent discourse, (No. 21 of THE PEOPLE,) avow that Immortality is necessarily known to the religious mind by intuition: but he states this as a universal fact, and I am not sure that he means more than 1 have above asserted.

viii. 24, 25.—Just before he had said: "Hope maketh not
ashamed, because the love of God is shed abroad in our hearts
by the Holy Spirit which is given to us." Rom. v. 5. He
cannot go without the inward witness, and does not really rest
on dogma. If we farther ask, what is the actual experience of
each faithful soul, it will possibly be found to bear a witness not
very different from the following.

The Soul which is wedded to its Infinite Lord, knows there is
no presumption in thinking that He cares for it. Day by day,
and hour by hour, it tells out its complaints, its wants, its
thoughts, its fears, mixed with the sweet breath of praise or the
sigh of dim longings, all understood by Him. Yea, He who
searcheth the heart knoweth what is the mind of the Spirit,
which pleadeth for the saint according to the will of God. Out
of a consciousness of permanent communion with the Eternal,
rises a practical assumption of its indivisible union with Him,—
a conception that it partakes of His nature, and can never be
forgotten by One, whose infinity embraces the least of those who
love Him. Yet in the ordinary, and perhaps the healthiest state,
there is no dwelling of the mind on its own prospects. When the
actings of love are purest, they rest most in the present,* in
which they are too fully absorbed to allow much of either speculation or anxiety concerning the future; as the child receives day
by day its father's tokens of affection, and feels, that sufficient for
the day is the good thereof. And in fact, if speculation concerning the future is attempted, it can take but one form;—the
hope of more Grace, more Holiness, better Obedience, purer and
deeper love, whether here or there, presently or in a distant age:
no other Heaven is within the power of human imagination. It
is not from the side of Self, but from parting with those who are
dear to it, that the Soul begins to *speculate* on a future world: and
when forced thus to speculate, and ask whether they and it will
ever cease to exist,—cease therefore to love, to serve, to praise,—
both mutual love and conscious blessedness must needs excite
the wish of immortality. Some may even have anxiety and intense longing : but most, I suppose, have a certain yearning, that
(if possible) their union with God may be made perpetual; that
is, not merely commensurate with earthly life, but stretching out
beyond into a real eternity; and the very possibility of such a
thing, (not as imposed on the intellect, but as apprehended by
the soul,) stimulates every holy effort. Faith also appears to gain
an ever-increasing confidence in the good will of God to perfect
us more and more; and it is very wholesome to nourish this ex-

* I have seen this quoted as a remark of Fenelon's.

pectation : for the higher thoughts we hold of our nature and our destinies, the more fervent will be our upward effort. Herein we discern some probability, (increasing with the strength of that Faith,) that the highest state which the soul here reaches, is not and cannot be meant by God as its ultimate and absolutely highest ; but that his work begun in it must needs go on towards perfection, unchecked by the limit which we call Death. That God should as it were elaborately train a soul for serving and loving Him, and then suddenly abandon his own workmanship, when its lineaments were beginning a little to exhibit the hand of the Divine Artist, appears a harsh and almost cruel thought. Undoubtedly, if we reason from the analogies of organic nature, we shall come to an opposite conclusion ; but spiritual action in many respects is quite peculiar, and especially in this, that we cannot conceive of God as tying himself (so to say) by general laws, so as to deal otherwise with *this* soul than He would have done if it had been the only soul in the universe. In organic life, we often suffer pain or loss, from the mere operation of general laws which take no cognizance of our moral state : that, I say, we cannot imagine to happen as to spiritual relations. Hence no *à priori* disproof is felt from the arguments of physiology :* it remains as a thing not manifestly refused by God. For this therefore, from time to time, the Spirit within pleads, and knows that it will be accepted in asking, even if the prayer be ignorant.—Still, unless some clear conviction can be gained, that the thing asked is *according to the will of God*, the soul cannot have confidence that the petition will be fulfilled ; and to ascertain this by direct vision, is (to me hitherto) impossible : for to our blind eyes many things seem easy, which the Perfect Wisdom knows cannot be granted ; and while the intellect hesitates on this point, the soul dares not to dogmatize. Confidence thus there is none, and hopeful Aspiration is her highest state. But then, there is herein nothing whatever to distress her : no cloud of grief crosses the area of her vision, as she gazes upward : for *if her Lord, infinite in love and wisdom, sees that it cannot be, she herself could not wish it.* While in such vigour of life as to have any insight into God's mind, she is also in vigour enough to trample selfishness under foot. In fact, it would not be selfish merely, but silly, to fret, that odd cannot be even, nor a creature be as its Creator ; and nothing short of difficulty insuperable as this, would lead to the refusal of so holy and simple a desire.†

* See Note 1 at end of this Chapter.
† See Note 2 at end of this Chapter.

H

The general conclusion to which I personally come, is, that the state of *Aspiration* to which alone I attain, is perhaps the very best thing for me, until some other conditions of soul are fulfilled, in which as yet I am deficient. If selfishness mixes unduly in my desires, might not a greater certainty (especially one impressed from without) benumb the outgoings of the spirit; just as human love is easily sated and flags, if it be not pure, as well as strong? The Honourable Robert Boyle somewhere says quaintly: "I hold a piece of meat to my dog, that he may jump at it; and the higher he jumps, the higher I hold it, to make him jump the more: even so does God hold out beyond our reach the soul's true aliment, eternal glory," &c. If the principle here hinted at be sound, a clear prospect of eternity may conceivably be the last reward reserved by God for faithful souls; imparted then, but only then, when He sees that it could not produce lapses into unconcern, irreverent self-conceit, with all its train of abominations, or foolish and wrong neglect of earthly interests. But in the same proportion to our hopes concerning self, are our hopes concerning all spiritually enlightened souls; all that are capable of obeying and rejoicing in God: and we have concerning them precisely the same comfort as concerning ourselves. If we can happily cast our own souls on Him who careth for us, there is surely no greater difficulty in so trusting Him for all who are dearest to us. Meanwhile, nothing but mischief can come from speculating how he will *punish* others; which really amounts to sitting in judgment over them ourselves, as though we could read the heart, and could measure sin and temptation. Let us not repine that we get no answer to the questions, Are there few that shall be saved? and, What shall come to yonder man? but suffice it, ourselves to live with God now, if haply we may live with Him to all eternity: or at any rate, let us love Him while we live, and live only to be conformed to His will. For if an eternity of holy obedience is infinite bliss, it can only be because every day of obedience is bliss. We therefore do not need the promise of such an eternity, as any bribe to be obedient and loving now: but either Heaven is an empty name and foolish delusion, or it is a Heaven on Earth to be God's true servants. In any case therefore it remains, to rest our souls on a faithful Creator, knowing that whether we live, we live unto Him, or whether we die, we die unto Him. Living therefore or dying, we are His.

NOTE 1, *referred to at page* 145.

In a splendid article on the Ethics of Christendom (Westm. Review, Jan. 1852) the writer denounces "the old Hellenic method of studying the problems of the universe by fetching rules from the *wider* sphere (therefore the *lower*) to import into the *higher*. . . . So long as this logical strategy is allowed, the Titans will always conquer the gods; the ground-forces of the lowest nature will propagate themselves, pulse after pulse, from the abysses to the skies, and *right* will exist only on sufferance from *might*."—For a fuller development of this extremely important subject, one must look with hope and desire to the same eminent pen.

NOTE 2, *referred to at page* 145.

† If I labour under an error, the reader will be most likely to see through it by my expressing the error more distinctly. I therefore add, that I cannot feel *sure*, that Eternity (in the future, as in the past) is not as much an incommunicable prerogative of God as Omnipotence or Omniscience. Thus one who presses us with the question: "*Ought we to be contented* without knowing our immortality?" seems to me in danger of exerting himself to make us *discontented with our creaturely position*. "By this sin fell the Angels." This thought the old Greeks expressed by θνητὰ δεῖ θνητὸν φρονεῖν,—"a mortal should have mortal ambitions."

CHAPTER VII.

PROSPECTS OF CHRISTIANITY.

IN the course of the last hundred years, the Christian name has begun to extend itself over many barbarous tribes: first over the Greenlanders by Moravian missionaries, since then, as a result of the unparalleled naval power of England, over many islands in the Pacific, and in certain parts of South and West Africa. But over the old regions of India and Arabia it has evidently but little power; and what is most startling of all, its prospects in Europe itself are externally darker than ever. In Spain, Italy, France, and Germany, it is hard to say that much belief of formal Christianity remains among the more educated part of the community, or to guess how deep a gross and fearful unbelief has penetrated among the lowest population of the towns. As for England and Scotland, it is notorious that a horrid heathenism has taken firm root in our town population also, and that millions have cast off all reverence for any of the claims of authoritative religion. Facts so widely spread over the face of Europe cannot be lightly treated. Churches are built, but that class does not come to them which has cast off the Christian yoke: ministers may be sent to seek them out, but it must not be hastily assumed that they will be successful: hitherto, experience is the other way, and the causes of spiritual difficulty deserve analysis.

The causes appear to me to be identical with those which encounter Christian missionaries in dealing with acute Hindoos or Mohammedans; namely, the unmanageable character of what are called *Christian Evidences*. The demands made on men's faith are indeed far greater than ever the Apostles made; for the Apostles did not take a Bible in their hands, and say to the heathen, "Here is an infallible Book: to believe that every word of this is dictated by God, is the beginning of Christianity: receive this, and you shall be saved." But now, although our teachers do not all assent heartily to this way of preaching the Gospel, yet few have strength of mind or plainness enough to disown it: and this claim of *Mechanical Inspiration* enables every bold and sharp-witted man to carry on an offensive war against the Christian teacher, who will soon find that he has more than enough to do in repelling the infinite objections to which he lies open. The war is thus carried away from the region of the Conscience and of the Soul into that of verbal and other criticism; and who can expect spiritual conversion from that?

But this is only the beginning of difficulty. *Doctrine* also has been built up into a system which aims at, but cannot attain, logical exactness. I need not enter into any questions of detail, and I barely hint at the Trinity and Incarnation, the Immaculate Conception of Jesus, his Vicarious Sufferings, the Pelagian controversy, and other matters which divide Arminians and Calvinists. No one, I think, can read the New Testament with fresh eyes, and not be struck by the fact, that the Apostles never encountered practical difficulty from the heathen or from the Jews on these points. There is not the slightest mark that they were assailed as polytheists or as contradicting themselves. It is evident that they did not hold as essential to Christianity any exact system of logical doctrine, which the opponent could attack as *il*logical. To recognize the authority and headship of Jesus as Messiah, was all that they expected of a convert; and this, not in connexion with any authoritative book that professed to set forth his words as an absolute law of truth. At least, during Paul's labours no such book existed. The convert gladly learned all the wise and holy thoughts which Paul had to impart; but while trusting his " private judgment" so far as to leave the faith of his fathers for Christianity, it did not occur to him to commit an act of moral suicide, by promising thenceforward to have no judgment of his own, but to believe everything that Paul told him.

There is no book in all the world which I love and esteem so much as the New Testament, with the devotional parts of the Old. There is none which I know so intimately, the very words of which dwell close to me in my most sacred thoughts, none for which I so thank God, none on which my soul and heart have been to so great an extent moulded. In my early boyhood it was my private delight and daily companion; and to it I owe the best part of whatever wisdom there is in my manhood. Yet after more than thirty years' study of it, I deliberately, before God and man, protest against the attempt to make it a law to

men's understanding, conscience or soul ; and am assuredly convinced that the deepest spiritual mischief has occurred to the
Churches,—nothing short of a stifling of the Spirit of God (with
few intervals) for seventeen centuries and a half,—from taking
the Bible (or New Testament), instead of God himself, as our
source of inspiration. Paul certainly did not contemplate this.
" Who then is Paul, or who is Apollos, but ministers by whom
ye have believed ?"   Paul was an inspired man ; but, in his view,
so was Timothy, Philemon, Onesimus; so was the meanest
Christian who was faithful. A spiritual man and an inspired
man were with him the same thing. Inspiration was not infallibility, nor did it consist in guaranteeing to them the contents
of a book. That the *writings* of the Apostles were more peculiarly inspired than their *spoken words,* is a fiction invented in
modern times for the service of controversy : while that the one
and the other alike were not only fallible but sometimes erroneous, an unprejudiced examination presently shows. Paul and
Peter came, once at least, into rude collision. The interpretations
of the Old Testament given in the New are very frequently
fanciful and mistaken; and the expectation of Christ's speedy
return in the clouds of Heaven to bring about the general judgment, is a manifest error which pervades the whole New Testament. When will men leave off the attempt to serve God by a
lie ? To varnish over these and other plain facts in zeal for God,
can only issue in confusion to our own work and damage to true
religion. A calm consideration will presently show one who is
not tied up from thinking, that as Paul or John might err in
astronomy or geology, so might they in history or logic or metaphysics : nay, that they necessarily held all the metaphysics of
their own age, without knowing that they did. In communion
with God, their souls imbibed many holy feelings, and put forth
holy actions ; and their reflective intellect shaped, into what we
call Doctrine, the perceptions of their spirits. Unless the intellectual and logical processes had been infallible, (of which we
have clear evidence before us to the contrary,) the resulting
propositions could not be divine and absolute truth, even if the
inspiration were the highest possible to human nature ; and when
they did not encumber their Gospel with such pretensions, or
elaborate an exact system of Divinity as a target for the enemy,
it is gratuitous in their modern followers to do this.

But let us suppose these two burdens cut away from the
shoulders of the Christian champion. He does not desire to
make the New Testament a law to the mind, nor has he any
Corpus of Divinity which he needs to uphold in entireness ; he

advances as lightly equipped as Priestley himself:—what may
we now expect from the true Theologian, when he attacks sin
and vice and gross earthliness?   If we form an *à priori* conception of the genuine champion of the Gospel from the New Testament, we shall say, that he is girt with the only sword of the
Spirit, the living word of God, which pierces to the dividing
asunder of soul and spirit, joints and marrow, and is a discerner
of the thoughts and intents of the heart.   In his hands it is as
lightning from God, kindled from the Spirit within him, and
piercing through the unbeliever's soul, convincing his conscience
of sin, and striking him to the ground before God ; until those
who believe, receive it, not as the word of man, but as, what it
is in truth, the word of God.   Its action is directly upon the
conscience and upon the soul ; and hence its wonderful efficacy ;
not on the critical faculties, upon which the Spirit is powerless.
Such at least was Paul's weapon for fighting the Lord's battles.
—But when the modern battle commences, what do we see ?   A
study-table spread over with books in various languages ; a
learned man dealing with historical and literary questions ; referring to Tacitus and Pliny ; engaged in establishing that Josephus
is a credible and not a credulous writer ; inquiring whether the
Greek of the Apocalypse and of the fourth gospel can have come
from the same hand ; searching through Justin Martyr and
Irenæus, in order to find out whether the gospels are a growth
by accretion and modification, or were originally struck off as we
now read them ; comparing Philo or Plotinus with John and
Paul ; in short, we find him engaged (with much or little success)
in praiseworthy efforts at Local History, Criticism of Texts,
History of Philosophy, Logic, (or the Theory of Evidence,)
Physiology, Demonology, and other important but very difficult
studies ; all inappreciable to the unlearned, all remote from the
sphere in which the Soul operates.   And are these abstruse
arguments the powerful and living word of God ?   Is it not
extravagant to call inquiries of this sort " spiritual," or to expect
any spiritual results from them ?   When the spiritual man (as
such) cannot judge, the question is removed into a totally different
court from that of the soul, the court of the critical understanding.   Nay, the Soul *may* not choose by her own instincts ; it is
a dishonesty to allow likes and dislikes to operate ; calm indiffer-
ence is required, not impulses *for* or *against* alledged historical
events : the question is one of external evidence.   How then can
the state of the Soul be tested, by the conclusion to which the
Intellect is led ?   What means the anathematizing those who
remain unconvinced ?   And how can it be imagined that the

Lord of the Soul cares more about a Historical than about a Geological, Metaphysical or Mathematical argument? The processes of thought have nothing to quicken the conscience or affect the soul. More words are surely not wanted, to show the intense opposition of all this to the Gospel as conceived of by St. Paul.

I have already had occasion to remark, how entirely independent of external evidence Paul felt himself to be, when he preached for three years without caring to meet the apostles, whose *senses* could give the best external witness to the resurrection of Jesus : and that he thus kept aloof from them, he many years after deliberately boasted, as among the proofs that his gospel and his apostleship came direct from God. I see not how to doubt, that he would have looked on an apparatus of learned evidences with the same contempt as on his Rabbinical books, and would have pronounced them all to be dross and dung. He would at all hazards have refused these weapons; for Saul's armour must needs encumber David. Nay, he would have espoused the cause of these modern Gentiles, who are so often " without God in the world," and for their sake would have vindicated a Gospel free from the embarrassments of critical erudition, level to their capacities,—or rather, addressed to the Soul; which is often as active and susceptible in the poorest and most illiterate as in the wise and great. What means *now* the declaration, "Unto the poor the Gospel is preached"? and what the boast,—"I came not unto you with excellency of speech, or of man's learning"? For concerning our modern Evidences, the poor and the illiterate cannot possibly judge, and the preacher cannot preach unless he is learned: so entirely has the Gospel shifted away from its primitive basis. And then, can we wonder that it is wholly bereft of its power to convince unbelievers?

Another important result of this unscriptural and unspiritual system is seen in the Christian Ministry. A minister in modern days is expected to excel others in what are called Theological accomplishments. Theology, one might have thought, was the Science of God; but no: it is the sciences of Biblical Interpretation and Historical Criticism. A person eminent in these becomes a Doctor of Divinity,—Sanctæ Theologiæ Professor. And yet these are topics, in which a man might obtain high ecclesiastical renown, though his conscience were seared and his soul utterly paralyzed. Though by courtesy called spiritual, the knowledge is simply secular ; and an immediate result of it is, that *youth*, however unspiritual, if only the critical and logical faculties have been developed, steps into the chair of the Christian teacher, and becomes ecclesiastically higher than *age* however spiritually exercised. Christianity has been turned into a LITERATURE, and therefore her teachers necessarily become a literary Profession. Previous to Ordination, they may be subjected to some literary ordeal; they may also be required to profess orthodoxy and to be morally respectable; but this is all that can be attempted in a public system. Thus in result, a national clergy cannot be expected to excel ordinary Christians in any spiritual qualities, but only in learning. How then can they be expected to exert any high spiritual influence? Many Dissenters imagine that this evil is caused by the Union of Church and State; but the same evils appear in their Academies and Churches: naturally not so glaringly, and yet in substance as truly. Age and spiritual experience are, with them also, subordinate to critical cultivation; and plainly because, with them also, Christianity has become a Literature.*

How opposed this is to every thing in primitive Christianity, not Paul alone testifies. By every writer of the New Testament it is manifestly presumed that the historical and logical faculties have nothing to do with *that* faith, which is distinctive of God's people. Everywhere it is either stated or implied that the Soul or Spirit of man is alone concerned in receiving or rejecting God's revelation. Unless we can recover this position, we have lost the essential *spirit* of apostolic doctrine; and then, by holding to the *form*, we do but tie ourselves to a dead carcass, which may poison us and disgust mankind.

To *keep* and to *get* Historical Faith, are different problems. He who has been educated in it and never has lost it, throws the burden of disproof upon others: he believes, till some refutation is shown him. Hence mere indolence of mind suffices to keep him in his father's (historical) faith: and without any such indolence, he is generally kept in it, if he have any keen feelings of the spiritual glories of Christianity. But if a man have no hereditary

* I have been thought here to undervalue mental culture and scientific accomplishment in ministers of Religion: but that is not my intention. I believe that the only *essential* qualities for them are Age and Spiritual Experience; nevertheless, it is of very high importance that a considerable fraction of them should *also* have a large and liberal cultivation; without which, the rest will become narrow and fanatical. But in the individual, as in human history, religion must be a Life, long before it can approximate to the character of a Science; and a knowledge of human nature in general seems to be far more valuable to a religious teacher than any special set of facts. Indeed much that is currently called Theology, appears to me suited only to bring barrenness, degeneracy, and contempt upon Religion.—(Second Edition.)

faith in it; if he was born a heathen or a Jew, or has cast off all
reverence for his national Christianity, from seeing so much
hypocrisy and worldliness in it, and knowing nothing of the
good;—then he casts the burden of proof the other way: he dis-
believes, until somebody shows him valid reason for believing
things marvellous and beyond his experience. It is absolutely
impossible to recover the tens of thousands who have learned
to scorn Christian faith, by arguments of erudition and criticism.
Unless the appeal can be made directly to the Conscience and
the Soul, faith in Christianity once lost by the vulgar is lost for
ever: what could the very chiefest of Apostles do to bring it
back? They never converted one soul by learned proofs; and
why should we dream that they would attempt it now, or could
succeed? If we continue to do as we are doing,—*if no action of
a totally new kind is set up,*—the present course of affairs must
go steadily forward, but with accelerated velocity, in proportion
to the increase of mental sharpness or physical destitution: a
real black infidelity will spread among the millions,—an infidelity
of the soul to God, of the heart to virtue,—until the large towns
of England become what Paris is. And as for the cultivated
and philosophic, what else will they become but poetical Pantheists? acknowledging intellectually a plastic Spirit or (as it
were) Life in the Universe, but just as empty of the moral affection towards God, which has been the great animating principle
of Christianity and of the highest Judaism, as if they were
avowed Atheists.

But it will be said: "What are we to do? we are not
Apostles, and how can we speak as Apostles?" I reply: if you
wish to be a follower of the Apostles, and can seize and keep
both the form *and* the life of their teaching,—well: do so. Imitate all the early preachers of Christianity. In teaching about
God and Christ, lay aside the wisdom of the wise: forswear
History and all its apparatus: hold communion with the Father
and the Son in the Spirit: from this communion learn all that is
essential to the Gospel, and still (if possible) retain every proposition which Paul believed and taught. Propose them to the
faith of others, *to be tested by inward and spiritual evidence only*;
and you will at least be in the true apostolic track.—If however
you meet (as I confess I meet) insuperable difficulties here, in
the attempt to hold fast, on such a basis, the *form* of their Gospel; then solemnly do I say, Oh God most High, let us not lose
the *Spirit* also! At present, we are trampling down the Spirit
in an attempt to retain the Form: with how little success even
as to that mean object, our countless divisions prove.

The tangle in which we find ourselves, and which (it seems to me) must be boldly cut, and can never be untied, is this :—*we cannot reason as the Apostles did, unless we could recover the Metaphysics and Logic of the apostolic age.* This is now to us a matter of erudition: with them it was a medium of all common thought to rich and poor alike, except to a few highly-cultivated men. Modern research and experience have wrought a revolution in all our notions of Evidence. We have been forced to choose between *easy* belief of miracles, and so admitting far more than those of orthodoxy ; or *difficult* belief, and so criticizing those of Scripture with a severity of which no Apostle dreamed. We are also far more scrupulous and fastidious in the sort of evidence which we can admit in each subject. We cannot take Astronomical proof of a Physiological proposition, nor Chemical proof of a Moral one: we have learned the divisions of the Sciences. But Plato did not hesitate to offer Grammatical proofs of the Soul's Immortality ; and the ancients in general were prone to give Moral proofs of Physical truth, or perhaps Physical explanations of Moral facts. We now know that though in their higher development the Sciences osculate, yet (to the human mind) their bases are quite independent, the specific facts of each being furnished by a specific sense or informant : and a result of this is, that the idea of Historical Religion is seen to involve as essential a contradiction as Historical Astronomy or Mathematical Religion. Every Science *has* a History ; but cannot *be* History, nor can History be it. As to Historical Religion, we find in it two incongruous elements, iron and miry clay. The iron is the pure morals and spiritual doctrine, of which the conscience and Soul take cognizance ; and this is at once the strong part and the precious part of Christianity : being concerned Eternal Truth. The miry clay is the historical element, of which the Soul can take no cognizance at all; which is concerned with with the accidents of Time ; which is to be dealt with by critical erudition (according to *our* notions of Evidence), and therefore is essentially out of the reach of the great mass of mankind.* How can we then include the latter element in Religion at all ? This mixture of the Historical with the Spiritual effectually forbids formal Christianity to be a pure spiritual system, and lames its spiritual energy.

* All the attempts to found historical fact on spiritual evidence, when analyzed, present an argument which runs thus : " It does my soul good to believe such and such external events ; *therefore* such events are historically true." This is speciously called " the argument which rests on the *adaptation* of the Christian scheme *to the wants of our nature.*" (For fuller explanation, see Chapter I. which is added to the Third Edition.)

That the metaphysics (or current philosophy) of early ages, and of the Apostles themselves, was here in irreconcileable opposition to ours, is clear beyond dispute. If an Englishman of this century, however devout and morally wise, were to declare that he had learned *by communion with God* the truth or falsebood of some external event, said to have happened in a distant time or place, (as a Virgin's immaculate conception, or somebody's impeccability,) he would be thought a hopeless fanatic or monomaniac.* It is a first principle with us that the spiritual faculties discern spiritual things *only*, and cannot teach worldly and external truth, which essentially demands the aid of the specific bodily senses.   Nor would it any the more satisfy us, if the person asserted that the knowledge was imparted to him in a supernatural trance or mesmeric rapture : for we should ask how he discriminated his revelation from a dream or dosing fancy ; and until he explained this, and gave us the means of testing and verifying the accuracy of this new faculty of his, his statement would go for nothing.   Now it is clear that in ancient times no call was made for this discrimination, nor for any verification at all.   A person who professed to have a vision was believed outright, provided that the moral and spiritual doctrine connected with it seemed satisfactory : for spiritual men then judged by the Soul *all* things that stood in any spiritual connexion, even those which in our view manifestly cannot be made independent of Sense or of the common Understanding.

And here, (if I meet with a reader of that stamp,) I may be told that our deviations from the old ways of reasoning are indeed lamentably great, but that we ought therefore to throw away our modern Philosophy, as false and impious, and adopt afresh the Philosophy of the Apostolic age.   This will be said seriously and devoutly by thousands of women, and by men of feminine understandings ; yet I do not hesitate to assert, that whoever holds this language, is (just in proportion to his influence) actively fighting against the souls of men—little as he knows it,—and helping to propagate heathen darkness.   He virtually tells us, that *we shall not have God in our Souls, except by the sacrifice of our Understandings.*   Hereby he does not any the more enter the

---

* Of late years a sect has been heard of, called the Lampeter Brethren, who are said to believe a certain Mr. Prince to be an Incarnation of the Most High.   Such pretensions however are rejected by all sound-minded persons *without examination.* We do not wait to ask whether Mr. Prince offers evidence by miracles, or from prophecy, or by eminent holiness of life, &c., &c., but we repudiate the idea as obviously and intrinsically incredible.

kingdom of God himself, but he hinders others from entering it. As the old Jews "pleased not God, and were contrary to men," forbidding the Gentiles to be saved, unless they would accept the law of Moses, so have these moderns a zeal for God, but not according to knowledge.

First of all, it is *wicked* so to sacrifice our understandings : and secondly, though possible in an individual case, it is quite *impossible* on a large scale.—It is a faithless thought, that God has so constructed our nature, that its different parts are essentially in conflict : and the result of such a wilful sacrifice of the understanding, might be a wretched, incurable, drivelling superstition, or even any amount of moral corruption, if the remonstrances of the understanding are thus put down by authority. It is not into modern English orthodoxy, nor into an enlightened Romanism, that such a sacrifice might plunge us; but into whatever is ugliest in the darkest Romanism : for the check to black superstition being once broken in pieces, we are left at the mercy of accident, as to how far we may go. To sacrifice the Understanding will never produce true Religion, but only Fanaticism. Now the Apostles and their contemporaries *made no such sacrifice.* They breathed the philosophy of their own century ; and if we are to imitate their spirit, we shall abide in ours, and not engage the two parts of our nature in a fatal civil war; which they neither did nor approved. The "vain philosophy" which Paul deprecates, is that which the Soul spurns as unspiritual,— namely, the pretence of a sanctification from Fastings, Ceremonies and Bodily *Exercise* or Asceticism : Coloss. ii. Nor has any man a right to invest with a divine sanction the philosophizings of Paul or of John. It is clear that Paul and Gamaliel, John and Philo, held common principles of logic and metaphysics; which belonged to each apostle by the accident of his age, and not by revelation from God.

But secondly, such a method of solving our difficulties is *impossible.* Within certain limits, the Will no doubt has controul over intellectual opinion, namely, when the evidence on which an opinion rests does not meet us everywhere, but in certain places only. Then we can purposely shun that evidence, and fill our minds with what is of opposite tendency; in which way men bring themselves sincerely to believe many things, which it is for their apparent spiritual benefit to believe or for their worldly interest to profess. But this power of the Will is not omnipotent. Three centuries ago it was able to sustain a man in the disbelief of the Copernican, and in the belief of the Tychonian theory; it is now, on the contrary, quite unequal to such an effect on a

mind which moves in educated or half-educated circles; because
the certainty of truth in the Copernican or rather Newtonian
system has permeated all cultivated thought: hence the Will
cannot avoid the evidence or hinder its effect on the judgment.
Precisely the same thing is true of those logical principles, which
pervade, as axioms, all modern accurate investigation. In every
step forward which the Sciences make, in all their harmonious
results, in all their practical applications, we have perpetual verification of the truth of the great principles by which their processes are animated: and the conviction of this has sunk deep
into the hearts of all, who, even as artizans only, behold the
achievements of practical science. It is thought a great thing
for a man to stake his life on the truth of his religious faith. It
is *not* a great thing, but a matter of every day, for common men
to stake their lives on the truth of scientific propositions; which
propositions would be quite uncertain, if any doubt rested on the
soundness of our scientific foundations. He who knowingly sets
Religion into contest with Science, is digging a pit for the souls
of his fellow men. Except the more ignorant or rash, all probably will allow this: a sufficient proof indeed of it is found in
the actual state of Theology. Why else would men load themselves with the unendurable burden called Christian Evidences ?
a mass of investigation, which, if it is to be calmly and thoroughly
judged, requires some ten years' persevering study from a cultivated intellect in its prime. Why all this effort for Theological
Colleges, and instruction in learned Divinity, except that it is
felt to the very bottom of our minds, that external miracles can
only be believed upon external proofs ? And this is a conviction
too profound, ever to be got rid of by any resoluteness of the
Will to return to a more infantine metaphysics.

Religion can never resume her pristine vigour, until she becomes purely Spiritual, and, as in apostolic days, appeals only to
the Soul: and the real problem for all who wish to save cultivated Europe from Pantheism, Selfishness, and Sensuality, (such
as flooded and ruined ancient Greece,) is,—to extract and preserve the heavenly spirit of Christianity, while neglecting its
earthly husk. Our Deists of past centuries tried to make religion
a matter of the pure intellect, and thereby halted at the very
frontier of its inward life: they cut themselves off even from all
acquaintance with the experience of spiritual men, and their religion necessarily vacillated between that of Plato and Aristotle.
Practical Christianity was as nothing to them, because they took
those divines at their word, who said that it all depended on historical faith;—which in fact is as needless, as it is confessedly

insufficient. Let this truth be avowed, and a preacher, animated by the spirit of Christ and Paul, will have plenty to say, alike to the vulgar and to the philosophers, appreciable by the Soul. Then he will be able to keep clear of Historical and other extraneous inquiries, taking for his guide through entanglements this single principle : to *render to the Understanding the things that belong to the Understanding, and to the Soul the things of the Soul.* Then he may speak with confidence, of what he knows and feels ; and call on his hearers, of themselves to try and prove his words. Then the conversion of men to the love of God may take place by hundreds and thousands, as in some former instances. Then at length some hope may dawn that Mohammedans and Hindoos may be joined in one fold with us, under one Shepherd, who will only have regained his older name of the Lord God. Then finally, the long schism of Jew and Gentile may be healed, and the hearts of the *fathers* may be turned to the *children,* ere God comes to smite us both with a curse.

I well know that (if this book be read) people will exclaim, that I am advising them to throw away Christianity *itself,* when I make light of its historical and miraculous side : and none will be more clamorous to this effect, than those who care little about that spiritual life which Paul lived, and which is here set forth as essential Christianity. Nowadays men are generally thought fanatical, whose souls are in sympathy with Paul's : and I feel certain that this book will meet with at least as much dislike (not to use a harsher word) because it lays down certain Christian experiences as matter of fact, as because it treats as unimportant those things which are indifferent to the life of the Soul. Answer to God, ye who think yourselves on the side of Paul and John ; who say of yourselves, " The Temple of the Lord, the Temple of the Lord, are *we* ;"—do you believe in Sanctification of the Spirit by Peace and Communion with God ? in the New Birth of the Soul by believing in God ? in the Free Grace of Him, who loved us before we loved Him ? in Justification of the sinner, in the midst of his sins, by simple Faith in God ? in the permanent Union of the believing Soul with God ? what know you of the love of God shed abroad in the heart by the Spirit, and of the Hope thence arising ? or of man's insight into the heart of God, when he has received somewhat of that Spirit which searcheth even the deep things of God ? of a Faith that overcomes the World ? of a Spirit that guides by a higher rule than Law ? Such sentiments and experiences (not propositions) are the true heart of Christianity : and if the reader hold them not, he may haply have the shell of Christian truth, but he has not the kernel. If he rightly knows them, he will not say, "They are all worth nothing, without a belief in Historical and Metaphysical paradoxes."

Alas! what extension of Christianity can be expected among our neglected millions, when men in high ecclesiastical places eagerly promote sacerdotal inanities! when zeal is called out for Episcopal Power, for Baptismal Regeneration, for Mechanical Apostolic Succession; nay, for Episcopal Revenues and lordly pomp; when the higher clergy are exposed to the taunt of loving the splendours and greatness of this world, and therefore of not having the love of God in them; when not only Mechanical Inspiration is ascribed to the Bible, but a power of Mechanical Consecration to the hands of Bishops and Priests; nor only immaculate truth to "all and everything" in the book of Common Prayer, but extreme importance to everything in the Rubric! The heart sinks at the infatuation of such extravagances, while sin and crime and hardness of heart are abroad among us. Meanwhile, it is well if the Soul's present union with God in peace and joy and sanctification is only secretly despised, and not denounced as hypocritical or fanatical rant, by those who display zeal for the Church and for the doctrine of the Trinity. Yet of what use would Baptism or Bishops or the Church or the Trinity or the promise of Heaven be to us, if the soul had here no union or sympathy with God? If earthly things have been tendered to us, and we receive them not, why should God show us things beyond the grave? and if we have not been faithful in that which is our own, who shall commit to us that which is another's? To rise to the full dimensions of the Jew, is surely pre-requisite for those who aspire to the stature of Christ; and even the Jew thirsted for God, found peace with Him, loved Him, rejoiced in Him, clung to Him. Yet, after the first blaze of apostolic Christianity, the heavenly flame instantly paled, the Churches declined, form and rule grew up, Bishops became proud, superstition increased, controversy raged, persecution began, this World became the prize for which the Churches fought, ecclesiastical dominion took deep root, darkness overspread the earth, polytheism invaded what should have been God's kingdom, and cruelty, sensuality, ambition and avarice hid beneath Priests' robes. Devout individuals there always were, whose spiritual life was independent of the prevailing system: but no public and visible ameliorations took place, except very partially, where a little Freedom was obtained; until the great Insurrection against Authority, to which the name of Luther has been attached. The Reformation brought about much good, till the forces of Free-

dom which animated it were again chained down; and then
commenced a new decay, and a sapping of spiritual faith, alike
in Germany and in England. Is it not historically manifest,
that *Authority* has been the bane of Christendom? Authority;
which, when established as a church-rule, means that we are to
prefer Sense to Conscience, ostensible presumptions to spiritual
insight; that we are to subject our mature to our immature
convictions, progressive knowledge to some fixed standard in the
past. To set up other men's inspiration as our law, is to disown that teaching of God, to which alone they owed their emi-
nence. Christians were certain to degenerate, the moment they
began to worship apostles and books and church-rules and pre-
cedent and tradition, and thus to sip at other men's buckets,
instead of drawing living water from the true fountain, God himself. Better would it have been to retain peaceably in the church
shoals of Judaists, Docetists, Gnostics, Cerinthians, Valentinians,
and every heterodox name which Theology hates, than to ac-
quiesce in the belief that all God's inspiration had been drunk
up by the apostles, and drive out into corners and overwhelm
with contumely (as we also now are apt to do) the only men who
might have secured that Freedom, without which there can be no
Justice and no Love in a community. So Christ's church, where
all were to be brethren and where no one was to bear rule, was
turned into a kingdom of this world, where the few ruled over
the many; while the many liked to have it so, and applauded
the cruel and wicked punishment of those who would not be
subject. So too the passions of princes and the struggles of
party have dictated rigid forms of orthodoxy, which secure no
one spiritual quality of soul, and which Satan would subscribe, if
occasion required. So now they strain out of God's ministry all
who have scrupulous consciences, and swallow down the world
unstrained; and while men frown or tremble at Free Inquiry and
stop their windows against the light of Criticism, they do not
blush to enunciate, that whoso receives not the words to which
they give assent, *hath not received the love of the Truth, that he
might be saved!* Might not one call on the Powers of Darkness
to rejoice, that Darkness calls itself Light, and religious England
believes it?

But alas, it is not the Church of the State only, that is paralyzed. None of the Churches, except in some small measure the
fanatical ones, address themselves directly to the Soul. Nearly
all the teachers of that Gospel, which once scorned the learning
of this world, confound worldly sciences,—the domain of erudition,—with spiritual knowledge and faith. They appeal to the

Intellect, not to the Soul, in order to establish a spiritual religion; and try to force propositions into the mind, instead of bidding the heart freely to expand in the light and glory and love of God.

Surely God has a noble army of faithful men, who would follow the right, if they did but see it; but many an old idol has to be broken, many a mental struggle to be gone through. Oh brethren, (if there be any whom I may dare so to address,) learn that inspired words were not meant as premisses for syllogisms, nor as ready-made weapons against heretics, nor as barriers against free thought and feeling; but as torches that kindle new souls, so that the *child* in the Spirit is as truly inspired as the *parent*: for the heart of man is still young; the Spirit of God has not died out. The Bible is a blessed book, rightly used: yet the Bible may be causing more spiritual evil than any other book, if by it you smother the Holy Spirit within yourselves, and condemn those who love God. A great revolution of mind is wanted. *The kingdom of God* is not meat and drink, nor sermons and sabbaths, nor history and exegesis, nor a belief in the infallibility of any book, nor in the supernatural memory of any man; but it is, as Paul says, *righteousness and peace and joy in the Holy Spirit.* And he who in these last is minded as Christ, is accepted with God, and shall at length be approved by men. For to the life of God neither belief in miracles availeth anything, nor unbelief; but a new Creation; and Faith that worketh by Love: and as many as walk after THIS RULE, peace shall be upon them and mercy, and upon the Israel of God.

THE END.

Woodfall and Kinder, Printers, Angel Court, Skinner Street, London.

WORKS
PUBLISHED BY GEORGE MANWARING,
(SUCCESSOR TO JOHN CHAPMAN,)
8, King William Street, Strand.

The Second Edition of
A HISTORY OF THE HEBREW MONARCHY:
From the Administration of Samuel to the Babylonish Captivity.
By FRANCIS WILLIAM NEWMAN,
Formerly Fellow of Balliol College, Oxford, and Author of " The Soul :
its Sorrows and Aspirations," &c.
{Large post 8vo, 8s. 6d.

" It is truly refreshing to find Jewish history treated, as in the volume
before us, according to the rules of sound criticism and good sense. . . . .
The publication of such a work will form an epoch in biblical literature in
this country."—*Inquirer.*

" The author has brought a very acute mind, familiar with knowledge
that is beyond the range of ordinary scholarship, to the task of combining
and interpreting the antique and fragmentary records which contain the
only materials for his work."—*Prospective Review.*

" This book must be regarded, we think, as the most valuable contri-
bution ever made, in the English language, to our means of understanding
that portion of Hebrew history to which it relates."—*Massachusetts
Quarterly Review.*

The Sixth Edition of
PHASES OF FAITH;
Or, Passages from the History of My Creed.
By F. W. NEWMAN.
With an additional Chapter on the Character of Christ, and a
Reply to the " Eclipse of Faith."
{Post 8vo, cloth, 3s. 6d.

" Besides a style of remarkable fascination, from its perfect simplicity
and the absence of all thought of writing, the literary character of this
book arises from its display of the writer's mind, and the narrative of his
struggles. . . . . In addition to the religious and metaphysical interest,
it contains some more tangible biographical matter, in incidental pictures
of the writer's career, and glimpses of the alienations and social persecu-
tions he underwent in consequence of his opinions."—*Spectator.*

" No work in our experience has yet been published so capable of
grasping the mind of the reader, and carrying him through the tortuous
labyrinth of religious controversy; no work so energetically clearing the
subject of all its ambiguities and sophistications; no work so capable of
making a path for the new reformation to tread securely on. In this history of the conflicts of a deeply-religious mind courageously seeking the
truth, and conquering for itself, bit by bit, the right to pronounce dog-
matically on that which it had heretofore received traditionally, we see
reflected, as in a mirror, the history of the last few centuries. Modern
spiritualism has reason to be deeply grateful to Mr. Newman : his learning, his piety, his courage, his candour, and his thorough mastery of his
subject, render his alliance doubly precious to the cause."—*The Leader.*

LECTURES ON POLITICAL ECONOMY.

By FRANCIS WILLIAM NEWMAN,

Author of " Phases of Faith," " History of the Hebrew Monarchy," &c.

Post 8vo, cloth.   Original price, 7s. 6d.; reduced to 5s.

" The most able and instructive book, which exhibits, we think, no less moral than economical wisdom."—*Prospective Review.*

" For a lucid statement of principles in a singularly compact and readable volume, we know of nothing comparable to this.   Any person familiar with the subject, and the writings upon it, will appreciate the union of fulness and brevity which distinguishes it; but only those who have some experience in lecturing can understand the amount of thought and dexterity required to keep such a subject within such narrow limits, and yet not have a tedious page. . . . . . The best manual or introduction to the science of Political Economy with which we are acquainted. . . . . . We send our readers to the volume itself, with our emphatic commendation."—*Leader.*

THE CRIMES OF THE HOUSE OF HAPSBURG

AGAINST ITS OWN LIEGE SUBJECTS.

By F. W. NEWMAN, Professor of Latin at University College.

Post 8vo.   1s.

" As in everything that comes from Professor Newman's pen, there are earnestness of tone, weight of reflection, and knowledge of the subject, on every page of this terrible little volume.   Those who are curious about royal crimes, or interested in the history of European constitutions, will find in Professor Newman's book, matter to hold their attention riveted from first to last."—*Athenæum.*

" To the doubter we earnestly commend the perusal of every line of the following chapter from Professor Newman's able review of the ' Crimes of the House of Hapsburg.' "—*Weekly News.*

" A serious and telling little work."—*Leader.*

" A brief but terse and energetic treatise."—*Literary Gazette.*

CATHOLIC UNION:

ESSAYS TOWARDS A CHURCH OF THE FUTURE,

As the Organization of Philanthropy.

By FRANCIS WILLIAM NEWMAN.

Post 8vo.   3s. 6d.

THE CREED OF CHRISTENDOM:
ITS FOUNDATIONS AND SUPERSTRUCTURE.

By W. RATHBONE GREG.

8vo, cloth, 10s.

"Will rank high with those critical and erudite works which have of late cleared up so many obscure matters in the history of religion, corrected so many false theories, dispelled so many errors, and done so much to bring into harmony, science and religion, the voice of Nature and the voice of God."—*Economist.*

"He appears to us to have executed his task with thorough honesty of purpose, and in a spirit essentially reverential—in a style clear, animated, and often eloquent, and, for one who disclaims the possession of learning, with no small amount of critical knowledge and philosophic endowment."—*Prospective Review.*

"No candid reader of 'The Creed of Christendom' can close the book without the secret acknowledgment that it is a model of honest investigation and clear exposition ; that it is conceived in the true spirit of serious and faithful research ; and that whatever the author wants of being an ecclesiastical Christian, is plainly not essential to the noble guidance of life, and the devout earnestness of the affections."—*Westminster Review.*

NEW WORK BY DR. DUNCANSON.

THE PROVIDENCE OF GOD MANIFESTED
IN NATURAL LAW.

By JOHN DUNCANSON, M.D.

Post 8vo, price 7s. cloth.

CHRISTIAN THEISM.

By C. C. HENNELL,

Author of "An Inquiry concerning the Origin of Christianity."

Post 8vo, 1s.

"This little work deserves very attentive perusal. . . . . It is a little book finely written, and, independent of the importance of the subject, as a literary production alone is well worthy of respect."—*Weekly Dispatch.*

THE POSITIVE PHILOSOPHY OF AUGUSTE COMTE.

FREELY TRANSLATED AND CONDENSED.

By HARRIET MARTINEAU.

Two Volumes, large post 8vo, cloth, 16s.

The following extracts from an article (understood to be by Sir David Brewster) which appeared in the *Edinburgh Review*, will give some idea of the aim and character of this celebrated work :—

" A work of profound science, marked with great acuteness of reasoning, and conspicuous for the highest attributes of intellectual power.   It comprehends MATHEMATICS, ASTRONOMY, PHYSICS, and CHEMISTRY, or the sciences of *Inorganic* Bodies ; and PHYSIOLOGY, and SOCIAL PHYSICS, or the sciences of *Organic* Bodies.

"Under the head of SOCIAL PHYSICS the author treats of the general structure of human societies, of the fundamental natural law of the development of the human species, and of the progress of civilization.   This last Section is subdivided into three heads—THE THEOLOGICAL EPOCH, the METAPHYSICAL EPOCH, and the POSITIVE EPOCH—the first of these embracing FETICHISM, POLYTHEISM, and MONOTHEISM."

Referring to the Astronomical part of the Work, the Reviewer says :—

" We could have wished to place before our readers some specimens of our author's manner of treating these difficult and deeply-interesting topics—of his simple yet powerful eloquence—of his enthusiastic admiration of intellectual superiority—of his accuracy as an historian, his honesty as a judge, and of his absolute freedom from all personal and national feelings. . . . . The philosopher who has grown hoary in the service of science longs for the advantage of such an historian to record his labours, and of such an arbiter to appreciate their value."—*Edinburgh Review.*

THE CATECHISM OF POSITIVE RELIGION.

TRANSLATED FROM THE FRENCH OF AUGUSTE COMTE.

By RICHARD CONGREVE, M.A.,

Author of "The Roman Empire of the West," &c.

One Volume, fcap. 8vo, 6s. 6d.

THEISM, ATHEISM, AND THE POPULAR THEOLOGY.

Sermons by **THEODORE PARKER**, Author of "A Discourse of Matters pertaining to Religion," &c.

A Portrait of the Author, engraved on Steel, is prefixed. Post 8vo, 9s.

The aim of this work is defined by its author at the beginning of the first Discourse as follows :—"I propose to speak of Atheism, of the Popular Theology, and of Pure Theism. Of each first as a Theory of the Universe, and then as a principle of Practical Life ; first as Speculative Philosophy, then as Practical Ethics."

"To real thinkers and to the ministers of the Christian gospel we emphatically say—Read them (Parker's books) and reflect on them . . . there are glorious bursts of eloquence, flashings of true genius."—*Nonconformist.*

"Compared with the sermons which issue from the majority of pulpits, this volume is a treasure of wisdom and beauty."—*Leader.*

"The method of these discourses is practical, addressing their argument to common sense. Atheism and the popular theology are exhibited in their repulsive relations to common life, while from the better conception of divine things, of which the writer is the chief apostle, there is shown to arise, in natural development, the tranquil security of religious trust, guidance, and comfort in all social duty, and the clear hope of the world to come."—*Westminster Review.*

TEN SERMONS OF RELIGION.

By THEODORE PARKER.

Post 8vo, cloth, 8s.

I. Of Piety and the Relation thereof to Manly Life.
II. Of Truth and the Intellect.
III. Of Justice and the Conscience.
IV. Of Love and the Affections.
V. Of Conscious Religion and the Soul.
VI. Of Conscious Religion as a source of Strength.
VII. Of Conscious Religion as a Source of Joy.
VIII. Of the Culture of the Religious Powers.
IX. Of Conventional and Natural Sacraments.
X. Of Communion with God.

"We feel that in borrowing largely from his (Parker's) pages to enrich our columns we are earning the reader's gratitude."—*Leader.*

"These Sermons are characterized by a lofty eloquence, a vigorous grasp of thought, an eclecticism which gives benignancy to the otherwise generally severe and sectarian aspect of religion, and are marked by an earnestness of zeal and piety, and which gives to literature of this class an attraction so necessary to enlist readers."—*Weekly Dispatch.*

A DISCOURSE OF MATTERS PERTAINING TO RELIGION.

By **THEODORE PARKER.** New Edition, post 8vo, cloth, 4s.

"Parker writes like a Hebrew prophet, enriched by the ripest culture of the modern world."—*Westminster Review.*

"There is a mastery shown over every element of the great subject."—*Prospective Review.*

THE CRITICAL AND MISCELLANEOUS WRITINGS OF THEODORE PARKER.

One volume, post 8vo, cloth, 6s.

THEISM,

DOCTRINAL AND PRACTICAL;

Or, Didactic Religious Utterances.

4to, cloth, 8s. 6d.

CONTENTS :

BOOK I.—*Theory of Religion.*—Animal Instincts—Human Instincts—Free Will—Man and Truth—God in Conscience—Spiritual Prayer—Science of Things Outward—Intuition and Verification—Axioms of Religion—Functions of Unbelief—Intellectual Pantheism—Rectitude of God—Truthfulness of God—Blessedness of God—The Love of God—Sin and Holiness—The Letter and the Spirit—Evil—Childish and Manly Virtue—The Moral and the Spiritual—Instruction in Virtue—Object of Teaching—Self-convicted Teachers—Individualism and Unity—Law and Mercy—Death—Enforcement of Rule—Faith and Foresight—Retribution—Divine Government—Collective Government—Faith—Special Providence—The Material and the Moral—Immortality of God's Beloved—The Infinitude of the Finite—Soul and Body—Worth of the Soul—Animal Development—Brotherhood of Men—The Alternatives—Future of the Righteous—Future of the Wicked—Prevenient Grace—Waters of Lethe—Modern Polytheism.

BOOK II.—*Proverbs.*—Abstract Truth—Religion—Right and Righteousness—Virtue—Social Virtue—Justice—The Passions—Pleasure—Conjugal Relations—Church and State—The Church internally—Sacred Books—Teaching and Public Prayer—Rebuke and Prophecy—Education—Short Creeds.

BOOK III.—*Religious Life.*—Call to God's Service—Postures of Devotion—Joy and Consolation—Deadness of Soul—Despondency of Providence—Modern Martyrdom—Perfect and Imperfect Virtue—Moral Contagion—Foundation of the State—Loyalty and Allegiance—Patriotism—Capital Punishment—Prevention of Crime—The Twofold Law—Pomps and Vanities—Luxury—The Elect—Political Expediency—Political Vacillation—The Order of Progress—Vitality of Sin—Strength out of Weakness—Lawful Obedience—Defensive War—Military Oaths—The Hardened Politician—The Considerate Politician—Truths—Oaths and Solemn Affirmations—Cleanliness—Rights of Animals—Adoration.

NOTICES OF THE PRESS.

" The book is full of deep truth and fine discrimination. . . . . On the Theistic Basis of faith there are few Christians who have not to learn from Mr. Newman."—*National Review.*

" The natural theology of this book . . . . . is for the most part well reasoned out from the evidence of facts perceptible to common experience. It establishes religion upon the solid basis of *the moral consciousness*, treating it justly as a matter of intuition, and no longer after the old manner as an induction of science . . . . Mr. Newman is more radically Christian than many have been who held most faithfully to the formal doctrine of a miraculous inspiration."—*Inquirer.*

" It is a book which abounds on every page with beauties of thought and expression ; it enunciates clearly profound and weighty theological truths ; it puts forth a multitude of penetrating yet kindly observations upon nature and humanity ; it infers numerous wise practical maxims, political and social ; it is unsparing in its rebuke of all kinds of hypocrisies. For the fit reader . . . . it will be read with infinite pleasure and with great profit. But the author does not intend his system to rest in speculation. He has brought himself face to face with religious superstitions, with social corruptions, with personal heart-delusions. He has traced the connection of various pests, which are an abomination to civilization, to error or defect in religious conceptions. He has set himself the task not of a critic but of a teacher . . . both to destroy and to construct."—*Westminster Review.*